The Seven Deadly Sins of White Christian Nationalism

RELIGION IN THE MODERN WORLD

Series Editors:

Kwok Pui-lan, Candler School of Theology, Emory University

Joerg Rieger, Vanderbilt University

This series explores how various religious traditions wrestle with the dynamic and changing role of religion in the modern world and examines how past changes reflect on today's critical issues. Accessibly and engagingly written, books in this series will look at secularization, global society, gender, race, class, sexuality and their relation to religious life and religious movements.

Titles in Series:

Not God's People: Insiders and Outsiders in the Biblical World by Lawrence M. Wills

The Food and Feasts of Jesus: The Original Mediterranean Diet, with Menus and Recipes by Douglas E. Neel and Joel A. Pugh

Occupy Religion: Theology of the Multitude by Joerg Rieger and Kwok Pui-lan

The Politics of Jesús: A Hispanic Political Theology by Miguel A. De La Torre

Modern Muslim Theology: Engaging God and the World with Faith and Imagination by Martin Nguyen

Race, Religion, and Politics: Toward Human Rights in the United States by Stephanie Y. Mitchem

The Hong Kong Protests and Political Theology edited by Kwok Pui-lan and Francis Ching-wah Yip

The Seven Deadly Sins of White Christian Nationalism: A Call to Action by Carter Heyward

The Seven Deadly Sins of White Christian Nationalism

A Call to Action

Carter Heyward

ROWMAN & LITTLEFIELD
Lanham • Boulder • New York • London

Published by Rowman & Littlefield
An imprint of The Rowman & Littlefield Publishing Group, Inc.
4501 Forbes Boulevard, Suite 200, Lanham, Maryland 20706
www.rowman.com

86-90 Paul Street, London EC2A 4NE

Distributed by NATIONAL BOOK NETWORK

British Library Cataloguing in Publication Information Available

Library of Congress Cataloging-in-Publication Data

Names: Heyward, Carter, author.
Title: The seven deadly sins of white Christian nationalism : a call to action / Carter Heyward.
Description: Lanham : Rowman & Littlefield, [2022] | Series: Religion in the modern world | Includes bibliographical references and index.
Identifiers: LCCN 2022011754 (print) | LCCN 2022011755 (ebook) | ISBN 9781538167892 (cloth) |9781538188316 (paperback) | ISBN 9781538167908 (ebook)
Subjects: LCSH: Christians, White—United States. | White nationalism—United States. | Christian conservatism—Political aspects—United States. | Religious right—United States. | Christianity and politics—United States.
Classification: LCC BR517 .H49 2022 (print) | LCC BR517 (ebook) | DDC 261.7—dc23/eng/20220711
LC record available at https://lccn.loc.gov/2022011754
LC ebook record available at https://lccn.loc.gov/2022011755

Dedicated to
Rob, Isabel, Kate, Cooper, Ramsey, Katie,
nephews, nieces, goddess children one and all

You are a light. You are the light. Never let anyone—any person or any force—dampen, dim, or diminish your light.

Release the need to hate, to harbor division, and the enticement of revenge. Release all bitterness.

Hold only love, only peace in your heart, knowing that the battle of good to overcome evil is already won.

John Lewis, *Across That Bridge: Life Lessons and a Vision for Change*[1]

1. New York: Hachette Books, 2017 (2012).

Contents

Acknowledgments   ix

Preface   xiii

PART I: IN THE BEGINNING   1

Chapter 1: Why This Book?   3

Chapter 2: What Is White Christian Nationalism?   19

PART II: THE SEVEN DEADLY SINS   41

Chapter 3: Sin as Our Collective Problem   43

Chapter 4: The First Sin: The Lust for Omnipotence   49

Chapter 5: The Second Sin: Entitlement   65

Chapter 6: The Third Sin: White Supremacy   77

Chapter 7: The Fourth Sin: Misogyny   89

Chapter 8: The Fifth Sin: Capitalist Spirituality   105

Chapter 9: The Sixth Sin: Domination of the Earth and Its Creatures   117

Chapter 10: The Seventh Sin: Violence   127

PART III: A CALL TO ACTION   141

Chapter 11: Questions and Call   143

Chapter 12: The First Call: Empowering One Another   149

Chapter 13: The Second Call: Embodying Humility   157

Chapter 14: The Third Call: Approaching the Blackness of God   165

Chapter 15: The Fourth Call: Empowering Women, Celebrating
    Sexuality, Affirming Gender Diversity   181

Chapter 16: The Fifth Call: Transforming Capitalism   195

Chapter 17: The Sixth Call: Belonging with Earth and Animals   209

Chapter 18: The Seventh Call: Breaking the Spiral of Violence   219

Notes   231

Resources and Selected Bibliography   253

Index   261

About the Author   275

Acknowledgments

Three friends worked with me on this project from its beginnings: Darlene O'Dell, Susan Lefler, and Anne B. Gilson, each a gifted professional writer and teacher herself. When I called them up and said, hey, we need to say something about what happened at the Capitol on January 6, they responded, yes, we do. We four white Christian women, three of us from the South, were troubled in our souls by the reticence of our liberal Protestant churches to get overly involved in "politics" lest too many good Christians be offended. After the Trump presidency, culminating in the shocking events at the Capitol, we decided it was time to risk offending. We set out to design a project considerably larger than this one book. Our project has been energizing and exciting, but it was too much for one book. We decided I should finish writing my part on "the seven deadly sins." I did, and this book has found its way to your hands.

I owe many thanks to friends and colleagues over the years who have helped raise my consciousness about power dynamics in the world near and far. There are way too many to name and, besides, I would doubtlessly leave some of the most important folks out. But you know who you were, and are. You were my teachers, all along the way, beginning at home and in high school and continuing right up through seminary. You were, and are, Bev. You were my coauthors of *God's Fierce Whimsy* (1985), a book that explored racial, ethnic, and sexual diversity in Christian theological education. You were my coauthors of *Revolutionary Forgiveness: Feminist Reflections on Nicaragua* (1986). You were my colleagues at the Episcopal Divinity School in Cambridge, Massachusetts, and at Union Theological Seminary in New York City. You were my sister priests, beginning with the other ten ordinands in the proudly infamous "Philadelphia Ordination" of 1974. You were, and are, my consciousness-raising group at Union Seminary—and, yes, we still meet over Zoom every month more than fifty years later.

You called yourselves my "spiritual parents," Dorothee Soelle and Bob DeWitt, and you surely taught me so much about the church and world. You were Reinhild Traitler-Espiritu of the Boldern Evangelical Institute outside Zurich. You were Angela Solling and your Clare community in Stroud, New South Wales, Australia; Angela Moloney, OP, and your Sophia community in Adelaide, Australia; Susan Adams and John Salmon in Auckland, New Zealand; Denise Ackermann in Cape Town, South Africa; David Conolly in Melbourne, Australia, and Jim Lewis in Charleston, West Virginia—the whole lot of you, white women and men doing your best to empower people of color, racial-ethnic minority and majority groups, as well as women and LGBTQ folks from one continent to another. And you certainly were count-less queer siblings in America and around the world who named our truths.

Most recently you have been my colleagues in the NAACP of Transylvania County, North Carolina, coconspirators in the work of justice. Your collective spirit has coauthored this book with me. There are many of you, and I can name only a few, mainly those I recall often standing, sitting, or kneeling in front of the courthouse on Moral Monday, as well as brothers and sisters on the Religious Affairs Committee: Sheila Mooney, Rosalynd Storer, Tommy Kilgore, Robert Kilgore, the late Curtis Cash, the late Michael Wainwright, Marty Wainwright, Kathleen Barnes, Joe Castro, Larry Goodwin, Linda Goodwin, Desmond Duncker, Maureen Copelof, Sylvan Copelof, Sue Sasser, Nancy Richards, Sam Edney, Deda Edney, Kathy Voltz, Lisa Rodke, Nora Johnson, Jeb Buffinton, Susan Lefler, Charles Lefler, Ian Cowie, Vanessa Cowie, Yang Li, Spencer Jones, Sue Barrett, Eleanor Mockridge, Peter Mockridge, the late Susan Sunflower, Nona Walker, Sue Null, Norene Carter, Doug Denton, Elly Andujar, Judy Nebrig, John Hobbs, Anne Gilson, Ellen Dozier, Diane Livingston, Bill Livingston, Jackie Jenkins, Rob Field, Mark Burrows, and Suzanne Comer-Barrett.

Jody Ralston, I've valued our walks and talks about matters in this book. And glory be, my sister priests, how I've treasured our ongoing strug-gles to navigate the treacherous, deadly patriarchal currents of the church we love and yet, each in our own way, so fiercely resist: Alla Renee Bozarth, Merrill Bittner, Ann Franklin, Anne Gilson, Barbara Plimpton, Gretchen Grimshaw, and Judith Davis. Interestingly, several folks who have been pow-erfully instructive to my awareness of the formative roles of Christianity on American society are not themselves Christians: Janet Surrey, Gerry Azzata, Kathleen Barnes, Robbie Heyward, Hilary Dirlam, and Sue Sasser. Often it takes some distance to notice what is going on right before our eyes. Thank you for helping sharpen my vision as a Christian in America.

My dearest friends and closest family at Redbud Springs, and nearby—in Brevard, Asheville, and Charlotte, North Carolina—know who you are. Know also that you're right here, page by page. Your love never fails to empower me to say what I believe must be said.

Deep appreciation to my friend and former seminary colleague Kwok Pui Lan for encouraging me to submit this manuscript to Rowman & Littlefield, where she is a series editor, and to her fellow editor Joerg Rieger for his thoughtful critique of what I have attempted in these pages. Special thanks for the creative communication with acquisitions editor Natalie Mandziuk, who helped me from beginning to end. Richard Brown and Jaylene Perez joined this editorial team later in the process. Likewise, various members of the publishing staff, like Sylvia Landis were wonderfully helpful. Also Joshua Schwartz and his team at Pubvendo were indispensable in getting the word out. Thank you, everyone. I was able to bring this project to a close only when I made myself stop writing in December 2021, four months after Natalie and I signed our contract. Otherwise the book would never have seen the light of day because new data pours in constantly in relation to the evils being spawned by the white Christian nationalism that threatens to destroy so much that we value—unless we act together boldly and strategically, now.

Finally, on a sad but hopeful note. I remember the late Desmond Tutu not only as a great Christian leader for our time and all time, not only in South Africa but around the world. I also remember him as a next-door neighbor and colleague when he visited the Episcopal Divinity School in 2002 as a visiting scholar. Mostly, I keep thinking about the story that ends this book, in which Sue Hiatt, my friend and colleague, weak from cancer, lay in her hospice bed in Watertown, Massachusetts. She had asked Bishop Tutu to come and bless her, which he did—and then he had asked her to bless him, which she did.

As Desmond Tutu slowly walked from her room, his head bowed, she thanked him for coming and said, "You give me hope that the truth will go on."

Preface

I'm a politically progressive, white Christian American woman in my late seventies, and I write urgently to those with ears to hear. Listen up, my friends! An Episcopal priest who identifies these days as a "Universalist Christian," I have written, taught, preached, and spoken publicly as a lesbian feminist theologian for most of the last fifty years. This book, from my perspective, is far and away the most important piece I have ever done.

I am writing primarily to *American Christians*. Those who are neither American nor Christian might find portions of the book engaging and even helpful, and I urge you to give it a try. I am writing to *white Protestant Christians*, though Roman Catholics and Orthodox Christians in America might recognize themselves here, and Black and Christians of color may find these pages ring true to some of their experiences of white Christianity and, surely, to large chunks of their experiences of America.

The book is also intended largely for those who are *moderate to progressive in their politics and spiritualities*. Whether we are Democrats, Republicans, independents, unaffiliated, participants in other parties, active in no party, or generally uninterested in politics, I am calling you to join in helping to preserve, protect, and defend our most cherished value—the love of God and of our neighbors, a love that generates justice, freedom, and compassion for all. This book is a call to action, a call for American Christians to get involved, to do whatever we can, each and all of us, to make "justice roll down like waters, and righteousness like an ever-flowing stream" (Amos 5:24 New Revised Standard Version).

The moral challenges and political hurdles we face in today's America have been simmering and bubbling here and there throughout our history as a nation. Nothing that we are witnessing in the twenty-first century is new. In the past several years, however, our problems have come to a boil. Today they threaten to destroy the constitutional foundations of our democratic republic and turn us into an authoritarian nation that most Americans and most Christians would come to despise, regardless of how conservative, moderate, or progressive we may be in our politics or our faith. If we love a God of justice and compassion, if we aspire to walk with Jesus as an advocate of friend and stranger alike, and if we wish to be a servant of the public good, the well-being of all, we must learn how to stand together—and be strategic in doing so. For most of us, this means supporting a political party that can win, not casting protest votes, much less sitting out upcoming elections at national, state, or local levels. It will take us all to turn things around, which we must if we value both the constitutional foundations of our country and the basis of our religious faith.

This book is based on a premise that Christians have particular roles to play in this process because, regardless of whether we are more liberal or conservative, Christianity has played a foundational role in American history. Much of American Christianity's role has been for good. Everything churches have contributed to making a nation of liberty and justice for all has been excellent. But much of Christianity's part in forging American history has been more problematic. The "seven deadly sins of white Christian nationalism" that are named and explored in these pages have distorted the American dream by thwarting, again and again, the movements among people to generate liberty and justice, truly for all of us, not just some of us.

As we walk a perilous path in today's America, Christians need to be mindful of a terrible moral and political threat to our country. "Christofascism" is a seductive form of authoritarianism taking shape among us in the guise of Christian faith and all-American values, especially the value of liberty, or freedom, even at the expense of the common good. The great German Christian theologian Dorothee Soelle coined the term "Christofascism" in the early 1980s while she was teaching theology at Union Seminary in New York City. Recalling her German homeland in the 1930s and 1940s, Soelle recognized in Ronald Reagan's America the seeds of something familiar. Digging from her past, she named as Christofascist the dangers she detected in Reagan's "America first" foreign policy, which was being built on stealth and lies. Soelle noticed that this expansionist foreign policy was being funded and bolstered at home by a "trickle-down" economics designed to increase the wealth of rich white Christian American males. She saw that trickle-down economics were not working—the rich were getting richer, and the poor were getting poorer. She saw that much like Hitler's regime had crafted its Aryan supremacism, anti-Semitism, misogyny, and military expansionism, the Reagan administration was waging domestic and international violence against Black Americans, gay men, feminist women, and others deemed either dangerous or useless to building the greatest nation on earth.

And Soelle saw also that Reagan and his lionizing of rich people in America was being supported enthusiastically not only by rich people but also by less rich, even poor, white Christians who were aspiring to make it in America, desperate to survive the very conditions that were resulting from trickle-down Reaganomics. All the while, these middle-, working-, and poorer-class Americans were being assured by their spiritual leaders, mainly conservative Christian evangelists, that upward mobility, spiritually and economically, was God's will for the patriotic faithful in a reliably white Christian nation. In the decades since the Reagan administration, many white American Christians have continued to be seduced by religious, business, and political leaders to vote against their own economic interests. In matters of economic justice, Christianity, capitalism, and the GOP have conspired as a most unholy trinity in the upper tiers of American power. Soelle realized, and warned, that such unholiness, and seduction of the masses in the name of God of rich white Christian men, is exactly what fascist leaders did in Germany in the 1930s.

Indeed, this is happening again today in Europe and other parts of the world, including the United States of America ("America" for short in this book). The unholy trinity of business, religious, and political interests presents us not only with an American problem but also a uniquely *Christian* challenge because our churches have allowed a latent authoritarianism in both church and state to fester theologically among us from the time of our origins as a nation. This has been especially the case since the Second World War, from which the United States of America emerged victorious. Our nation quickly became not only a rich and proud nation but the richest and proudest nation on the planet—a nation whose wealth and power has deep roots in white supremacy, misogyny, capitalist spirituality, and the other sources of evil named in these pages as "the seven deadly sins of white Christian nationalism."

This book in your hands explores these sins and calls us all, especially those of us who are Christians and Americans, to some urgent moral work of spiritual renewal and social transformation. Can America be made great again—or, in some ways, deeply good and thereby great for the first time? It's up to us.

Carter Heyward
January 2022

PART I

In the Beginning

Chapter 1

Why This Book?

"The fathers have eaten sour grapes, and the children's teeth are set on edge."

(Jeremiah 31:29 English Standard Version)

Soon after the insurrection at the U.S. Capitol on January 6, 2021, this book began to take shape. My family and friends had been stunned as we watched hundreds of rioters, their makeshift gallows rising above them, attack both the Capitol itself and those there to protect it. We had watched in dismay as video showed the torture of police officers and how close the insurrectionists had come to breeching the chambers of a sitting Congress. With the rest of the nation and much of the world, we had witnessed insurrectionists carrying Confederate flags alongside wooden crosses, wearing "Camp Auschwitz Staff" sweatshirts, and wrapping their arms around copies of the Bible. We had seen angry men draped in Trump flags bowing in front of a cross. We had been shocked as this mob smashed windows, yelled obscenities, destroyed the camera equipment of journalists, formed nooses from the cords, and yelled, "Hang Mike Pence!," all in an attempt to overturn the 2020 election results. We had watched in disbelief at the flaunting in real time of white supremacy and other death-dealing dynamics of hate in front of, and inside, the U.S. Capitol, which Abraham Lincoln had named "the people's house." Later we learned that some of the rioters had defecated inside legislative chambers.

Nearly all the insurrectionists were white, which no doubt helped them live long enough to have their murderous rampage downplayed by a former president and his political party. Trump's people hope that most Americans and most Christians will simply move on and not hold it against the "Grand Old Party," which, in this historical moment, is composed largely of white Christian men and the women who play along with them.

And make no mistake. The January 6 attack was a Christian affair. As Jeffrey Goldberg reported in the *Atlantic*, "The conflation of Trump and Jesus was a common theme at the rally." Goldberg discussed a moment of exchange he had with an insurrectionist from Texas, noting that the violence was beyond what could be explained "through the prism of politics" but was "psychological," "theological," and "eschatological." The man, Goldberg reported, believed this attack was part of the End Times. "It's all in the Bible," he told Goldberg. "Everything is predicted. Donald Trump is in the Bible. Get yourselves ready."[1] This man was not alone in his cultlike devotion.

Witnessing neo-Nazis, Proud Boys, and other hate groups lie, destroy property, and torture others in the name of Jesus, many of us knew deep in our bones that this moment was not an anomaly in U.S. history. We realized that its violence has roots deep in our national story. We also knew that the groups attacking the Capitol, like hate groups before them, were relying on most Americans and most Christians to provide them with legitimacy either by trivializing or shunning any connection with and responsibility for the insurrection. Furthermore, as research in the months after the attack has shown, many of the insurrectionists were not members of hate groups but were just average, mainstream American citizens. This has led commentators "to raise concerns about how extremist ideologies have moved increasingly into the mainstream."[2] The dramatic display of the large cross in the midst of this pageant of scorn and terror had been impossible to miss. We had watched this drama unfold in the name of the Christian God. As Anthea Butler wrote, "[These] evangelicals [were] not naïve individuals who were taken advantage of by a slick New York real estate mogul and reality TV star. They were his accomplices."[3] The time had come for other Christians to speak out—not only on behalf of this nation but more importantly on behalf of a God of justice, love, and peace.

WHAT ABOUT AMERICANS WHO AREN'T CHRISTIAN AND CHRISTIANS WHO AREN'T AMERICAN?

Why should anyone who isn't a Christian, or perhaps even an American, have any interest in a book that focuses almost entirely on being both Christian and American? People of other spiritual traditions, or none at all, and people from other countries might well read this book and ponder how it may also reflect how their religious tradition or philosophy has been shaped by similar dynamics to those we name as foundational to white Christian nationalism. For example, to what extent are American Jews, Muslims, Buddhists, pagans, or people of other traditions being co-opted and conditioned by what is named in these pages as the sins of white Christian nationalism? How might

Christians in Australia, South Africa, Brazil, and South Korea, for instance, experience their own political cultures as being shaped by one or more of the same, or similar, "seven deadly sins of white Christian nationalism"? Perhaps you will need to consider sins or simply failures in your own religious or national cultures. If you are American but not Christian, it still might behoove you to understand a bit more about how the underbelly of your country in many ways has been formed by the sins of white Christian nationalism.

People who are neither Christian nor American may or may not resonate with the Christian feminist foundations and questions I raise as they are shaped explicitly around liberative interpretations of scripture for Christians in America today. But here in parts 1 and 2, you might see yourselves, your religious traditions, and practices; as well as sharpen your senses of the insidious nationalism that is creeping around the world. For neither Christianity nor America has a monopoly on the social dynamics that generate evil.

POINTS OF PERSONAL ENTRY AS A WHITE SOUTHERN CHRISTIAN WOMAN

This rest of this chapter is a highly personal reflection on how my interest in matters of white Christian nationalism has been forged in the course of my life. I am including this material not because my personal journey is any more engaging than yours, but rather to spark you to think about how *your own experiences* have been influenced by the dynamics of white Christian nationalism. Our lives, after all, provide the basis of our politics as well as our spiritualities. The more boldly we share our stories, the more we are encouraging others to do likewise. The more honestly we share our values and our concerns, the better able we become to envision some significant reformations of our nation and of our Christian lives. This book is a call to such reformation.

In this spirit, I urge you to read this chapter with an interest not only in *my* life but also *your own.* Take mental notes as you go. Stop and think. Talk with a good friend: How have events in your life helped create *your* identity, *your* values, and how *you* view the current state of both the United States of America and the Christian Church or whatever your religious or spiritual community may be? Talk to each other and tell the truth.

Talk about Race

It never crossed my mind growing up that the church I loved was not just part of the problem but a major part of the problem of white supremacy in America. As a white Southern Christian girl-child, growing up in a home in Charlotte, North Carolina (the context is important), where both parents conveyed a moderately open, but still traditional, Southern—and Christian—view of race relations, I suppose I was rather precocious to raise questions at home about white privilege, not in that language, of course. I asked my parents why it was that Bessie, the Black woman who helped take care of me, lived in another part of town in a tiny house that didn't look as nice as our small frame house in a working- and lower-middle-class white neighborhood. I don't recall their answer.

And I was baffled, at age four or five, when Bessie walked away from me and our house and never came back in response to my having been singing the jingle "Eeny, meeny, miny, mo, catch a n----, by his toe . . . " while jumping rope with my best friend, another little white girl. My parents were shocked when I told them and, for the first time, they told me that people like us (meaning: nice white people) never, ever, used the "n-word," because it was cruel and unkind.

Why, then, I asked, does God allow white people to treat "colored" people in cruel and unkind ways? Why, why? I was one of those kids who always wanted to know why. To the best of my memory, Daddy said something like, "Sugarplum, God doesn't like it. God doesn't want white people to be cruel to 'colored' people." I must have pressed on: "Well, why don't *we* do something about it?" I think I recall my parents hugging me, but I also have a fuzzy memory of them looking at each other and shaking their heads. The message I got, whether or not spoken, was that there was nothing we could do, and that we ought to be sorry about it, and I was. Sorry, sad, and puzzled.

Talk about Gender

Meanwhile, up in the apple tree in our side yard, I was having regular chats with my imaginary playmate, "Sophie Couch," a "colored" girl my age who was just as concerned as I was about not only race relations but also what we girls could be and do when we grew up. Girls, not boys. Sophie was the first feminist voice in my life. Of course, she was my own better angel, my own little reservoir of wisdom. Why does a child concoct an imaginary friend in the first place? Probably because she needs someone to talk to, someone who understands her, another kid, somebody like her, more or less.

Until recently, I hadn't given much thought to how Sophie Couch's Blackness was shaping my female consciousness. And yes, I do believe that Sophie was, in fact, an inspired level of my consciousness as a girl-child and that she reflected some "colored" wisdom trying to reach, teach, and stretch my little white girl awareness of what was what. Not that I could be or become Black, but that I could, and should, begin to reflect on race as well as gender, and think about racism and sexism, and incorporate lessons from people of color into my white privileged life, even as a female, and even as a child.

Talk about Class

Then there was the matter of class, perhaps the most baffling matter of all for most Americans and most Christians in America. I was a white girl-child in a muddled middle- or working-middle-class Christian family. Who knows what class my family was? They certainly didn't. They spoke of themselves as upper-middle class, but I came to realize years later, as an adult, that in terms of class, my parents were more aspirational than realistic. We were, I believe, plain old middle-class white people in the mountains of North Carolina. Later in this book, we will be highlighting capitalist spirituality as a significant problem among Christians in America. As a child I knew nothing firsthand about social or economic class because I was never hungry, homeless, or without access to health care or good public education.

My father had picked cotton on a farm in South Carolina where his father was the manager of a mill. Later, Daddy had played shortstop on a minor-league baseball team before joining the army and serving in the Pacific during World War II. Mama had been born into a fairly prominent family in Charlotte, North Carolina, where her father had owned a wholesale tobacco company and her mother had belonged to various ladies' clubs and cotillions. Bob Heyward and Mary Ann Carter met on a blind date during one of Daddy's leaves in 1943; they married on another such leave in 1944; and I was born in 1945. At the end of the war, my father took a job as a salesman for Esso (later Exxon) Oil and my mother was a homemaker. As their first of three children, I was the apple of their eyes, they each would tell me, and I never had any reason to doubt that I was a most beloved little girl. When I was a child, my two great passions were for animals and God, probably in that order.

Talk about Animals

Early on, I knew beyond any doubt in my little girl mind-body-spirit that the giant spirit man, very old and very white, who everyone called "God," had as much to do with the box turtle and black snake in the yard as with any human being. I've already mentioned my "colored" playmate Sophie Couch as one of the first God bearers into my consciousness and deepest sense of self. I say "one of" because as far back as I can remember it was the animals, not only our dogs, but also turtles, snakes, frogs, crawfish in the creek that ran behind the house, hoot owls, robin redbreasts, and bluebirds who godded for me. Filled with God, they became conduits of the sacred.

I don't recall any lessons from the animals about race or gender—those lessons came first and foremost from my own imagination in the form of Sophie Couch. As Sister Angela, an Anglican nun, priest, and beloved friend, would ask me fifty years later as we sat together over tea in a tree house in her monastery in the Australian bush, "What is imagination, dahling, if not a window into God?" Was it God who was teaching me about race and gender through my imaginary playmate? Was Sophie Couch my most direct line to God? My parents, Bob and Mary Ann, who I believe never contradicted Sophie, also taught me explicitly about gender and race, though it was a little later. I was probably six or seven when I began to hear from my parents about what girls could and could not do. For example, girls could not be priests, they said, because girls were the wrong sex. "Gender" was called "sex" in those days, and sex was not spoken of in our home, regardless.

Talk about Abuse and Violence

When, at about age five, I was molested—touched inappropriately, not raped or hurt—by Jeff the yardman, everybody freaked out, especially Police Chief K, who shot several times over Jeff's head, making him run for his life, and yelling, "If you ever come back into this county, there'll be one dead n----r." Jeff hadn't hurt me, but his behavior had puzzled and scared me—taking me into the garage, giving me prizes from Cracker Jack boxes, asking me to touch his penis, touching me lightly, telling me not to tell, saying what a sweet girl I was. When I mentioned this to Mama one day as she was helping me bathe, she phoned Daddy, who hurried home from work in the company of Chief K who had Jeff with him and was pushing and shoving him around, calling him a n----r, and making him run. My parents didn't press charges, I guess because they wanted to protect everyone from the publicity a trial would have generated in our small mountain community.

Once they were confident that Jeff had not raped or hurt me physically, they wanted us all just to forget. They told me it would be better if we never talked about what had happened, even among ourselves, and we never did talk about it, never again, my parents and I—

until sometime in my midtwenties, when I was home from seminary and fresh from a consciousness-raising group in which we women seminarians had been sharing our sexual secrets. Mine was Jeff.

Talk about Secrets and Silence

When I told my parents I'd discussed Jeff with my seminary friends, they asked why. Why would I bring this up twenty years later? Had more happened than they realized? Had my experience with Jeff left me emotionally scarred? Is this what had made me a lesbian? I remember saying to my parents, as we sat on their screened porch in Charlotte in 1971, something like this: No, Jeff didn't hurt me sexually. Nobody hurt me sexually. The worst part of what happened was watching Chief K shoot at Jeff and call him a n----r. I hated that I had precipitated this incident by telling them about Jeff, because he had not hurt me and he did not deserve to be shot at and screamed at using that ugly, scary word.

The big lesson for me from that incident was in witnessing the violent hatred of a Black man. As a child, I believe I had not only been terrorized by Chief K's gunshots but also by the fact that he, a white man, was shooting at a Black man and in his fury calling him a n----r. Even as an adult, I don't think I felt myself to have been primarily a victim, but rather a witness to a violent incident of racism. The other big lesson for me was in the silencing of what had happened, the sweeping away into a void the sexual abuse of me, a girl-child, as if this event could somehow disappear, become a nonevent, which in a way it did. Looking back, I ask myself—how *did* my parents' silencing me in this context contribute to the shaping of my sexuality not so much as a lesbian but as a woman, a girl, a child, a female in a world in which so many men assume the right to do whatever they wish and whatever they can—with the bodies of women and children? Why *not* talk about this with your daughter, and with each other! Why for God's sake, do we not speak of hard things with the people we love most?

From these snippets, it's not hard to pull out threads of white supremacy and a violent masculinity that are twisted together. Instead of being consciously examined and untwisted insofar as possible by frightened parents and a puzzled child, these thick, knotty threads were swept secretly and silently under a carpet of assumptions that hold white Christian nationalism in place even among kind, good, intelligent Christians like Mary Ann and Bob Heyward and their children, beginning with their first child, a girl, me.

Off and on throughout my life, certainly throughout my professional work as a teacher, priest, and theologian, I have asked myself, and my students, what are the assumptions that hold the destructive, damaging parts of Christianity in place—white supremacy, sexual violence, and the silence so often cultivated to cover up secrets so that we can appear to be something we are not—invulnerable and perfect? With Jewish feminist poet Adrienne Rich, I believe to the bottom of my toes that our lies, secrets, and silences[4] play a major role in upholding what we will examine as the seven deadly sins of white Christian nationalism. We learn too well, we white Christian Americans, simply not to talk about, not to notice, perhaps not even to remember the parts of our lives that are the most embarrassing or shameful, the parts that seem somehow strangest or out of sync with how we see ourselves, the parts other people don't want to hear about or think about even if we do. I hope that, as you read, you will reflect on your own stories—where you have encountered white supremacy, misogyny, and others of the sins we will be exploring. The reason for telling these stories, mine and yours, is to help us experience the embodied, incarnate, real-life character of both good and evil

SILENCES ARE BROKEN, POWER-OVER DYNAMICS LAID BARE

From the Jeff incident, I learned that good girls don't talk about strange or scary things that happen to their bodies. This silence began to lift as a result of the women's movement. Beginning in the 1980s, I had dozens of women students, and a few men as well, who spoke about their sexual abuse at the hands of trusted family members, friends, ministers, teachers, employers, and other adults. In 1991, my students and I were inspired by the brave testimony of Anita Hill against her boss Clarence Thomas, who—despite her testimony—would be confirmed by the Senate as an associate justice of the Supreme Court. Almost three decades later, Christine Blasey Ford would testify against Brett Kavanaugh, who she said had sexually assaulted her when they were teenagers. As in the Clarence Thomas situation, the largely male United States Senate drew a gentlemen's circle around Brett Kavanaugh and confirmed him to a lifetime appointment on the Supreme Court. Many accusers of former United States presidents and many women and children who tell of their abuse at the hands of powerful men, from presidents and bishops right on down the power lines, continue to be either ignored or besmirched. This happens habitually in deference to the power of men in authority who are usually, not always, both white and Christian, men who take what they want because they want it and can usually get away with it.

The incident around Jeff was a moment in which I saw white supremacy, white hatred, white violence, with my own eyes and heard white supremacy with my own ears. At age five, I assumed there was nothing my family or I could do about it because it's just the way it is, especially among angry, powerful white men with guns, strong white men who assume that with their "n-words" and their guns, they are protecting little white girls like me, but from what?

I don't doubt that Chief K was interested in protecting me from violence and hate. And yet, given his treatment of Jeff, with his hateful language and his gun, what was he protecting me from? Violence? Seriously? In protecting me from abuse by a *Black* man, the police chief was scaring me out of my socks and terrifying me of life among violent *white* men. Yes, Jeff had scared and puzzled me, and this sadly abusive man needed to be held responsible for his crime. Justice needed to be served, but—and this is a huge, definitive "but"—in the Jim Crow South in 1950, justice in this situation would have been impossible. Had it become known that a Black man had molested a white girl, Jeff probably would have been lynched by a bunch of white men, maybe even my father's friends in the small Southern town, though I cannot bear to imagine such a thing.

CHRISTOFASCISM ON THE RISE TODAY

Three-quarters of a century later, Mama and Daddy are among the angels or somewhere in the realms beyond. Chief K is there too or somewhere else in the mysteries of God, and so too are Jeff and Bessie. Over the years, Sophie Couch has grown with me into Sophia, a full-blown spirit of liberation and healing, transcending race, gender, sexual identity, religion, culture, class, species, planets, and stars. And here I am—a white Southern woman, not far from eighty years old, with strong "Universalist Christian"[5] roots, white hair, lined face, dimming vision, full of questions and ideas—thinking about Christian nationalism, *white* Christian nationalism, which we will explore more fully in the next chapter. Let me quote sociologists Andrew Whitehead and Samuel Perry in describing Christian nationalism as a "cultural framework—a collection of myths, traditions, symbols, narratives, and value systems—that idealizes and advocates a fusion of Christianity with American civic life . . . [and] includes assumptions of nativism, white supremacy, patriarchy, and heteronormativity, along with divine sanction for authoritarian control and militarism."[6] Is this not exactly what Trump and his cronies have meant by "making America great again"?

This book excavates the dubious prospect of "making America great again"—a white, patriarchal, Christian, militaristic bastion of unregulated capitalism. In it we will examine several central theological themes embedded in American history and culture, themes generated and secured in large part through Christianity, transparently in its white evangelical manifestations but also through its mainline Protestant, Roman Catholic, and Orthodox organizations, as well as the Mormon Church. No Christian church in America is exempt morally or politically from responsibility for the perpetuation of white Christian nationalism, from the so-called founding of this nation by European Christians to the January 6, 2021, assault on the U.S. Capitol, led by Christian nationalist rioters and their supporters within the government, including the president and members of Congress.

This book in your hands may matter more than others I have written on similar themes[7] because this particular moment in our history is uniquely urgent for American Christians. We are facing today an onslaught by evil forces that, in the early 1980s, German Christian political theologian

Dorothee Soelle named as "Christofascist."[8] Soelle was commenting on how she perceived Ronald Reagan's "America first" populism and his willingness to bow to the unholy trinity of military, economic, and Christian priorities, which were emerging as a white Christian nationalist agenda. Soelle understood the Reagan agenda to be signaling ominous Christofascist possibilities. These themes threw her back forty years into what had happened in her native Germany: social control being exercised through violence; capitalist obsession with the individual's possession and increase of wealth; and the sanctity and purity of the traditional white patriarchal family as exemplified by conservative Christians.

Christian Anti-Semitism[9]

In Hitler's Germany, the country's economic woes after the First World War had been linked to the presence of Jews. This violent scapegoating was steeped in the anti-Judaism of the Christian Bible,[10] which, over centuries of Western history, had morphed into the violent anti-Semitism that produced the Holocaust. Jonathan Greenblatt, head of the Jewish Anti-Defamation League in America, warns that "it could happen here."[11] Indeed, a hatred of Jews is latent in American society. Anti-Semitism has raised its evil head repeatedly in the slaughter of Jews by avowed white supremacists and Christian nationalists. Following the 2018 murders at the Tree of Life Synagogue in Pittsburgh, Pennsylvania, Isabel Fattal, a staff writer for the *Atlantic*, detailed a number of mass and other notorious murders of Jews in America—simply because they were Jews.[12] Christians need to be clear that, in America, anti-Semitism is perpetuated through several of the deadly sins explored in these pages—specifically, the sins of omnipotence, entitlement, white supremacy, capitalist spirituality, and violence. The chant by white men, probably mostly Christians, marching in Charlottesville, Virginia, in the summer of 2017 signaled the hateful and Christofascist substance of the anti-Semitism lurking throughout Western Christian history and manifest shamefully in contemporary America: "Jews will not replace us."

In my lifetime as a Christian in America, no evil has been subtler and more invasive to the well-being of all people than this anti-Semitism. Where do young white Christian men even get the notion that, somehow, Jews will "replace" them? Replace them where, and how, and in what senses? There's Henry Ford, an example of a prominent American who warned about Jews taking over American businesses; Charles Lindbergh, the famous aviator, who blamed Jews for America's entry into World War I; American expatriate poet Ezra Pound, who joined the fascists in Italy during World War II; and T. S. Eliot,[13] with whom I wrestle with personally, because like many American Christians, ever since reading his poetry in college, I have admired him. Over the years I've had a number of conversations with Jewish friends and colleagues about this evil toxin that infuses the veins of all societies with deep Christian roots. Working as a Christian theologian, I have come to realize what most theologically educated Christians do, to our great sorrow: that Christianity itself has long planted anti-Jewish seeds, beginning with the errant accusation that "the Jews killed Christ," when in fact the Romans killed the Jewish Jesus along with others whom they considered criminals in the Roman state. From Christianity's earliest days, Christians have sought to scapegoat "the Jews" for whatever social ills may be present, especially economic woes. The wrongful accusation and lynching of Atlanta business-man Leo Frank in 1915, followed by the rise of the KKK, was a reflection primarily of bad Christian teachings, every bit as wrongheaded and violence instigating as Christianity's attachment to whiteness.

As a structure in America, perhaps we can imagine anti-Semitism as an off-shoot of white supremacy, in which "the Jews" have often been treated much the same way as Native, Black, and other Americans of color. Of course, the history of anti-Semitism reaches back historically into Mediterranean and European cultures in which, from time to time, Christians and Muslims have blamed and fought "the Jews" as well as each other. But in America, which is the focus of this book, we need to realize that Jews have often been targets of the hatred and violence similar to that which has targeted Black and other Americans of color. Like other victims of white Christian nationalists, Jews continue to be scapegoated in the name of Jesus.

It's important that we realize that this is happening even now. Look at the hostages taken at Congregation Beth Israel in Colleyville, Texas, near Dallas, in January 2022, as this book was being edited. Although the hostage taker was neither Christian nor American (he was a British Pakistani), the fact that Jews were singled out and taken hostage reflects the anti-Semitism that too often plagues our nation and is stirred by white Christian nationalists like those in Charlottesville ("Jews will not replace us") and at the U.S. Capitol on January 6, 2021 (the "Camp Auschwitz" logo).

Terrorism in Christofascist Guise

Americans of my generation have seen a great deal of struggle for social change, through the civil rights movement; the anti–Vietnam War protests; the women's and LGBTQ movements; protests against American-sponsored anti-socialist coups or attempted coups in Cuba, Guatemala, Chile, and Nicaragua to name a few examples; antinuclear protests; increasingly vibrant green and climate movements as floods and fires rage out of control around the world; a relentless global pandemic; and the tragic implosion of Afghanistan. Over the course of my lifetime, there has not been much letup in demands for social change and cries for social action among Americans. But the rapid rise of fascist-inspired authoritarian governments around the world since the turn of the new century has been stunning in Europe, Asia, Latin America, and the United States of America. Christofascism is peculiarly American due to the driving force of right-wing Christians in shaping authoritarian public policy.

Although I've been speaking, teaching, preaching, organizing, witnessing, and writing against the various components of Christian nationalism for about fifty years, until recently, I've seldom used the term "Christian nationalism," much less "Christofascism." Like other liberation theologians, I've spoken of Christian "supremacy," "imperialism," "arrogance," "oppression," "domination," and certainly anti-Semitism in discussions of the church's all too common stance toward people who are not Christian as well as dissidents and minority voices within the churches. I also have long assumed that many Christians, including myself in my teens, have believed that America—because of the religion of the majority of its European "founders"—has always been implicitly a Christian nation, this despite the Establishment Clause of the First Amendment to the Constitution.

During the past few years, the term "Christian nationalism" has emerged as a critical code on the left for the merger of Trump's MAGA nativism with the Christian Right's agenda to make America *white* again and to secure the sexual and economic headship of men over women in white Christian families as well as in the society at large. I don't believe most Christians personally aspire to be "Christian nationalists," although certain religious and political voices on the far right of both church and state might find the term endearing because it can make them feel as if they are, in their words, "owning the libs" like me and many readers of this book. But most conservative evangelical Christians, like all mainline and progressive Christians, would resent being dubbed "Christian nationalist." They would interpret this correctly as an indictment of their pandering to white supremacist, anti-Semitic, anti-Muslim, sexist, homophobic, and other oppressive activities and attitudes that are fracturing even our aspirations to be a unified people, at peace with each other across our ideological divides.

Be aware, however, that there are those on the far right—and their numbers are increasing—who are proud Christian nationalists, unapologetically fascist in their politics. Neo-Nazi terrorist David Lane launched the American Renewal Project (ARP) in the early 2000s to "engage the church in a culture war for religious liberty, to restore America to our Judeo-Christian heritage, and to re-establish a Christian culture."[14] Today, the ARP's organization in North Carolina, where my family and I live, enjoys the enthusiastic support of the state's lieutenant governor and at least two of its congressmen, Mark Walker and Madison Cawthorn. These Trump loyalists along with dozens of other Republicans in the U.S. Congress are delighted to embrace a Christian nationalist identity. If the ARP were not politically conservative and did not flaunt its Christian identity, if for example it were a Muslim movement to take over America, it would have long since been branded a terrorist organization by the United States Department of Homeland Security.

REFUSING TO SIMPLY GAZE OUT THE WINDOW

But Christians do not have to be on the far-right terrorist fringes of our common life, nor do they have to be insurrectionists seeking to restore Donald Trump to the presidency, to share in the responsibility for the perpetuation of white Christian nationalism. Christian churches—conservative and liberal, though in different ways and to varying degrees—have driven the growth of white Christian nationalism throughout our history. Many conservative evangelicals and fundamentalist Protestant Christians, as well as Roman Catholics, Eastern Orthodox, and Mormons, often have contributed explicitly, sometimes proudly, to the perpetuation of race- and gender-based oppression in America life. At the same time, many white Christians—Episcopalians, Presbyterians, American Baptists, Lutherans, Congregationalists and others, as well as moderate Catholics and Orthodox—who have not wished to be associated with white supremacy or male gender domination, nonetheless have refused to join, much less lead, publicly in social struggles against injustice throughout much of American history. In response to white Christian nationalism, our great collective sin, we who have grown up in white churches, often in politically moderate or liberal congregations, has been our complicity through silence. In our silence, we moderate to liberal white Christians bear much responsibility for the perpetuation of white Christian nationalism in America.

In one of his novels exploring theological and ethical dimensions of the Holocaust, Elie Wiesel suggested that as bad as the killers were those who looked out their windows, watched, and did nothing as the boxcars carried Jews to the death camps.[15] Since childhood, I have recoiled against simply gazing out the windows of my white Christian middle-class American life. I have been determined not simply to shake my head in sadness and frustration about the injustices festering all around us. I have wanted to speak up and speak out in whatever pulpits I've had access to in my writing and speaking— often, as a priest, literally in pulpits. Yet, like many academics and clergy, I've lived a privileged life in most ways and, despite my fierce desire to participate in changing the world, I have spent much time "gazing out the window" and admiring those on the front lines of social struggle. As an activist-teacher-priest-writer, some of my work has been stronger and more uncompromising than other parts. Some of my messages have been angrier, some gentler, some more scholarly in traditional style, some freer in style, some the rantings of a mad woman who imagines herself prophetic, some steeped in pastoral assurance that if we just love one another all will be well.

CONSCIOUSNESS RAISING FOREVER

Dorothee Soelle, who would become a close friend and colleague, asked me in the moment we met in 1976 how on earth, if I were seriously interested in justice making, I could be an Episcopal priest—meaning an avowed member of a rather precious profession in an economically privileged largely white American church. Looking back, I realize how seriously to heart I took Dorothee's question. I heard it as a vocational charge. From that time on, for the next fifteen years or so, my work as a priest and teacher reflected an effort, professionally and personally, to reconcile being an Episcopal priest with being not only a feminist, a lesbian, and an antiracist white woman but also a radically *human* being on a planet where our species is basically unnecessary—and certainly most threatening—to the survival of the earth.

From the 1980s and early 1990s, at least six factors interacted to raise my political consciousness as an American, a Christian, and a white middle-class lesbian woman: One was my first real introduction to the Holocaust. Through studying and teaching the writings of Elie Wiesel, I realized that most Christians in Europe and America had failed to take the Holocaust seriously as a genocidal assault on Jews, a moral travesty with deep historical roots in Christian anti-Semitism. A second influence on my spiritual and political formation was my involvement with Christian base communities in Nicaragua and with the Nicaraguans who found themselves under so-called "covert" attack by the United States–sponsored "contra."[16] A third contribution to my continuing education was a deepening camaraderie with increasing numbers of Black, brown, and Asian women as faculty colleagues and students in religion and theology, women who often became my friends and always became my teachers.[17] A fourth, and closely related, set of experiences that sparked my consciousness was my heightened exposure to different cultures, conditions, languages, and perspectives in the course of traveling, as a theologian and activist, to different parts of the United States and world, meeting with varieties of people, including Indigenous and minority religious communities.

A fifth experience that empowered me to hear and see what was really happening around me was my coming to terms with being an alcoholic and, with the help of Alcoholics Anonymous, stopping the drinking of alcohol that heretofore had numbed my sensibilities to the sorrows and horrors of oppression as well as the joys of healing and liberation in the world.

A sixth factor shaping my life during this period was a sobering offshoot of my early recovery from alcoholism. I had a difficult experience in psychotherapy, a source of personal shame at the time, in which neither my therapist, evidently, nor I realized that I was recovering addict who needed spiritual encouragement, not psychiatric treatment. I could not seem to extricate myself from this professional relationship as it was battering my senses of confidence and competence. This painful relational conundrum—which my partner and other loved ones saw clearly at the time and encouraged me to break away from—became a window for me into dysfunctional power-over manipulations that can become the basis of any relationship, including professional ones.[18]

A few empowering, beautiful friendships of loved ones (you know who you were), were steady, foundational resources during my processes of becoming, I trust, at least a little wiser during the 1980s and 1990s, my "midlife" stretch. These processes were of course simultaneously professional and personal, spiritual, and political, and the relationships that encouraged them were forever. My consciousness and my life, and the lives of my closest friends, were in flux.

By the time of my fiftieth birthday in 1995, I had been sober for a decade. My head and heart were increasingly clear. I had seen quite enough of my country's disingenuous and violent maneuvering at home and abroad, and I had had quite enough of our mainstream—moderate to liberal—Christian churches' silent complicity. In conscience and common sense, I could not ignore the obvious: neither the United States of America nor mainline American Christianity was seriously committed to living up to the morally righteous rhetoric of its own foundations: Liberty and justice for all? Hardly. Love of neighbor as self? Not so much.

DARING TO IMAGINE, WE MUST TRY

During the last twenty years or so, my vocation has become amazingly multilayered and open to evolving questions about what on earth I am doing—writing, speaking, helping care for humans and horses and other creatures, sometimes a sacramentalist or prophet or pastor, always a white antiracist feminist cisgender bisexual lesbian woman. Very much alive, though gradually coming apart, as an older but not yet ancient human being whose life is one small speck of matter in time and space, embedded here for a while longer among countless species of creatures great and small. I am filled with wonder and gratitude and, as ever, a passion for justice.

My theological work has become ever more intersectional, based in the premise that everything is connected, whether or not we realize it.

Systemically and personally, matters of gender, race, class, culture, species, et al. are unable to be understood, much less helpfully addressed, if approached as isolated phenomena. And while no one will ever fully apprehend the breadth, depth, and strength of the connective tissue among the many "isms" like racism and sexism, the more fully we realize that the connections are there, whether or not we notice or understand them very well, the more truthful and honest our lives can be.

I offer this book as an urgent, honest call to a process of reformation that, only if we do it together, can reach far beyond any of our lives on this planet. I write to encourage study and action among Christians and other Americans who know that something is wrong and has been for a very long time. I know that you sisters, brothers, and siblings know that changes are needed in American Christianity. I know that many of you want to help stir and deepen our national conscience so that we can figure out how to work together—we Americans, we Christians, and others whoever you are. I know deep in my heart and with every cognitive power in my brain and body that, if we dare to exercise our moral courage and good common sense, we can begin to re-form our democracy into a union more perfect than anything Abraham Lincoln could have imagined. I know that, for the sake of God and this country, we must try.

Chapter 2

What Is White Christian Nationalism?

It becomes clearer by the day that the foundations of our democracy are seriously under attack not simply by a mob of Trump-inspired rioters at the U.S. Capitol but also by the large Republican minority in Congress and the man from whom they take their marching orders, the former president. Moreover, the democratic fabric of our nation's highest ideals from the beginning—flawed, partial, and unrealized though they have been—is being shredded by the silent complicity of the majority of our fellow Americans, many of them Christians—liberal, moderate, conservative Christians, Black, brown, Asian, Native, and mainly white Christians. Just like me and most readers of this book.

Like many Americans, I have been pondering connections between American Christianity and the contemporary political situation in the United States for quite some time—especially in conversations since the 2016 election. White Christian nationalism is a movement spawned by white Christian Americans to superimpose their conservative religious values on the leaders and laws of the United States of America. It is not new, and it is not entirely white. Los Angeles, California, talk-show-host-turned-politician Larry Elder, North Carolina's Lt. Governor Mark Robinson from Greensboro, and evangelical pastor Mark Burns of Easley, South Carolina, reflect a vocal Black presence among American leaders who most enthusiastically espouse white Christian nationalism. It is ironic, but obviously true, that some conservative Black Christians, and other Christians of color, can erase from their minds and memories the racist violence embedded, and active to this day, in the white supremacist foundations of Christian nationalism.

White Christian nationalism didn't begin with Trump's administration or even with the strong influence of the revered Christian evangelical leader of the twentieth century, Billy Graham, who was special counsel to every U.S. president from Harry Truman to Barack Obama. The movement is rooted in the presumption that certain Christians—in the United States, especially over the past seventy-five years, white conservative evangelicals—are spiritually obligated to use their powers of persuasion, and coercion, if necessary, to shape and eventually lead the government of the United States in all three of its branches—executive, legislative, and judicial. This narrow, militant Christian vision of a great and righteous nation, insisting on its own definition of righteousness, means to exclude other religions, dissenting political opinions, and all who live and think outside its view of Christianity and of what a truly Christian nation should look like.

Hence, white Christian nationalism is inherently authoritarian, not democratic. Free and fair elections are the chief enemy of Christian nationalism because the leaders of state do not want all people to vote, only those who agree with them. This pivots us back to the insurrection at the U.S. Capitol on January 6, 2021, where an authoritarian leader and his followers refused to accept the results of a free and fair election—only because their man had lost. This was much in keeping with long-standing assumptions among Republican strategists. Four decades earlier, in 1980, Paul Weyrich, a chief architect of both white Christian nationalism and the modern GOP, told an audience of evangelicals meeting in Dallas, "I don't want everybody to vote. Elections are not won by a majority of people. They never have been from the beginning of our country, and they are not now. As a matter of fact, our leverage in the elections quite candidly goes up as the voting population goes down."[1]

A BRIEF HISTORY

Strong threads of white Christian nationalism can be detected throughout U.S. history, beginning with the attitudes and actions of white Christian Pilgrims and Puritans toward the Native peoples who lived in the Americas in the seventeenth century. The Christian assumption that the Indians were "heathens," unworthy of respect and undeserving of life or liberty on their own terms, was the first major white Christian nationalist assault on America, a violent movement that eventually would lead to the Trail of Tears in the mid-nineteenth century.

As early as 1619, the first Africans had been transported in chains to become slaves for the first settlement of white British settlers in Jamestown, Virginia.[2] This was the first of many unspeakably violent middle passages across the Atlantic of human chattel from West Africa to the eastern coast of the new American colonies. Like Native Americans, the Africans would be deemed heathen by their Christian masters and unworthy of treatment as human beings. In slavery, white Christian nationalism continued to burrow itself into American soil.

Almost two centuries later, with Native Americans and African slaves established as less than fully human—the opposite of white man's view of himself—the white male "founders" would declare, in 1776, a Declaration of Independence for the colonies. A decade later, they would craft a Constitution in shared belief that the United States would be governed by white men of European descent, mostly Christian, who would shape the new nation according to the values they had brought from Europe. The race and gender of the emerging republic's leaders did not have to be stated. White Euro-American males simply assumed themselves to be the rulers of the new nation, although the Declaration's framers, including slave owner Thomas Jefferson, may have intuited expanded interpretations of the phrase "all men are created equal."[3]

One of the most significant and prescient values enshrined by the founders of the nation was that the American colonies would have no official religion.[4] In other words, America would not be a Christian nation, even though most of its leaders were white Christian men. Irrespective of religion, white wealthy men could share in ruling the new country, because unlike in England, America's leaders would not be beholden to any King or "established" religion. The U.S. president's religion, or lack thereof, was not deemed relevant to the founders of the United States (yet we've never had a non-Christian president). All Americans could live free of religious tyranny because their government would have no interest or say in their spiritual life. This was spelled out in the establishment clause of the First Amendment to the Constitution. Going forward, at least in theory, neither the United States government nor any particular religion would be obligated to the other.

From the beginning, therefore, America has been a complicated case in relation to white Christian nationalism. On the one hand, the white Christian men who first arrived in this new land in 1607 brutalized Native men and women as less than human and as unworthy heathens. The violence of the early European settlers against Native or Indigenous Americans and Africans was steeped in assumptions both about Christianity, in which non-Europeans and non-Christians were less than human, and about America, which was being established by white men for white men. On the other hand, almost two hundred years later, on December 15, 1791, the framers of our democratic republic crafted the First Amendment to the U.S. Constitution, in which they signaled an official distance between the government of the United States from the beliefs and moral practices of Christians and other religious believers.

Because of the long-standing legal tradition of separating church and state, America has not been an easy target for white Christian nationalists. Still, throughout our nation's history, many white Christians with traditional, conservative values in realms of family, race, culture, gender, sex, and the economic rights of the individual white male have sought to bring American law—and the whole of American culture—into alignment with their own religious values. Arguably the most consequential example of this effort over the past two centuries of American history was the expansionist movement that flew under the banner of Manifest Destiny. John L. O'Sullivan, editor and Democratic politician, coined the term in 1845, proclaiming America's "manifest destiny to overspread and to possess the whole of the continent which Providence has given us for the development of the great experiment of Liberty and federal self-government entrusted to us."[5]

Spiritual Motives

Because such Christians have believed that America has always been in fact a Christian nation, even if not by legal mandate, it follows that new Americans ought to be Christians, or so the reasoning goes. These devotees to the shaping of America by Christian values like the sanctity of the nuclear family and the headship of its father often have believed that it is their moral duty to make America a more fully and explicitly Christian nation.

A *spiritual* devotion to keeping America great is currently in ascendance and has been, from time to time, throughout American history. A "great America" is, by definition, a country dominated by white affluent men who, for the most part, are conservative Protestant Christians, with conservative Catholics, Orthodox, and Jews permitted alongside as long as they support the political, spiritual, and economic aims of conservative evangelical Protestantism. This strong spiritual devotion not to any one church but rather to a strong, godly America is one-half of the historical impetus for white Christian nationalism. Its threads can be traced to the founding of this nation—never officially but no less strongly in the framers' assumption that a providential God had led the settlers to the American shores and had been continually at work shaping a godly nation.

Throughout the first couple hundred years following the arrival of Pilgrims and Puritans on the Atlantic coast, American settlers embodied a sturdy determination to make the most of the new land and eventually the new nation that they had "discovered" and taken away from the Native peoples. A prevailing attitude among the settlers was that only an almighty God could have enabled them to subdue and sanctify the new continent. Such a God, in whose almighty image the white male settlers and founders saw themselves, knew no bounds in relation to territorial expansion and domination of land and people.

In the nineteenth century, two major turning points in white Christian nationalism took place: One was the arrival of the Industrial Revolution with its machinery, including trains, which revolutionized transportation and the American economy, lightening the burden of working men and horses. The other was the Civil War, which brought an end to the economic institution of slavery and revealed a struggle between theological assumptions about the nature of God in whose image all—or only some—men are created equal. These developments pushed white Christian men into spiritual reckoning. Not having to do the work of machines, Christian men feared that they, or their sons and grandsons, were in danger of becoming too soft, losing a sense of their manhood. With the Confederacy's defeat, many Southern white Christian men—and their sympathizers in the North—lost confidence in the God whom they had believed would give them victory over the Union troops, who were fighting to deprive them of their slaves and, thus, their livelihoods as well as their culture and ultimately their faith. This confluence of the fear that machines were replacing men, and the fear that the South's devotion to a slavery economy and culture was a "lost cause," generated a new breed of white Christian nationalist evangelists at the dawn of the twentieth century: white men devoted to preaching and teaching about a God who had chosen America to be his country, an America singled out and blessed by an omnipotent Father God.

Into the midst of America's dominant white cultural mood slid a former major-league baseball player. Billy Sunday was the most famous evangelist in America in the early decades of the twentieth century. He is said to have remarked that any parade or procession marching behind an American flag and the Christian cross could only be good. Most of Sunday's preaching took place in highly emotional revivals in tents and other outside venues, where he would run from one end of the speaker's platform to the other, sometimes sliding toward the podium as if it were a base on a ball field. He believed that individualism, capitalism, and patriotism especially in a time of war were essential to God's plan for America. Billy Sunday was not, however, entirely devoted to conservative policies, such as child labor and eugenics. In fact, his authentic Christian zeal was probably more basic to his life's ministry than his devotion to the country or its economic system; nonetheless he preached enthusiastically that God had bestowed special rights and privileges on the individual white Christian American male.[6]

At about the same time, in response to the inequities of the Gilded Age and the momentum of labor unions that were growing stronger, the latter part of the nineteenth century and early decades of the twentieth had given birth to the social gospel movement. This group of progressive white Christian theologians and ministers included Baptist pastor Walter Rauschenbusch who, in 1917, set forth the theological foundations of the movement in *A Theology for the Social Gospel*.[7] Believing that God intends the kingdom of God to take shape on earth through collective human efforts for justice, the social gospel movement encouraged the government of the United States to assume responsibility for the economic opportunities and well-being of all Americans, still assumed legally to be white people, principally men. This liberal religious movement had contributed some momentum to the 1932 presidential victory of Franklin Roosevelt over Herbert Hoover, under whose conservative economic policies the United States had been plagued by the Great Depression of the late 1920s.

Economic Motives

If half of the impetus for white Christian nationalism in twentieth-century America was genuinely *spiritual*—as in the evangelistic efforts of conservatives like Billy Sunday and liberals like Walter Rauschenbusch—the other half was *economic*. The most intense, methodical push by business interests for a Christian nation took root in a fierce reaction among business leaders against the New Deal economics of President Franklin Roosevelt in mid-twentieth-century America. Throughout the 1940s and 1950s, a campaign against the progressivism of the New Deal was waged by economic and religious leaders in alliance with each other. In the words of industrialist Alfred Haake, speaking in 1945 to the National Association of Manufacturers, "Religious leaders must be helped to see that their callings are threatened. . . . The collectivism of the New Deal, with its glorification of the state, is really a denial of God."[8]

While a case can be made for either group—business executives or Christian evangelists—as leader of the "spiritual mobilization" movement, the fact seems to have been that religious spokesmen like Rev. James W. Fifield Jr., pastor of the prominent First Congregational Church of Los Angeles and economic leaders like J. Howard Pew of Sun Oil Company realized that they needed each other to successfully market their respective products: religious growth and economic prosperity. For example Pew warned Americans against social and political liberalism: "A large percentage of ministers in this country are completely ignorant of economic matters and have used their pulpits for the purpose of disseminating socialistic and totalitarian doctrines."[9] Working in tandem, conservative Christians and business leaders organized political resistance to Franklin Roosevelt's populist, socialist economic expansion of the federal government's role and hostility also to his wife Eleanor's relentless drive for racial and gender justice.

As a result of the spiritual mobilization movement of the 1940s and subsequently the "freedom under God" celebrations in the 1950s, Congress added "under God" to the previously secular Pledge of Allegiance in 1954. Throughout the federal government, Christian religiosity was in vogue. Billy Graham's "Crusades" popped up everywhere across the nation. Religious and economic interests had merged in an immensely popular and, for white people, a less violent version of what Americans are experiencing today, the white Christian nationalism of the 2020s.

On a personal note: In 1959, as a fourteen-year-old Christian girl seeking spiritual meaning, I attended a Crusade and "gave my life to Christ" in the Charlotte, North Carolina, Coliseum. I don't remember who I was with at the time—my parents maybe, because both admired Billy Graham, or maybe a couple of my friends, who were also devout Christian girls. In any case, my decision was a spontaneous response to Graham's charisma. No one accompanied me from my seat to the front of the stage into the midst of an enthusiastic crowd of seekers. I recall being given a flyer with some information, I assume, about what believers in Jesus Christ should do next. I have no memory of what the flyer said or of how it all ended, other than that I was happy enough to have attended the Billy Graham Crusade, given my life to Christ, and been up close to the immensely charming and compelling white male evangelist.

During the 1930s and 1940s, the white Christian nationalist movement had grown in popularity through the power of radio evangelists like Charles E. Fuller, whose *Old Fashioned Revival Hour* at its peak was broadcast on more than six hundred stations, and the founding of conservative Christian colleges like Bob Jones University in Greenville, South Carolina. Democrats and Republicans, richer and poorer, for the most part Christian and almost entirely white, came together for parades, sporting events, and holiday celebrations in 1950s America to salute and celebrate "one nation under God." Public figures with amiable images, representing corporate and religious America, could march together and stand on podiums side by side, almost always white men—Jimmy Stewart, Billy Graham, Walt Disney, J. C. Penney. Added to these cultural icons was the handsome figure of General Douglas McArthur, who had been scorned by President Harry Truman. In the early 1950s, McArthur had become a symbol of the U.S. war machine, able and ready to defend his country. In white Christian America, being a tall, white, good-looking, macho, Christian man is always a plus, and it turned the stately looking general into an icon of conservative Christian America.

Christian Nationalism in America since 1950

In 1982, Austrian school economist and leading figure in the Christian reconstructionist movement Gary North wrote:

> We must use the doctrine of religious liberty . . . until we train up a generation of people who know there is no religious neutrality, no neutral law, no neutral education, and no neutral civil government. Then they will get busy constructing a Bible-based social, political, and religious order which finally denies the religious liberty of the enemies of God.[10]

This section on characters, events, movements, and decisions spanning almost three-quarters of a century is meant to highlight some of the factors in American history that have evoked either strong affirmation or emphatic condemnation by those who are most fully invested in the basic premise of white Christian nationalism—that America is meant, by its "founders" and by God, to be a nation led by, and accountable to, conservative white Christian men. This section, like most chapters in this book, could be expanded into a book of its own. My choices of which people, social struggles, and court rulings to name here have been determined by my choices of which sins to explore in part 2. Many other significant dates, people, and movements could have been named.

J. Edgar Hoover and the McCarthy Hearings

White conservative evangelical Christians, supported by the alliance of corporate interests and Republican politics, have continued to mount an intense battle for America's families over the past seventy-five years.[11] The 1950s were a happy moment for these white Christians in America. Nonetheless, a stable postwar economy, combined with public crusades and celebrations of a God who had blessed America, provided the perfect backdrop for the anti-Communist, pro-Christian witch hunt launched by Wisconsin senator Joseph McCarthy, with the encouragement of the paranoid FBI director J. Edgar Hoover.

Over several decades, and buoyed for a brief period in 1954 by the McCarthy hearings on un-American activities, Hoover took it upon himself to clean up America, to rid the nation of subversive elements, including Communist sympathizers and American socialists, homosexuals,[12] and Black leaders. All were caricatured as threatening not only to America as a nation but also to conservative white Christian principles that were steeped in allegiance to an all-powerful God, an unchanging stable country, and the centrality of the patriarchal nuclear family.

The Civil Rights Movement

Against the reactionary racism, sexism, heterosexism and classism of J. Edgar Hoover's agenda, the civil rights movement that had been growing behind the scenes of white America for a long time launched itself publicly in Rosa Parks's strategic refusal on December 1, 1955, to go the back of the bus in Montgomery, Alabama. The civil rights movement became the central force for change in America for over a decade—until the assassinations of Malcolm X on February 21, 1965, in New York City, and three years later Martin Luther King Jr., on April 4, 1968, in Memphis, Tennessee. The

March on Washington on August 28, 1963, became a symbol overnight of civil rights, and King's "I Have a Dream" speech became an icon of what the movement was all about.

Many white Americans, including Christians, participated in the civil rights movement, believing it to be, as it was, a vibrant, morally motivated, struggle for equal rights and freedom for Black Americans. By the time of his violent death, Dr. King had been hailed as a hero by nearly all Black Americans and many white Americans too. That he was a Christian leader, a preacher, a man of faith in Jesus, made an enormous difference to white and Black Americans' perceptions of not only his courage but also his moral integrity. Martin Luther King seemed to be like American Christians in all the ways that matter most, including being Christian.

Malcolm X and Muhammad Ali

Malcolm X had been perceived differently, at least through white eyes. He was not like us, and not like Dr. King. Most white Americans continue even now to be unaware of his significance and his appeal, especially to Black Americans in the North, many—like Malcolm himself—who had converted from Christianity to Islam. White Christian Americans did not understand this, and still to this day do not. Why would any patriotic American convert from Christianity to Islam?

Despite the fact that Malcolm X was one of the chief architects of Black Americans' refusal to make peace with their own oppression, his conversion to Islam moved him beyond the pale for most white Christian Americans, even liberals. A year before the assassination of Malcolm X, heavyweight boxer and soon-to-be Vietnam War resister Cassius Clay converted from Christianity to Islam and was given the name Muhammad Ali by Elijah Muhammad, head of the Nation of Islam, better known among most Americans as Black Muslims. In the 1960s, most white Americans feared Malcolm X for calling Black people to armed struggle against their "white devils" oppressors—and feared Muhammad Ali for refusing to fight against the people of Vietnam who, as he noted in a press conference, had never called him a "n----r."[13]

Indeed. Why would a Christian convert to Islam if not to destroy everything good about America? This was, and is, a very white question. All along white Americans have had trouble grasping the horrors of white supremacy, the violence that white people actually have done to Black bodies and souls. That is why white American Christians cannot comprehend either the logic or the morality of a choice to convert from Christianity to Islam. We have great difficulty acknowledging that Black people might well be attracted to a religion that not only does not demonize or degrade their Blackness but moreover lifts up their Blackness as holy.

Through most of American history, white Christians have claimed to be against most armed struggle and violence (hence, against Malcolm X). They had no trouble, however, condemning Muhammad Ali for refusing to take up arms against the Vietnamese. It all depends on who targets whom. For white Christian nationalists, armed struggle even against fellow Americans is a worthy undertaking if the targets are Black, brown, Asian, Native, queer, feminist, Communist, socialist, liberal, atheist, Jewish, Muslim, Buddhist, pagan, or some "other" sorts of people deemed hostile to conservative white male–dominated American Christian interests. In later chapters, we will examine some intersections of violence with other deadly sins of white Christian nationalism.

The Vietnam War

Not long after the passage of major civil rights legislation in the mid-1960s, President Lyndon Johnson found himself in big trouble over his failure to end America's ill-begotten war against Vietnam, a small country in Southeast Asia that Johnson and Presidents Eisenhower and Kennedy before him had feared was in danger of falling into the Communist orbits of China and Russia, thus becoming a gateway into Communism for other small Asian countries. It took twenty years (1955–1975), the loss of more than three million Vietnamese people, and the deaths of more than fifty-eight thousand American soldiers, for the Vietnamese Communists, inspired by Ho Chi Minh (1890–1969), to win the war.

The loss of the Vietnam War was a significant setback to the rise of white Christian nationalism in America. Symbolically, the loss of this major war against Communism—or socialism, as most Americans wrongly equate them—signaled America's military vulnerability. America and our allies had won World War II by using planes and bombs and long-distance weaponry. In Vietnam, we were not very apt as guerilla warriors, fighting on foot, navigating alien terrain, needing to win not only hand-to-hand combat but also the minds and hearts of the people in villages and countryside. America's loss of the Vietnam War was a huge blow to our national pride as a military force to be reckoned with around the globe.

Moreover, for some conservative American Christian fundamentalists, their nation's defeat by Vietnam punctured their faith in a God who, they believed, had blessed America and was always on our side. How could a godly nation have lost that war? Our loss in Vietnam at the hands of non-Christian and non-white Communists was an assault on the most basic of our white Christian nationalist sensibilities. Worst of all, many Americans blamed our defeat on the rebellious youth culture of godless liberal idealists who had taken to the streets of our cities to mount protests and even, in some cases, to side with America's enemy: "Ho, Ho, Ho Chi Minh, Viet Cong are gonna win!" was a common chant among anti–Vietnam War protesters. The American government, peopled primarily by middle-aged white Christian men, Democrats and Republicans alike, was angered by the offensive, sacrilegious rebellion on the part of America's youth, sometimes their own kids. And we young Americans were even angrier at the president's and Congress's failure to stand for justice and peace, not only in our own nation but across the Pacific in Vietnam, values rooted in the aspirational American dream of seeking liberty and justice for all.

Looking back, as one of the young people of that era, I believe the turmoil of the Vietnam War and the protests against it in American streets shook the foundations of white Christian nationalism. From the mid-1970s on, those committed to building a white Christian America—conservative business, Christian, and political leaders together—had to redouble their efforts to beat back the "elites"—that is to say, liberals, young people, African Americans, academics, artists, Jews, Muslims, and people of other spiritual traditions. The elites were those who believed that we often knew better than our leaders what was good and right not only for the United States of America but also for the rest of the world. From the end of the Vietnam War to this day, white Christian nationalists have been dead set against the liberal elite.

That was almost fifty years ago. Much has happened in the last half century to secure both the aims of white Christian nationalism and its opposition among Americans. We could think together about what difference in this history has been made by such signature events as the 1972 Watergate break-in and the fall of President Richard Nixon in its wake. We could think about the Supreme Court's 1973 *Roe v. Wade* decision, which sparked a firestorm of misogynistic reaction against the empowerment of American women. We could consider how the feminist, womanist, and LGBTQ movements of the 1970s, 1980s, and 1990s affected ongoing tensions between the "make America white, male, and strong again" proponents and the rest of us. We could ponder why public worries about the proliferation of nuclear weapons, the growing epidemic of gun violence in America, and the climate change challenges facing the whole earth today do not seem to interest those Americans most devoted to keeping America white and Christian. Most of these issues and questions we will return to in later chapters.

Brown v. Board of Education (1954) and Roe v. Wade (1973)

In the latter half of the twentieth century, two Supreme Court decisions in particular enraged proponents of white supremacy and women's rights.

Brown v. Board of Education ruled in 1954 that segregated public schools are unconstitutional, and *Roe v. Wade* determined in 1973 that women have a constitutional right to abortion without undue government restriction. Both of these legal rulings were far reaching in their practical, life-changing implications for Americans of all races and cultures and for American women and girls. But these rulings also made a lasting impact on America's political landscape, in which racial segregation and male control of women's bodies had previously been held sacred and simply assumed by significant numbers of American Christians.

In the wake of the *Brown* decision in 1954, many conservative American Christians set out to find ways around having to send their children to integrated schools. Private secular as well as religious schools and, later, the homeschooling movement came to life as a result of the court's decision to integrate schools. And while abortion had never been a contentious political issue and had previously been supported by as many Republicans as Democrats, the passage of *Roe v. Wade* became a political football which the Republican Party decided to run with in the aftermath of the Civil Rights Act (1964) and the Voting Rights Act (1965), which had legally toppled white conservative America's last defenses against "Black power." It is worth noting, as this book enters its final editing, two urgent matters: (1) the failure of the U.S Senate to enact voting legislation that would safeguard the votes of Black, brown, elderly, and other marginalized Americans; and (2) the Supreme Court's likely overturning of its own 1973 Roe v. Wade decision, thereby endangering the lives and well-being of American women and girls. Both of these contemptuous actions—by the Senate and the Supreme Court—reflect the power of white Christian nationalism in contemporary America.

The Reagan Administration

No single presidential election and administration in the last seventy-five years played a greater role in setting the stage for the heralding of capitalist spirituality—the idolatry of the individual and his right to wealth and power—than the 1980 victory of Ronald Reagan and his widely acclaimed "trickle-down" economic theory. This neoclassical theory, which was being taught by the Chicago school of economics and embraced by Reagan and UK prime minister Margaret Thatcher, assumed that an unregulated market would produce great wealth that, in turn, would trickle down to the unwealthy majority of citizens. Reagan's trickle-down economic policies were the Republicans' answer to Franklin Roosevelt's New Deal. Beginning in 1981 and lasting until the election in 2020 of Joe Biden, even America's Democratic presidents—Bill Clinton and Barack Obama—in order to win, had to cozy up to the wealthiest Americans so as not to offend the corporate interests that Reagan and his Republican Party had cultivated. "Reaganomics"—the policies of keeping taxes low on corporate America and regulations few on American businesses—planted seeds for the rise of poverty and alienation among working white Americans, which was also a fertile ground for white Christian nationalism. By the late 1980s, American Republicans had become experts at scapegoating Black Americans and other people of color for the rising anxieties of poor and working-class white Americans who were unable to enjoy the upward mobility they had long believed was their due.

Abolishing the Fairness Doctrine[14]

In 1987, Congress abolished the Fairness Doctrine of the Federal Communications Commission (FCC) that had been established in 1949 to ensure that both or all sides of controversial issues would receive fair treatment in broadcast media. In doing away with this doctrine, the door was opened to savvy broadcast gurus like Rush Limbaugh and media giants like Rupert Murdoch to gather the money necessary to take up as much time and broadcast space as possible. There is ongoing debate about whether to attempt to revive the Fairness Doctrine, and whether, or how, this could happen in the age of the internet and social media like Facebook. Democrats, including Senators Chuck Schumer of New York and Debbie Stabenow of Michigan, have advocated a consideration of its renewal. There is no question that the elimination of such legal, enforceable guidelines by the FCC has had major implications for the prevalence of fake news, the spread of lies, the promulgation of conspiracy theories increasingly in the mainstream of American politics and American media, and the cultivation of white Christian nationalism's high media profile.

9/11 and the Wars in Afghanistan and Iraq

I was honestly surprised to learn that, according to the Pew Research Center,[15] the terrorist attacks on America on September 11, 2001, made no significant difference on Americans' attitudes toward religion, either our own religions or those of others. Twenty years after the attacks, *Christianity Today* reports that Christians and other people of faith became neither more nor less observant in their practices.[16] Reflecting on these observations, I realize there has seemed to be relatively scant commentary on either the religious or political repercussions of 9/11. Certainly, it was neither the beginning nor the end of terrorist attacks on American soil by religious extremists from either outside or inside our country. But 9/11 was without a doubt the most dramatic assault on Americans at home by outside forces, and it has played a massive role in

shaping our consciousness. As Americans, we were horrified by the sudden-
ness, shape, and scale of the violence. We were stunned by the use of com-
mercial airliners as missiles, and the events of the day showed us the extent
of our vulnerability as a nation, as Americans.

As Christians, many of us—more liberal as well as more conservative—
had to reckon with our faith at least momentarily. Many of us probably
wondered, though few of us asked out loud, where was God on the morning
of September 11, 2001? We assumed God was with all the victims—but who
were all the victims? Surely the victims of this terror attack were the people in
the planes and buildings that toppled and their families, but were the victims
not also Islamic people throughout the world, including the families of the
terrorists?

Remarkably, media-hungry evangelists blamed America's liberals for the attack:

The Rev Jerry Falwell and Pat Robertson set off a minor explosion of their own
when they asserted on US television that an angry God had allowed the terrorists to succeed in their deadly mission because the United States had become a
nation of abortion, homosexuality, secular schools and courts, and the American
civil liberties union.[17]

It was no doubt hard for conservative evangelical Christians to imagine
the role of God in the September 11 attacks. What on earth was God doing,
and why? These questions had to be pressing against the assumption that God
has blessed America, that America is somehow God's chosen land. Those
Christians most dedicated to their image of America as a white Christian
nation would have been badly shaken—and surely emboldened in their desire
to rid America of its enemies, including darker peoples, Muslims, "foreigners," and others whom they deemed to be ungodly or unpatriotic. I had little
doubt then, and still today, that Falwell and Robertson were speaking on
behalf of other white Christian nationalists.

By far, America's most significant and lasting response to the 9/11 attack
was to wage war in Afghanistan in our search for Osama bin Laden—whom
we captured and killed in Pakistan in 2011—and to remain in Afghanistan
for twenty years. It was almost as if we forgot we were there, which the
American people more or less did when President George W. Bush made the
foolish decision to invade Iraq, supposedly seeking to destroy "weapons of
mass destruction," which actually did not exist. The war in Iraq, launched in
2003, ignited a firestorm of reaction against America throughout the Middle
East. More than at any time since Vietnam, America's image abroad—as a
gratuitously violent bully—was widely shared by friend and foe alike.

The two wars waged early in the twenty-first century—in Afghanistan and Iraq—have shaped the minds, bodies, and hearts of a couple of generations of young American men and women. Many millennials (born after 1981) got to know these wars personally, some serving multiple rotations over the years. At least five thousand American soldiers lost their lives, and many thousands more returned home badly wounded mentally as well as physically.

Among the lessons learned by soldiers is how to use weapons, how to be part of a team, and the importance of showing respect for authority and following the command of superiors. Still another lasting and important lesson from war is how to be a faithful friend. Throughout American history, such lessons have served veterans and their county well, because they are important lessons when exercised in reasonable, humane, and moral ways. From the wars in Afghanistan and Iraq, however, many veterans came home terribly disabused—angry about what they had experienced, confused about why they had been there, and feeling out of place or lost upon reentry into a country that had little to offer them in terms of work, security, or hope for the future.

More than anything, 9/11 and the wars it spawned cemented our perceptions as Americans and Christians of an "us vs. them" view of both our nation and, perhaps to a lesser degree, our religion. For the past twenty years, we have acted like a nation afraid—of brown and Black immigrants, of "others" who are not like "us"; a nation ripe for picking by a con artist politician seeking fame and fortune who came promising to build a big, beautiful wall to protect us from those "others" bringing crime, disease, and destruction to America. Donald J. Trump and his base of true believing white Christian nationalists was a toxic gift from 9/11 to the American people.

Obama's Election and Presidency (2008–2016)

One primary event that must be named here as we review the history of white Christian nationalism in America is the election in 2008 of Obama as America's first Black president. We should not underestimate the fear and horror struck by the election of Barack Hussein Obama in the hearts of every man and woman in this county who could not imagine living under the authority of a Black president. What had happened was unthinkable and unacceptable to a minority of American citizens, including many white Christians. Much of what has happened in American politics since the inauguration of Barack Obama in January 2009 has been motivated at least in part by the refusal of significant numbers of American Christians to accept even the possibility that the stranglehold of white male power on America might be broken.

Domestic Terrorists: Hate Groups, Online
Connections, and Violent Lone Rangers

It should come as no surprise, according to the Southern Poverty Law Center,[18] that hate groups, including white nationalist groups, proliferated under both the Obama and Trump administrations, but for different reasons. In reaction against Obama, hatred rose out of fear and fury about the audacity of having a Black man in the White House; under Trump, this same white hatred was stirred by the president to secure his own power. During the Trump presidency, in-person meetings of groups devoted to white supremacy, misogyny, homophobia, anti-Semitism, anti-Muslim and other forms of hate began to ebb, probably because more hatred and disinformation has become available online and it has been less risky to meet online than in person to plan activities. Hate group watchdog organizations such as the Southern Poverty Law Center and the Counter Extremism Project warn, however, not only of online organizing but also of the violent "lone ranger" activities of right-wing shooters and bombers like antigovernment activists and Iraq War veterans Timothy McVeigh and Terry Nichols, who in 1995 bombed the Oklahoma City Federal Building, killing 168 people, including 19 children. More recently, in 2015, twenty-one-year-old Dylann Roof massacred nine black worshippers with whom he had just joined in Bible study in the sanctuary of Charleston's Mother Emmanuel Church, and in 2020, Kyle Rittenhouse, a seventeen-year-old white boy, shot three people, killing two of them, in Kenosha, Wisconsin, during the protests against the police shooting of a young Black man, Jacob Blake.

During the insurrection at the Capitol on January 6, 2021, groups like the Proud Boys, 3 Percenters, Boogaloo Bois, and others who have been embraced by Trump and his coterie, signaled a public "f---you" to what Obama had stood for—making America a more diverse, inclusive, and just nation in which Martin Luther King Jr.'s dream of a nation might actually come true, a nation in which "little black boys and black girls will be able to join hands with little white boys and white girls as sisters and brothers."[19]

KEY SUPREME COURT DECISIONS IN THE
EARLY TWENTY-FIRST CENTURY

Citizens United (2010): Decision on Unlimited
Money in American Politics

The always dynamic, often tense, relationship between church and state in America changed dramatically for the worse in January 2010, when the

Supreme Court of the United States ruled, in *Citizens United v. The Federal Elections Commission*, that there is no limit to the amount of money that corporations can contribute to political campaigns. The effect of *Citizens United* has been to unleash massive outpourings of money by corporations and the wealthiest people in America into the political process to persuade politicians to do their bidding—mostly "dark," unacknowledged—are living in a nation today in which big money sets political agendas, picks legislators, and essentially buys their votes. *Citizens United* has enabled big money to set the stage, choose the actors, and write the script for American presidents, legislators, and judges.[20]

To understand how *Citizens United* has affected the rise of white Christian nationalism over the past decade, it is important to realize that white Christian nationalism has become increasingly an effort to achieve power—political and economic power. Flaunting a love of Jesus or declaring faithfulness to God's Word have become means by which white Christian nationalists reach their goal, which is not heaven but rather to leverage wealth and power to control the nation via its elected officials, their legislation, and their appointments of judges and Supreme Court justices. We need to understand that having and giving large sums of money to powerful people is how Americans—including American Christians—amass power and over time secure control of the government, the economy, and the culture.

Lawrence (2003), *Windsor* (2013), and *Obergefell* (2015): Decisions on Gay Rights

In each of these cases, the majority of the Supreme Court sided with those seeking to expand rather than limit the constitutional rights of lesbians, gay men, and bisexuals in America. In the 2003 *Lawrence* case, the court struck down sodomy laws that had made gay sex illegal. Ten years later, in its 2013 *Windsor* decision, the court struck down the portion of the Defense of Marriage Act (DOMA) that had denied federal recognition to same-sex marriages. And in 2015, the *Obergefell* decision held that all states must permit same-sex marriage and recognize same-sex marriages that have taken place in other states. Taken together, these three decisions by the Supreme Court, stretching only a little over a decade, were like a turbulent sea building up and then crashing like a tsunami upon conservative Christian values in America and shattering the hallowed tradition of marriage. Nothing except women's reproductive freedom and gun safety efforts have sparked such fierce resistance from the Christian Right and its political allies throughout federal and state governments.

Heller (2008) and *McDonald* (2010): Decisions on the Second Amendment

Along with women's reproductive freedom and LGBTQ rights, nothing has sparked such fierce resistance from the Christian Right and its political allies throughout federal and state governments than efforts to secure gun control in America. The Second Amendment and what it's taken to mean—"my right to bear arms"—has generated massive support among a hefty minority of Americans, including white Christian nationalists. The Second Amendment supporters were emboldened by the Supreme Court's *Heller* decision in 2008, in which the majority granted a resident of Washington, DC, the right to own and keep a gun in his home. Two years later, in its 2010 *McDonald* ruling, the court basically reaffirmed this same right to residents of Chicago. Although the Supreme Court's gun decisions have been narrow and by no means have given gun owners legal permission to own or bear any arms they wish anywhere they wish, Second Amendment advocates act as if they can do exactly that. With Trump's three appointments to the Supreme Court between 2017 and 2020, the court is likely to expand gun rights if given a chance to do so.

The Second Amendment continues to be a major political and legal priority for the most extreme right-wing Americans, many conservative Christians among them. For such Christians, the right to bear arms tends to signal "my" right to be free, "my" God-given right, "my" right to protect myself and my family. Among those most determined to protect the Second Amendment from any gun measures, there is no creative tension between the rights of the individual to bear arms and the rights of the larger community to be safe from gun violence. The individual has the rights. The larger community is nothing more than a bunch of gun-toting folks at a church picnic.

Shelby County (AL) v. Holder (2013): Decision on Voting Rights

In a closely divided decision, Chief Justice John Roberts sided with his four most conservative colleagues to vote that a particular section of the 1965 Voting Rights Act was unconstitutional. The court ruled as unconstitutional the specific criteria that had been used since 1965 to determine which counties and states were in compliance with the voting rights mandates that had been established by Congress. Essentially, Justice Roberts, writing for the majority, said that the criteria that Congress deemed necessary in the 1960s and 1970s were outdated, no longer needed to ensure voting rights. However, in the 2020's, as white supremacists in more than two dozen states are attempting to unravel our electoral processes for the purpose of suppressing Black votes, it is obvious how terribly wrong the majority of the SCOTUS was in the *Shelby* case.

Hobby Lobby (2014): Decision on a Christian Family's Right to Deny Birth Control Insurance to Its Employees

In its 2014 *Burwell v. Hobby Lobby* case, the Supreme Court ruled 5–4 in favor of Hobby Lobby, a craft store owned by a Christian family who, on the basis of religion, had objected to paying for insurance to cover women's birth control. In a blistering dissent, Associate Justice Ruth Bader Ginsburg wrote:

> Would the exemption . . . extend to employers with religiously grounded objections to blood transfusions (Jehovah's Witnesses); antidepressants (Scientologists); medications derived from pigs, including anesthesia, intravenous fluids, and pills coated with gelatin (certain Muslims, Jews, and Hindus); and vaccinations . . . ? Approving some religious claims while deeming others unworthy of accommodation could be "perceived as favoring one religion over another," the very "risk" the [Constitution's] Establishment Clause was designed to preclude. . . . The court, I fear, has ventured into a minefield.[21]

Ginsburg writes that the court may be "perceived as favoring one religion over another"—Christianity. Indeed. What Ginsburg does not say here explicitly, but what her long tenure on the bench as an advocate for women warned, is that the Supreme Court of the United States has revealed its misogyny, its transparent contempt for women, in the *Hobby Lobby* decision. In 2014, five men—four of them white Catholic Christians—interpreted the U.S. Constitution so as to handicap American women. This particular case—both the Christian family's complaint against having to pay for women's birth control and the Supreme Court's agreement with this family—painted a picture of white Christian nationalism in action. Ginsburg feared the court had "ventured into a minefield."

Vigilante Justice for Texas Women

In 2021, with three new conservative justices on the Supreme Court, Ruth Bader Ginsburg's fear, which she voiced in her 2014 dissent to the *Hobby Lobby* decision, is being realized beyond what would have been the now-deceased justice's wildest dreams. What would she think of the high court's granting permission in 2021 to Texas's system of vigilante justice, in which citizens are encouraged to track down women who've had abortions as well as people who've helped them and sue each woman and helper for $10,000? I can hear RBG's spirit in the dissent Sonia Sotomayor, her gutsy colleague, to the *Whole Women's Health v. Jackson (TX)* ruling: "Presented with an application to enjoin a flagrantly unconstitutional law engineered to prohibit women from exercising their constitutional rights and evade judicial scrutiny, a majority of Justices have opted to bury their heads in the sand."[22]

THE PANDEMIC AND THE BIG LIE

There is no way of overstating the significance of COVID-19's arrival in America sometime late in 2019 or its trivialization by the president of the United States, who was far more concerned with his 2020 election prospects than with whether his fellow citizens lived or died. Even with a benefit of doubt—that he failed to realize the seriousness of the pandemic—Trump's dismissive behavior toward Dr. Anthony Fauci and everyone else trying to solve the medical and economic problems brought on by the virus was a moral travesty. His self-centeredness in relation to the COVID crisis was amplified in his refusal to accept defeat by Joseph Biden in November 2020 and, subsequently, in his pushing of what has become known as the Big Lie: namely, that he, Donald J. Trump, did not lose the election but rather had it stolen from him by Biden and a cabal of corrupt Democrats.

As this book is being completed, both the global pandemic and the Big Lie live on, the latter exacerbating the toll of the coronavirus on the American people and the rest of humanity. Following their leader, many of Trump's most devoted followers refuse to take COVID seriously, shunning the vaccine, balking at being asked to wear masks for the protection of others, and thumbing their noses at the most reliable public health care providers and researchers in America and around the world. As for the rest of world, Trump's people, like their man, make it plain that they don't give a damn. America first! White Christian nationalism may be one of few survivors at the deadly intersection of COVID with the Big Lie.

We need to be clear that, in this dismal context, the traditional Republican Party is gone. The party of Lincoln, Teddy Roosevelt, Eisenhower, and more recently the Bushes, McCains, and Romneys has morphed into Trump's insurrectionist Republicans who are holding Americans hostage to their white Christian nationalist agenda. Today's Republican leaders are seeking to replace American democracy with an authoritarian, one-party system inspired by Russia's Putin and other autocrats around the world—and especially today, by Viktor Orban, the prime minister of Hungary. Once an atheist, more recently a self-proclaimed Christian (what can we make of that?), Orban celebrates an increasingly repressive Hungary as an "illiberal democracy," in which only certain people can vote and only certain people can win elections. He has risen to power largely through his intensely racist, anti-immigration policies that have been denounced by Pope Francis and by Hungarian-born George Soros. Orban and his followers cannot afford to be too publicly outspoken against the leader of the Roman Catholic Church, since they need Catholic support. But Orban has made no attempt to disguise his hatred of the liberal Jewish philanthropist Soros, in fanning flames of anti-Semitism and other forms of anti-immigrant bigotry in and beyond Hungary. Like Hungary, America will become an "illiberal democracy" if we do not act to stop this authoritarian slide into white Christian nationalism.

Moving on now into considering the seven deadly sins of white Christian nationalism, our challenge in this study is to try not to bury our heads in the sand—which is what white Christian nationalists would have us do. The Supreme Court of the United States may be ready to fall in behind those most determined to make America white and male and arrogant again. But whatever the high court does, and whatever actions the executive and legislative branches of our government may take, you and I have work to do, moral work with major implications for social change and transformation.

In 2020, Beth Moore, an esteemed leader in the Southern Baptist Convention, tweeted, "I do not believe these days are for mincing words. I'm 63 ½ years and I have never seen anything in these United States of America I found more astonishingly seductive and dangerous to the saints of God than Trumpism. This Christian nationalism is not of God."[23] Indeed this Christian nationalism is not of God, and it continues to grow stronger in America and in much of the world. This is the climate in which American Christians must figure out how most effectively to seek justice, love mercy, and walk humbly with God (see Mic. 6:8)—and how, in this work, to remain wise as serpents and innocent as doves (see Matt. 10:16).

PART II

The Seven Deadly Sins

Chapter 3

Sin as Our Collective Problem

It's time to talk about sin—ours, often through no fault of our own. While frequently not at personal fault, we share personal responsibility for helping heal our society that has been shattered by sin. Try to think of the chapters that follow not as "blaming" or "shaming" but as a wake-up alarm from the Spirit. No doubt this book could be caricatured as an attack on the GOP. Not at all. It is an attack on the seven deadly sins of white Christian nationalism, which have captured the hearts and minds of increasing numbers of contemporary Republicans but which fester among us all, regardless of political party. In truth, if taken to heart, lessons from these pages could help liberate all political parties and partisans in America. As many public figures have recently declared, we are all in this together.

Recent headlines in the United States include stories of Roman Catholic bishops trying to deny the Eucharist to President Biden and Southern Baptists arguing about whether their church—the largest and most socially conservative of the major Protestant denominations in the United States—is straying too far from the Bible by cautiously opening to questions about racial and gender justice. No doubt the Roman Catholic bishops and Southern Baptist conservatives believe that they are doing God's will, that in fact it is God's Spirit that propels their protests against abortion, women's rights, and the LGBTQ community.

From the perspective of most moderate and liberal Christians, like most readers of this book, such Catholic and Protestant actions, successful or not at this time, reflect ongoing resistance among many Christians to social justice in America. This chapter probes the underpinnings of this resistance—and names these underpinnings as "deadly sins." But dear readers, the deadly sins that we see so clearly in the Roman Catholic bishops and in Southern Baptist leaders are driving us as well. The sins we will be exploring are ours, not just theirs.

As has been shown earlier, much of the responsibility for our country's malaise lies at the feet of white Christian nationalism, the political goal and spiritual path of a significant number of American Christians and a major moral challenge today to all Americans who love both God and country. I am proposing that white Christian nationalism is a sinful movement rooted in seven interactive sins of a significant segment of white Christian Americans to superimpose their conservative religious values on the leaders and laws of the United States of America. More importantly to the readers of this book, I am proposing that these sins have been cultivated and held in place by all Christian churches in America.

As noted in part 1, in American history, these sins reach back into the seventeenth century and the earliest days of European settlement on the East Coast of the continent, when white European men, mainly Christians, assumed the prerogative to build a world of their own choosing on American soil. Their effort, steeped in an assumption that they and their progeny were the natural builders of the nation, stretches over four hundred years into this moment in which American historians such as Heather Cox Richardson and Jon Meacham are among a growing chorus of citizen-observers warning that our democracy is at stake. Their concern is urgent. Echoed and expanded in these pages, it was sparked by two specific ongoing contemporary events: first, the refusal of the former president and his followers to accept the legitimacy of the 2020 election and, second, his party aggressively seeking to suppress the votes of Black, brown, and young people so as to secure the Republican project to safeguard the white Christian character of this country.

Part 2 explores sins that have undergirded white Christian nationalism's hold on the imaginations and aims of significant numbers of American Christians over the course of our history, and especially during the last seventy-five years. During this period, notably since World War II, major political tensions have been ongoing between leaders like Franklin Delano Roosevelt and Martin Luther King Jr., who have wanted to make America a more just and inclusive nation, and those who have tried to keep the country largely in the hands of white Christian men, people determined to hold on to the American past. These are the men and women who have responded enthusiastically to the challenge of several American icons, including Charles Lindbergh and Ronald Reagan as well as Donald Trump, to "make America great again." Groups like Focus on the Family, universities like Bob Jones and Liberty, think tanks like the Heritage Foundation, the Family Research Council, and movements like the Promise Keepers—organized by white Christian men, with men of color scattered among them, and women in auxiliary groups—have not been shy in promoting spiritual warfare against what they believe to be the sins of secular humanism; feminism; same-gender marriage; environmental protections; government regulation of private businesses; and the full equality of Black, brown, other Americans of color, and, of course, immigrants arriving from Black, brown, and Asian countries.[1]

WHAT DO WE MEAN BY "SIN"?

For most Christians, conservative and liberal, *sin is human activity that separates us from God. It is an assault on the love of God. Sin shatters whatever goodness we might otherwise affirm and embrace.* Some Christians believe that sin originates in an evil presence or force sometimes called Satan or the Devil. Other Christians, though they may use such terms metaphorically to represent the presence of evil in history, believe that evil originates in human beings' wrong choices. Many Christians, especially conservative evangelicals, focus on sin as an individual's disobedience to God. Other Christians emphasize the social, collective root of sin as it describes a destructive dimension of the human condition, a curse structured into human society. From this perspective, sin is not simply or primarily an individual's wrongdoing. Sin belongs to the whole community. This is close to what Augustine, the Christian bishop of Hippo (in northern Africa, today's Libya) meant by "original sin," a condition common to all, which Augustine believed was passed on through sexual lust and activity. While I emphatically do not accept Augustine's theology of sexual sin as the foundation of humanity's separation from God, I concur with Augustine as well as many liberation, feminist, womanist, and queer teachers, leaders, and pastors in contemporary Christianity, that *sin is first and foremost a collective condition that shapes us individually and drives our personal choices to do right or wrong.*[2]

Understanding sin primarily as collective rather than as the personal fault of individuals is not how the seven deadly or "cardinal" sins were first enumerated by the Desert Fathers, a community of Christian monks in Egypt in the fourth century CE.[3] The sins of pride, greed, wrath, envy, lust, gluttony, and sloth were named as needing constant vigilance by Christians lest we easily fall into them. But we are not primarily concerned in this book with lapses in realms of personal behavior, such as sloth/laziness, gluttony, and sexual lust, as damaging as these can be and often are in our lives and personal relationships. Certainly, our individual failures of moral judgment and our personal wrongdoings play parts in shaping the larger fabric of our life together and thereby contribute to our collective sin, rendering it harder for us to choose love over fear, compassion over contempt, and kindness over hatred. The Desert Fathers' understandings of our seven deadly sins might well be taken to heart by any Christian trying to live a good and decent life through which we personally can contribute to the strength and beauty of God's movements in history.

The emphasis of this book, however, is on our collective attitudes and behavior, our social sins that undergird our structures of systemic oppression and evil—and that give shape to our personal faults and failures. With this in mind, I have taken the liberty of naming seven deadly sins that are social, systemic, and structural, not simply personal failures. *The sins set forth here cannot be blamed on any one person, past or present, but rather constitute the moral foundations of white Christian nationalism.* I invite you to gaze with me at these deadly sins, which are at the root of the ongoing assault on American democracy, and which have been spiritual sources of our chief problems as Americans over our entire history.

If the word "sin" alienates or disturbs some readers as too "religious" or "Christian," you might think of sin as a formidable psychosocial impediment to our shaping a justice-loving world—a boulder we encounter along the way that blocks our passage and turns us back or causes us to crash. Or you might think of sin as a wrecking ball used by prevailing institutions and powerful people to smash apart possibilities for our collective healing and liberation as a society. Or think of sin as an attitude—usually deeply embedded in our lives, often a pattern of behavior we have inherited or cultivated—that lures us away from doing whatever is right and good, by whatever if any names we may know the sacred source, or sources of such goodness, justice, and love. We Christians usually refer to this sacred source as God. But you don't have to believe in God, certainly not in the theistic God hailed by most Christians, to believe in sin as an impediment to our doing whatever is just and good in our life together.

None of us is ever fully aware of how sin has shaped—and is shaping—us, but all seven deadly sins have played major roles in making us who we are as individuals, as communities, and as a nation. This is true whether we are more conservative or liberal in our spiritual or political commitments. It is also true whether we are white or Christian, because the sins are structured as so foundational to our common life that they infuse even the air we breathe,[4] affecting everyone, regardless of our races, genders, sexualities, classes, religions, politics, or other forms of identity.

From the beginning, the seven deadly sins have torn at the fabric of our goodness and our greatness. Even in those situations where America's moral vision has been brilliant—Abraham Lincoln giving the address at Gettysburg, Eleanor Roosevelt's display of solidarity with Marian Anderson, Rosa Parks's strategic refusal to sit at the back of the bus—the sins are working among us collectively, ripping at the fabric of who we are when we are rightly related, jerking at us, scaring us, and discouraging us from doing the right thing. The sins are at the very heart of what is wrong with the United States of America today, and they are unfortunately at the core of much of what the churches, both liberal and conservative, teach us—often unwittingly, usually without much thought, and always without wisdom. These sins are being exploited today by Republican politicians, championed by Christian leaders in collusion with the Republican Party, and ignored or minimized by many

Democratic Party leaders and members, as if there is nothing that can be done about these grave spiritual, moral, and political mistakes.

SINS OF THE HUMAN SOUL AND
SINS OF AMERICAN HISTORY

In framing this presentation, I have wrestled with how we might best understand not only each sin but also how the sins are related. How do they function? Is one more important than the others? Is there really a "first" sin and a "second" and so forth? Are some worse than the others? I believe there is no "worst" among the seven deadly sins and so, in terms of importance, there is no first or last. The numbers could be interchangeable. Which sin is worst or most important depends on the real-life situation in which humans and other creatures find ourselves. Moreover, the sins cannot be viewed as parallel. They don't look "alike." They can't be lined up like colors of crayons or flavors of ice cream in a store. Not only can they not be ranked in importance or sorted out neatly for presentation, they interact, functioning together, twisting in and out of each other through our nation's history, each making the other more tenacious in the evil it generates.In our lives, both collectively and individually, the sins might be imaged as an alchemist's brew, in which it becomes impossible to tell which sin is which. Is the woman raped because she's female, or Black, or poor? Is the man lying in the water because he's poor or rich or brown or white or because the hurricane got him or because a passerby mugged him or because he killed himself?

Sin is complicated, as is the evil that it spawns. Folks sometimes ask—how do sin and evil fit together? A couple of examples may help clarify not only the connection between sin and evil but also the interactivity of the sins: The American institution of slavery was an evil spawned and held in place by deadly sins of omnipotence, entitlement, white supremacy, and capitalist spirituality. Rape is an evil generated by sins of omnipotence, entitlement, misogyny, violence, and often also by white supremacy and capitalist spirituality. Metaphorically, sin is to evil what fire is to a burning house, or what a tsunami is to a ravaged coastal town. Sin is the attitude, the assumption, the driving force, behind the evil, which is the real-life consequence of sin.[5]

On the basis of this understanding, this is how I have organized the presentation of the seven deadly sins:

The first two sins, and the last—omnipotence (the lust for power-over); entitlement (not knowing our place in God's world); and violence (a deadly addiction)—I have named *sins of the human soul*. These sins are not only deadly. They are not uniquely American. They are universal to humankind. They relentlessly twist their way through the other deadly sins. When slaves sang of "the sin-sick soul," we cannot know exactly what this may have meant to individual slaves, but surely their experiences, at the very least, reflected the deadly sins of white supremacy, capitalist spirituality, and violence in America.

The other sins we will explore I have named *sins of American history.* These sins are not uniquely American, and they take different forms throughout the world. But the sins of white supremacy, misogyny, capitalist spirituality, and domination of the earth and its creatures have taken particularly odious shapes in America. Because the United States of America is such an economically and militarily powerful nation, these particular sins, which are shaped by the sins of the soul, have made them among the most deadly on earth. There are no forces on the planet any more destructive in global impact than America's deadly sins of white supremacy, misogyny, capitalist spirituality, and the domination of the earth and its creatures.

The seven deadly sins constitute a toxic spiritual brew that continues to poison even our finest aspirations to become a democracy of liberty and justice for all Americans, much less a light to the nations.

OUR CALL AS CHRISTIANS

We who are Christians in America have a particular responsibility—and opportunity—to take stock of these sins. Whether our theologies are more conservative or liberal, and regardless of our political ideologies, we truly are heirs to the same set of spiritual and moral challenges.

Bear in mind that we do not need to seek uniformity or consensus in how we might best respond to the seven deadly sins. We surely will not come up with exactly the same answers if we remain faithful to the spiritual foundations of our respective traditions. For example, I am a Universalist Christian and liberal Episcopalian for whom Jesus is a brother and a friend, not so much a Lord and Savior according to traditional understandings of these images. As such, I no doubt struggle with sins of omnipotence and entitlement differently from how most of my more traditional Protestant, Catholic, or Orthodox Christian siblings might—and certainly very differently from how my born-again Christian neighbors would. But the sins are ours, not just mine, or yours, or those of others who are not "like" us, whoever we are.

I hope this book will inspire us to pray or meditate and think together about what we can do as American Christians to help restore what is best about both our nation and our religious communities. To do this in honest, intelligent ways, we need to look at where we have gone wrong.

Chapter 4

The First Sin

The Lust for Omnipotence

In the realm of American politics, we cannot in good faith lay all the blame for the deadly sins—including the lust for power-over—on one political party. Over the course of American history, partisan tides have ebbed and risen, repeatedly, provoking reactions and counterreactions. In the normal course of affairs, especially in liberal democracies like the United States, it's what politics is all about, as here in America and elsewhere around the world, particular parties and popular movements gain and lose traction. The ups and downs of partisan interests can be—and have been at times—a vibrant, constructive dynamic in the functioning of democracies like ours. From my perspective, it would be a good thing if Republicans and Democrats, and other parties as well, would work together to forge political compromises whenever and wherever possible. Now and forever.

The problem we face today—and it is has become a major crisis for our nation—is that one of our two primary political parties, the Republican, has morphed into a tool of authoritarian oppression under the spell of a former president who has made no effort to conceal his own lust for omnipotence, his determination to hold and keep power-over this nation and its people.

Today's Republican leaders may be motivated by their fear of Trump's base. Right-wing militia and other groups of hostile actors, after all, threaten literally to damage or kill those they believe are not faithful to Trump's agenda. Or Republican leaders may be holding fast to their corporate- and media-driven assumptions that Democrats really are a bunch of socialist wackos, often weird, sometimes violent, and usually unpatriotic on behalf of our own self-promoting interests. Some Republicans may truly fear that America is in danger of losing its cultural moorings to those people (Democrats) who have no respect or appreciation for all that has been forged as truly American over centuries by some remarkable white European men—Jefferson, Hamilton, Madison, Adams, et al.

Following the Republicans' filibustering—procedural blocking—of the Democrats' efforts to pass voting rights legislation on January 19, 2022, American historian Heather Cox Richardson reported that Senate Minority Leader Mitch McConnell (R-KY), in assuring reporters that Democrats' concerns about Black voting were misplaced, said that "African American voters are voting in just as high a percentage as Americans."[1] You may need to reread this statement to catch the shameful implication of McConnell's words: that we don't need more African American voters because, after all, they are not the real Americans who should be voting and governing this country. This terrible assumption is no doubt driving Republican zeal to suppress the vote in the 2020s and beyond. The Republican resistance to voters of color is indeed a shameful throwback to the racism of the post-Reconstruction and Jim Crow periods in American history, when Democrats managed to terrorize recently freed slaves, their children, and their grandchildren by suppressing their votes; intimidating them from striving to participate fully in America's civic, business, and political life; and punishing them whenever they succeeded in large numbers as in Wilmington, North Carolina, in 1898, and Tulsa, Oklahoma, in 1921.

Some Republicans surely know better than to believe that Democrats are out to destroy America, or that Democrats are always wrong about everything, but these Republican leaders are simply not courageous or strong enough to stand against their party. Congresswoman Liz Cheney (WY) and Congressman Adam Kinzinger (IL) are exceptions to this, as were any number of Republicans who worked at the state levels in Georgia, Michigan, Pennsylvania, Arizona, and elsewhere on behalf of election integrity in 2020. There are strong, sane, moral voices in the Republican Party—but we seldom hear them.

Today's Democrats also have problems, but ours is not that we have wed ourselves to a person who is hell-bent on our allegiance to his own personal agenda, the country's well-being be damned. Our primary challenge is that the contemporary Democratic Party has not figured out how to maximize the benefits of being the big tent it aspires to be—and which it actually is. The Democratic Party is a big tent in two senses:

First, the Democrats are a party of identity, racial, ethnic, religious, sexual, gender, and cultural diversity. Democrats welcome racial-ethnic minorities, people of different religions, cultural traditions, and languages; feminists and

LGBTQ persons; and others whose very beings challenge the monopoly that white straight Christian men historically have held in government affairs.

Second, the Democrats try to make space for a diversity of opinion and priorities in relation to issues and policies. The party tries to make space for progressives like Bernie Sanders (VT) and Alexandria Ocasio-Cortez (NY) and also more moderate or "centrist" Democrats like Joe Manchin (WV) and Kyrsten Sinema (AZ). But the Democrats haven't yet found a way to forge compromises between and among themselves and settle for policies that will never make everyone happy.

In this moment, the progressives seem better at compromise than their more moderate colleagues. Why might this be? Could it be because throughout American history, certainly over the past century, liberal Americans have learned that compromise is key to making any movement at all in the public realms of a nation that "leans right" historically in its economic, cultural, and political sensibilities?

Democrats have received a great deal of criticism, especially since the 2006 election, for not having a strong enough strategy to reach white rural and working-class voters as well as Latinx communities, who are often Roman Catholics with traditional views on gender roles, sexual diversity, and abortion. In this politically complex situation, Democrats critique the Republican outreach to poor and working-class white people and to immigrant communities, like Hispanics, as a cynical ploy to garner votes rather than an honest interest in helping either poor white people or marginalized ethnic groups.

The GOP's political strategy should not deter the Democrats from moving full speed ahead to forge policies that actually would enhance life for working-class Americans, rural Americans, and immigrant communities in America. The Democrats should play up such policies proudly and publicly rather than defensively. There should be no backing off by Democrats when it comes to engagement with rural and working-class America. There should also be no apology from the Democratic Party, but rather major efforts to organize and educate people from all demographics around matters of moral and historical urgency, none of which will be solved quickly: voting rights, universal health care, public education, economic fairness, women's reproductive freedom, and gun safety.

There is another major issue that neither of our political parties has done crackers about: America's place as the world's premier military power and its wildly excessive military budget that dwarfs our domestic needs and the budget to care for our people and earth. The buildup of the military industrial complex, which President Eisenhower warned seventy years ago[2] could become a problem, moves far beyond the scope of this book. But it is important to note that the growth of our military and its overlap with corporate power and white Christian nationalism, and the failure of either of our major parties to address it, has roots in all the deadly sins we'll be considering. Neither Democrats nor Republicans have done much to address this huge and major global challenge since the Second World War.

Do both of our two major parties have good people in them? Of course. Do both have corrupt scoundrels? Yes. There have always been people of integrity and scumbags in both, and all, parties. Truth tellers and liars. Honest brokers and men and women who'd steal your last cent, your bank account, or your identity. People who spend their lives saving those in trouble and those who spend much of their lives tearing down and destroying the lives of others.

Both this chapter on omnipotence, the lust for power-over others, and the book as a whole are not focused on individual characters, except insofar as—like the president and members of Congress, like our bosses and our bishops—they claim to represent us collectively. The seven deadly sins are basically collective, corporate problems that too often mute us individually and leave us personally at a loss as to what to do as individuals in our local churches, families, schools, workplaces, neighborhoods, and organizations.

OMNIPOTENCE AND THEOCRACY

Most Christians know that we get in trouble when we mistake ourselves for God. That is exactly what the first deadly sin reflects—our mistaken perception of ourselves as all-powerful, having power-over other humans and over creation itself, and we justify this by imagining ourselves to be "in the image of God." I would go further and suggest that our understanding of God as omnipotent is itself problematic—not because it is not true, but rather because most humans tend to equate "power" with "power-over"—having control over someone or something.[3] In the last part of this book, we will consider an alternative way of thinking about God and power. For now, we need to recognize that most Christians in America believe not only in a God with power-over us and all creation but, moreover, imagine that we ourselves are made in the image of this omnipotent God. Our troubles as human beings often begin in our quest for omnipotence, to have power and control over others. This desire for power-over is the first deadly sin.

In America, the drive for social, economic, and cultural power-over others took hold and metastasized when Christians first arrived in the new land. From the bringing of enslaved Africans into Jamestown in 1619 right up through the insurrection of Christian zealots at the Capitol in 2021, untold numbers of American Christians have been afflicted by a lust for power-over not only other groups and individuals but also over the nation's economy, its culture and language, its symbols and stories, and how we understand our collective past, present, and future as a country. Taken to its logical outcome, this drive for power-over others in the name of the Christian God leads toward a theocratic state, in which the Christian God rather than human citizens are believed to rule over America.

What happened on January 6, 2021, shocking and distressing as it was to most of us, was not extraordinary in the context of the long-standing goal of many American Christians to dominate the government and culture of the United States, much as they believe an omnipotent God controls all history. As noted previously, from early in American history, many Protestants and, more recently, some Roman Catholics as well have longed for the day when America at last would become a Christian nation, in their own image of what would constitute a Christian nation. Former attorney general William Barr and former national security adviser Michael Flynn are examples of those who seem to be wishing for a Christian theocracy, a nation governed by God rather than by people.

In 1985, Canadian writer Margaret Atwood's *The Handmaid's Tale* introduced readers to the theocracy of Gilead in what was once the United States of America.[4] Those citizens of Gilead who do not support the actions of the Christian leaders—referred to by Atwood as the Sons of Jacob—are systematically demolished. Interestingly, the people of Gilead are never seen attending church, which suggests that, for Atwood, the faith of the theocratic leaders and their followers is not especially important. What matters is only the people's obedience to the Sons of Jacob and their unquestioning conformity to the laws of Gilead.

Were such a phenomenon actually to be achieved—the takeover of our nation's laws and leadership by a movement of Christian zealots—it would be a theocracy, in which leaders of the nation would maintain that they govern on behalf of God, not on behalf of themselves or the people they serve. Beneath their godly rhetoric and rules, the leaders of such a theocracy would be determined to amass as much power-over people's lives, work, love, and money as possible.

Those who would oppose them or even raise questions about their values would be treated as enemies not simply of the government or of the religious leaders, but rather as the enemies of God. In such a theocracy—contemporary Iran is a good example—the religious leaders would be the supreme rulers, under whose headship the government would conduct the business of the nation. The name of the game would be power—specifically, the wielding of power-over the people of the nation, who would have little say in how the government runs and no significant say in who runs it.

THEOCRATIC STRATEGIES TO
OVERTHROW DEMOCRACY

Democracy, or government by and for the people, has been the basis of how the vast majority of Americans have envisioned the foundation of our nation. Although we have never had a perfect democracy, and there have always been groups of people left out—races, religions, genders, other groups—creating a more perfect union has long been the patriotic dream of most American citizens.

Today, more than at any time in American history except the Civil War and its aftermath, our democracy truly is at stake. This is because Christian theocrats, who have been gaining in strength for decades, are on the rise, and because theocracy is the archenemy of democracy. Democracy cannot be allowed to thrive if a nation is to be led by people acting on behalf of God. This is what happened in Iran in 1979, when fundamentalist Shiite Islamists took over the nation under their supreme leader, the Ayatollah Khomeini.

This is similar to what the insurrectionist Republicans are attempting in the United States today. They are trying to take over the government of the United States. Although Trump is at the center of the power-over plays being made by his followers, he will be increasingly expendable in determining the outcome of his white Christian nationalist agenda. Despite his popularity with his base, the theocratic agenda neither began nor will end with him. I would imagine that many of you, like me, are sick and tired of Donald J. Trump—his lies, his flags, his smirk, his egomania, his political manipulations, and most of all his gratuitous cruelty and hatefulness toward anyone and everyone in his way. Who wants to read another word about this ugly man? Not I. And yet, we ignore to our peril the evil that he and his people are spreading like fertilizer over our common life. We must regard this behavior as a serious threat to our democracy. These people are doing everything they can to reconstruct America as a theocracy in the image of an omnipotent white male capitalist God. As this book is being written, Trump and his GOP cult are using two overlapping strategies to accomplish their goal.

THE BIG LIE

The first strategy toward current efforts to establish a Christian nationalist theocracy is the Big Lie, which refers to the insurrectionist GOP's efforts to convince Americans that the 2020 election was stolen from their leader, who himself concocted this lie in his repeated warnings leading up to the election that, if he didn't win, it would be because the election was stolen from him.

He had made the same declaration in his 2016 run against Hillary Clinton. This claim, which most Americans see as transparently bogus and manipulative, evidently hooked his true believers, underscoring their devotion to this dangerous man and feeding his insatiable hunger to be up front and center on every stage.

After taking some time to assess not the moral travesty of the assault on the Capitol, nor its danger to our democracy, but rather only its political value to the Republican Party, GOP leaders in Congress—led by Kevin McCarthy and Mitch McConnell—launched an effort to keep themselves and their party in power by playing along with the Big Lie. Knowing full well that it is not true, they nonetheless have been willing to let Republicans, including millions of conservative Christians, believe that the 2020 election was stolen by Joe Biden, Kamala Harris, and the Democrats.

They spread this lie largely through silent acquiescence to Trump in the face of overwhelming evidence by Republican state officials throughout the nation, as well as rulings by dozens of judges, including Trump appointees, that there is not, and never has been, a shred of evidence that the 2020 election was stolen. Christopher Krebs, director of the Cybersecurity and Infrastructure Security Agency in the Trump administration, was fired by the former president in November 2020 shortly after he tweeted that claims of election fraud were unsubstantiated. A few weeks later, Krebs wrote, "The 2020 election was the most secure in U.S. history. This success should be celebrated by all Americans, not undermined in the service of a profoundly un-American goal."[5]

The dismissal of Krebs signaled the beginning of attacks by Trump and his followers against election officials in several swing states won by Biden who had declared that the elections in their states had been conducted fairly without significant problems, much less widespread fraud or miscast ballots that would have altered the outcome of the presidential election. Nonetheless, thousands of Republicans leaders at federal, state, and local levels are falling all over themselves in their efforts to curry favor with Trump's voters, including large numbers of conservative Christian voters.

SUPPRESS THE VOTE, SUBVERT THE RESULTS

The insurrectionists' second strategy is this: under the ruse of trying to "stop the steal" in future elections, the fanatical wing of the Republican Party, which has pretty much taken over the whole party,[6] is making a desperate bid throughout the states to suppress the votes of Black, brown, and young people in future elections. These Republicans believe that voter suppression, transparently aimed at groups they fear will vote largely for Democrats, will help them win future elections. Only by winning these elections by whatever means necessary—including denying people of color and young people their constitutional right to vote—do these Republicans assume they might be able to wield power-over the people for the foreseeable future. Furthermore, at least a dozen states with GOP legislatures are designing ways of discounting votes that do not serve the interests of the majority party.

This strategy is lifted right out of late-nineteenth-century efforts by white Southern Democrats in cahoots with sympathetic Northerners to deny social, economic, and political power to freed slaves.[7] Today's GOP hopes to secure for years, possibly decades, the power of white straight affluent male Christians over everyone else via the laws and prevailing customs set in place long ago by white Christian American men. As set forth earlier, this white Christian nationalist aim on the part of many conservative evangelical Christian Americans is not new. It can be traced back at least as far as the coalition forged between business and Christian leaders to weaken the social and economic impact of Franklin Roosevelt's New Deal, which had been created in the 1930s to lift up Americans in the wake of the Great Depression.

Only in an increasingly white Christian nationalist American theocracy would Trump's Republican Party be able to control where Americans would live; who would be admitted to our country; what languages we would speak in public; what versions of American history schoolchildren would study; whom Americans would be permitted to marry; which religions American leaders would be permitted to practice; and how American citizens would be permitted, or not, to exercise our freedoms to speech, religion, birth control, abortion, reproductive choice, the ownership and regulation of guns, voting rights, and the rights of all Americans to clean air and clean water, fair housing, food security, health care, and good public education.

CAN FOLLOWERS OF JESUS SUPPORT A WHITE CHRISTIAN NATIONALIST THEOCRACY?

The question for Christians, whether we are more liberal or conservative in our spiritual paths, is how the Christian tradition has played into these theocratic aspirations. To what extent does Christian theology support, or even encourage, a power-over form of civil government, shaped on hierarchical Christian principles?

From the beginning there has been tension in Christianity, as in most movements and organizations, between those who advocate a more hierarchical (power-over) model of leadership and those who espouse a more communitarian (power-with) model. The early church was not basically hierarchical, but it became increasingly so as it grew both larger in numbers and closer, over the first four centuries, to the Roman Empire. From Jesus's life and those of his earliest disciples and followers, including Paul, the young church was at its core a communitarian movement among equals. Its only true head was Jesus who, while alive on the earth, had not claimed or sought to exercise power-over his followers but rather to empower them to do what he did: to heal, teach, perform miracles, pray, and practice love for neighbor and stranger as manifestations of God's love.

According to traditional biblical teaching, the risen Jesus ascended into heaven (Luke 24:50–51), thereby shifting the attention of Christians from earth to heaven in what might be described as the early church's first hierarchical move. Yet the early church remained largely a horizontal effort of outreach, with some bishops and other leaders, but largely communities of people exercising different gifts and talents. Historian A. M. Schor contends that the young church's gradual loss of its more egalitarian and communitarian efforts was a major blow to the movement which Jesus himself had initiated. The more institutionalized, hierarchical church came into being during the fourth century CE, as the church and the Roman state reached a settlement that gave Christianity its first formal "nationalist" relationship to a political state.[8] While it would most certainly not be accurate to describe the Roman Empire as a theocracy, the empire did give Christianity its first proximity to political power.

How do we understand these Christian origins and the church's development through its first centuries in relation to American Christianity's alliances over time with the very principalities and powers that both Jesus and his disciples had to contend against? Is such a theocratic goal, steeped in power-over aspirations, not exactly what the founders of the United States were hoping to avoid?[9] Could there be anything more alien to both most of the founders of the United States and Jesus of Nazareth than a theocratic form of government, in which religious leaders—Christian or other—tell the civic leaders that they must obey them and their laws, keep their customs, and honor their spiritual traditions, in order either to be faithful to God or patriotic Americans?

A CONVERSATION BETWEEN CHRISTIANS
ABOUT JANUARY 6, 2021

I had a chance to talk with Ross (not his real name), the pastor of a conservative Baptist church in our community in the North Carolina mountains, about the January 6 insurrection not long after it occurred. He and I had both been appalled by the large cross in the crowd at the riot—but for different reasons. Ross said that the cross had no place in the riot because Christians shouldn't care who's in the White House, only who sits on the throne [of Jesus]. I too was horrified—and I *do* think Christians should care who's in the White House. I was horrified because of the violence and hatred on display that day, at least a significant part of it being done in the name of Jesus, hence the presence of the large cross, which disgusted me too, as it did Ross.

This little story is instructive because Ross and I agreed that the cross had no place at the Capitol on January 6. We also concurred that Christians had no business trying to overthrow the government of the United States, no business wielding power-over other people, literally beating and killing them to try to stop Congress from certifying the election. We most certainly agreed that the January 6 riot at the U.S. Capitol was despicable behavior, especially among Christians who had the audacity to carry the cross of Jesus into the midst of their violent Trump-inspired temper tantrum.

It is noteworthy that Ross was not alone in his view. According to Molly Olmstead, writing for *Slate* the day after the insurrection, a couple of prominent Southern Baptist leaders, among others, were critical of both what happened at the Capitol and of Trump's role in it. Olmstead reported:

> Most Christian leaders in prominent or formal positions of power either stayed quiet or spoke out against the violence—and a couple even came close to disavowing Trumpism itself. Southern Baptist Convention president J.D. Greear on Twitter asked the president to "condemn this mob" and called the peaceful transition of power "part of honoring and submitting to God's ordained leaders whether they were our choice or not."[10]

She continued:

> R. Albert Mohler Jr., the president of the Southern Baptist Theological Seminary in Louisville, Kentucky, spoke at length about the day's events and made the boldest statement against the president, calling "the cult of personality" the "greatest danger to the American experiment." Mohler, who had opposed Trump four years ago, supported the president's reelection bid.[11]

Two weeks after these statements were made, more than five hundred evangelical Christians issued an open letter decrying "radicalized Christian nationalism," arguing that the religious expressions by insurrectionists during the January 6 attack on the U.S. Capitol are "heretical" and a "perversion of the Christian faith."[12]

Ross maintains almost a year later that his concern is still not primarily with who the president is. But it would appear that many evangelical Christians who may, or may not, have echoed Ross's apolitical sentiment on the evening of January 6, 2021, have since thrown their support behind Donald Trump. Whether or not they had voted for Trump in 2020, and however strongly they may have condemned the January 6 event, as many evidently did, many evangelical Christians have since that time bought into Trump's Big Lie that the election was stolen from him. Moreover, according to a poll conducted by the nonpartisan Public Religion Research Institute in October 2021, three out of ten Republicans believe that violence may be warranted to save our country; and almost three out of ten believe that God has a special role for America in human history.[13] Like the GOP leaders of the House and the U.S. Senate, it would appear that, months after the insurrection, the majority of conservative Christian leaders have revised their opinions of this violent attack and are now playing it down as no big deal or perhaps as a staged performance by the leftist phantom group Antifa or even by the FBI. After all, among the majority of Americans, it would hardly serve the political interests of Republicans to call attention to a violent assault on the U.S. Capitol by rioters who had been called together by Republican operatives that likely included members of Congress, people in the president's circle of advisers, and, we might assume, the president of the United States.

Distancing themselves from January 6, 2021, Republican leaders—including conservative evangelical pastors—have cast their lots with Trump and must convince voters that theirs is a party of patriotic Americans and good Christians. This being so, leaders like Albert Mohler, J. D. Greear, and other Christian conservatives who were ambivalent about Trump's presidency prior to the Capitol riot seem not to be aligning themselves publicly with Trump or the GOP at this time. Perhaps Mohler, Greear, and my friend Ross, while they are conservatives who usually vote Republican, are waiting to decide if their backing of Trump's insurrectionist party in the final analysis may outweigh their support of what they fear to be the immoral and socialist policies of the Democrats.

I personally believe that most conservative white American Christians are probably torn about how they feel and how they vote. On the one hand they know that Donald Trump is not a good person, at many levels; on the other hand, they believe that Republican policies correspond to their long-standing beliefs—about abortion, guns, taxes, and most of all about the horrors of socialism, against which business executives and Christian leaders have been stirring fear and hatred for more than a century. As individuals, conservative Christians aren't all that different from other Americans, including progressive people of faith and nonreligious persons. However, unlike most Americans, those who have fallen under the spell of Trump and his lieutenants like Steve Bannon and Michael Flynn would likely follow Trump to the gates of hell. These true believers seem to have lost their ability to think critically about, understand, or perhaps even care what is actually happening to our country at this time or what their roles in this drama may be. Many of these are folks who, Trump himself conjectured, would vote for him even if he shot someone on Fifth Avenue.

Should Trump and his followers succeed in seizing power via vote suppression and other devious manipulations, many who are either enamored with Trump or are trying to defeat the dangerous Democrats will rue the day they closed their eyes and minds to the demise of democracy. Like citizens of other countries that have fallen into the hands of authoritarian leaders, whether fascists like Hitler, Communists like Stalin, or fascist communists like Putin, most people supporting Trump today will be at a loss to explain their remarkable, damning lack of good judgment and moral bankruptcy to their great-grandchildren.

What about American Liberals' Support for
Acts of Resistance and Revolution?

Here we must remind ourselves that Christians on the left of the political spectrum, people like me and many of you, have tried repeatedly to stop our government from acting in ways that run counter to our values. In the 1960s, my college classmates and I yelled out angrily in the streets of Lynchburg, Virginia, protesting the racist policies of the local newspaper. Later in the decade I was arrested for sitting in at Columbia University, in a demonstration against the university's real estate grabs in relation to its Black and brown neighbors in Harlem. In the 1970s, I marched in Washington, vigorously protesting this country's shameful participation in the Vietnam War. In 1983, along with other teachers and seminarians, I was arrested in Groton, Connecticut, for protesting the blessing of the Trident nuclear submarine—cynically named "Corpus Christi" (Body of Christ) by the Reagan administration. Alongside many liberal Christian and other religious activists, including my mother and siblings, I marched in Washington on behalf of gay and lesbian rights in 1993. Many Christians and people of other faith and moral traditions supported all of these demonstrations and many other protests and witnesses, up to this day, on behalf of abortion rights, environmental protections, immigration, the treatment of Asian American and Pacific Islander women, Black Lives Matter, and other matters of social justice.

In a similar liberal spirit, many Christians and other religious activists in America condemned the successful 1973 coup in Chile that ousted democratically elected socialist President Salvador Allende. This Chilean insurrection had been engineered by General Augusto Pinochet and sponsored by our own CIA because Pinochet, an avowed fascist, was dead set against the socialist government of Allende. Our government continued to support Pinochet despite the fact that he was a ruthless man under whose violent thumb thousands of journalists, teachers, young people, and other social dissidents were tortured and "disappeared." Pinochet would rule Chile with the full support of the United States government for the next seventeen years. Apparently, it was not a stretch for the American government to support a right-wing fascist, whereas it had been untenable to support a democratically elected socialist. Several years later, many American Christian activists and people of other faith traditions, who had supported Allende and condemned Pinochet, applauded the overthrow by the left-wing Sandinistas of the corrupt reign in Nicaragua of the right-wing dictator Anastasio Somoza who, like Pinochet, had been propped up by American political, military, and economic interests.

What then is the difference between our celebration in 1979 of the overthrow of a corrupt and ruthless dictatorship in Nicaragua and our horror in 2021 at our fellow citizens' attempts to overthrow what they believed to be a stolen presidency by Joe Biden and the Democrats? Is it simply that the Nicaraguan coup was waged by "our side" and the Capitol insurrection was staged by "the other side"? Bringing this tension closer to home, how might we have viewed a coup attempt by Democrats in 2017 to overthrow the presidency of Donald Trump? Bear in mind that many Trump supporters believed that the Mueller Commission was an effort to delegitimize the president—in effect, an attempted coup—which it was not.[14]

Do liberal Christians support power-over maneuvers when they are on "our side"? Clearly our experiences and history in this country would affirm that, yes, many of us can and we do. Unless we are absolute pacifists, opposed to all military activity—and I am not—most Americans and most Christians try to support revolutionary efforts that our values and senses of justice and fairness lead us to believe are being waged to create greater justice-love in the world near and far.

Among Christians, as among people of other faith and spiritual traditions, our values have roots in particular, often diverse, worldviews. Some Christians strongly oppose the death penalty. Others do not. Many Christians believe that wars can be just—World War II, for example—whereas other Christians are absolute pacifists. Christians—right, left, and center—have particular experiences and views of God, and particular understandings of how our views and values can be most faithfully embodied—incarnated—in human history and on this earth. Therefore, whether on left, right, or somewhere in between, Christians normally support actions undertaken on behalf of what we ourselves believe God is doing in history.

Here are some of the criteria that I rely on to make such judgment calls. Be clear that I do not make such calls in a vacuum nor simply inside my own head and heart. My moral sensibilities are shaped by a long line of teachers, mentors, priests and prophets, forebears, siblings, friends, and other believers in a Great Spirit that moves the struggles for justice and compassion generation upon generation. As you read, I urge you to ask yourselves by what criteria *you* judge the morality of protests and movements for social change.

- Is this action, this protest, this revolutionary movement, *steeped clearly in a commitment to make our society more inclusive of those who have been left out*?
- *Will it empower greater numbers of people* to live in justice and peace?
- *Does it challenge historical wrongs* such as white supremacist laws and voter suppression; misogynist treatment of women, including contempt for our bodily integrity and reproductive options; homophobic violence against LGBTQ siblings; economic injustices such as food insecurity, homelessness, inequality in health care and educational opportunities for all children; depletion of earth resources, and disregard for the environment, including climate change?
- Does the action move us closer to our images of the realm of God in which there is "neither Jew nor Greek . . . slave nor free . . . male nor female, for [we] are all one in Christ Jesus" (Gal. 3:28 ESV), or does it exacerbate our divisions? Another way of asking this question is, *does the revolutionary action evoke our better angels*, which *strengthen our empathy and evoke our compassion*, or does it release our demons, which stir greater division and deepen hatred among us?
- Will the action secure power-over relationships between the government and the people, or *will it generate more power-with dynamics between leaders and the common people*?
- Is this action being *undertaken in a spirit of revolutionary nonviolence*, led by the spiritual heirs of Martin Luther King and John Lewis, Dorothy Day and Delores Huerta, Rosa Parks and Jonathan Daniels?

WHERE ROSS AND I PART WAYS, YET STAY CONNECTED

Although my neighbor Ross and other Southern Baptist leaders might still agree that the January 6 insurrection was a deplorable event, I suspect these men would not agree with me that power-over relationships normally have no good place among Christians. Most evangelical Christians insist that, as their Lord, Jesus Christ has all power-over them and over other believers, whereas I would say that, as a brother and spiritual companion, Jesus shares power-with me, as his sister, and that—from a Christian perspective—our "power-with-ness," or mutuality, is a gift and a sign of the Holy Spirit. This critical distinction will be explored in part 3.

So while there is a big difference between Ross's and my experiences of Jesus, I have a sense that, like many Christian pastors and other conservatives as well as more liberal Christians, Ross would not affirm the wielding of power-over by those who insist that because they are acting on behalf of God, all other people are wrong and are enemies to be kept at a distance or, if need be, destroyed. Even though Ross sincerely believes in evangelizing people to become Christian in the way he understands what being a Christian means, I do not believe he personally would affirm a Christian theocracy as the American way. This is because I do not believe Ross wants a government—even a Christian government—to dictate his own, his family's, and his congregation's ways of being either good Christians or good Americans.

I know Ross and he knows me—we try to be good neighbors—and I do not see him personally as a white Christian nationalist. However, I do see the Christianity he preaches and his Christian worldview as infused by basic tenets of white Christian nationalism and the seven deadly sins that undergird it. This is because white Christian nationalism and its seven deadly sins work systemically, crossing all Christian churches, to shape and secure the structures of American Christianity and American society.

The problems spawned by white Christian nationalism are not Ross's nor my personal problems to solve as individuals, although we are affected by them personally to the detriment of who each of us is. The seven deadly sins are systemic, collective challenges with twisted roots burrowed deep in American soil. They face all American Christians and can only be uprooted by our collective commitments, in Jesus's words, to "go and sin no more" (John 8:11 New Living Translation).

POWER-OVER TO MAINTAIN PURITY

One of the chiefs and most offensive aims of white Christian nationalism and the insurrectionist Republicans is to maintain *purity* of race, religion, culture, sexuality, and gender identity. "Purity" is a strange-sounding concept to many contemporary ears. It's an ancient religious and cultural concept, built on superstition and traditions of protecting undefiled, clean, safe, life-giving substances like blood and water, substances often bestowed with sacred powers to heal, bless, preserve life, and perpetuate goodness.[15] Purity concerns have a long, sordid, violent history in America, especially in relation to white supremacist and misogynistic views of Black people, other people of color, and women. These will be explored in later chapters.

At this point, let us just say that when people are committed to the preservation of purity, there is no room for those who pollute or soil the American nation and its conservative Protestant, Catholic, or Orthodox brands of Christian religion. With the preservation of purity as a sacred goal, there is no space for any form of leadership except power-over—precisely to keep tight control and mete out punishment to offenders, those who would pollute what is otherwise pure. To maintain purity as a spiritual, social, and political goal, patriotic American Christians must keep tight control of their government, their communities, their families, and themselves. This is the basis of theocracy.

In *The Handmaid's Tale*, Margaret Atwood portrays the nation of Gilead as having been created by an obsession with the purity of white people in what used to be the United States of America. This scenario may seem over the top, just as George Orwell's *1984* might appear to be just good imaginative fiction. But Orwell and Atwood were not simply fiction writers. They were writing prophetically to those who take democracy for granted, people like us, open-minded, moderate to progressive citizens, many of us people of faith, many of us white Christians who cannot imagine such nonsense or blasphemy as the worship of our own "blood," our own race, or our own gender.

But beware the role of religion, especially Christian religion in the United States! That is Margaret Atwood's warning that authoritarianism, even fascism, is not far away in democratic societies whenever the lust for omnipotence, for power-over people, rather than a commitment to power-with them, becomes the obsession of the leaders of both church and state. This is not far from where we are today with one of our two major political parties and a significant segment of conservative Protestant and Catholic Christians.

Chapter 5

The Second Sin

Entitlement

The first deadly sin was about power, trying to exert power-over others. The second is about privilege—not knowing our place in the world of God and assuming that we are entitled to whatever is best or most. Both of these sins stand in stark contrast to the Christian call to neighbor-love as the basis of a good life and to the ever-unfolding American dream that all persons should have opportunities to flourish—to enjoy life, liberty, and the pursuit of happiness. Millions upon millions of Americans and Christians strive for these goals and struggle to make space for others to do the same. This is as it should be, and we should be proud of this. Although no one can live these commitments perfectly or even very well all the time, our lives reflect efforts to live in this way. Still for centuries, American Christians, especially white people (historically, men) of economic privilege, have confused pride in ourselves, our country, and our spiritual traditions with a sense of entitlement.

"Entitlement" refers to a deeply embodied assumption that, in the nation or in the church or wherever we are, our rightful place is on top, our prize is first, our rank is best. It's as if someone owes us this special place of privilege. Moreover, we easily assume that both our country and our brand of Christianity are more deserving of whatever is good than other nations and religions are. We fall into imagining that America and Christianity are closer to God, blessed by God in ways that other nations and religions are not. Entitled by God, many white American Christians, especially those who prosper economically, believe that we are "born to the purple," as the saying goes, a reference to British royalty. It's no accident that Episcopal bishops wear purple shirts. Please notice that I include myself in this indictment of entitlement, because there is no question that, as a white Christian who has been a liberal Episcopalian for most of my life, I have lived as a person of privilege in America, though not as much as had I been a white heterosexual male.

Here's how it works: From birth, or through the luck of timely connection with more entitled people, men and women of privilege assume they are naturally on top. They assume they have been chosen by God or by fate or simply by nature to rule. They are positioned, usually not by choice but by who they are, to look down on the rest of the nation and world and on people of other spiritual traditions as fundamentally lesser beings who are not as entitled, privileged, or lucky. More than others, entitled American Christians deserve the good life, lots of liberty (freedom), and a right to pursue happiness pretty much on their own terms. Leaders of both the United States of America and the Christian Church historically have fallen into this most grievous sin.

Moreover, Christianity heralds itself not only as the best but, sometimes, in Roman Catholicism and a number of Protestant traditions, as the only right religion, the only true path to God. In America and throughout the Christian world, Roman Catholics and most conservative Protestants have assumed that not only is their religion the only true religion, but more fundamentally that their God is the only true God. All other images, names, and experiences of god are false, and believers in any deity other than the Christian God, as they understand him, are dabbling in idolatry. In this spirit of entitlement, Christian certainty about our one and only true God has taken an inestimable toll on human and created life, from the Crusades to the Middle Passage and chattel slavery to the Trail of Tears to the Holocaust. The second deadly sin of white Christian nationalism, entitlement, breeds terrorism as surely as a similar assumption about privilege and power in other fundamentalist religions.

As for America, our chosen leaders, regardless of party, declare this country to be the world's premier nation, exceptional in almost every respect. Some are empirically true—America is the richest and most militarized nation on Earth, and America produces some of the best scholars, scientists, writers, artists, and athletes in the world. But neither America nor any country on the planet is best at everything. I doubt that many other nations—except today maybe Russia and China—spend much time worrying about it, at least not since the era of colonialism and imperialism. Yet being best and only has been an obsession among American political and military leaders since the end of the Second World War. Regardless of political party, American leaders have boasted about our country needing always to be regarded by Americans and others as the strongest, most righteous, and most enviable nation on the planet. Those Americans who have proposed that we regard ourselves as one among many excellent nations have risked being caricatured as unpatriotic.

What makes such religious and national arrogance aggravating to people who are not Christian and those who are not Americans is that, for so long, both Christians and Americans have demonstrated repeatedly that we do not know our place in the world. Our relentless boasting, in the manner more of kids' athletic competitions and high school cheerleaders, reflects a determination to win at all costs. In military, economic, psychosocial, political, and spiritual contexts, the Christian Church and the American nation have joined hands historically to demonstrate to everyone watching that, together, not only are they best but, moreover, they will win. They will win wars. They will win economic competitions. They will win everything they aim to win because God is on their side.

This is America's Christian God, of course, the one who always wins, because He is best—note the gender and the capital "He," which are not irrelevant here. He makes America best, and He helps America win, because America is Christian and because Christian America is His chosen nation. In this way, American and Christian identities reinforce each other, each making the other better than any other nation or religion on earth. This circular reasoning has buoyed and strengthened both the Christian Church and America in their often symbiotic identities. In much of its history, always with the blessing of Christian leaders, America has won its wars and grown its economy. By the end of World War II, the United States of America was acknowledged pretty much around the world as the greatest nation on earth. Truly exceptional. The best. Since that time, for the past three-quarters of a century, American Christianity has bested other great nations and religions of the world in generating the major idolatry of advanced global capitalism, with China nipping at our heels in this competition.

Doesn't that prove that believing ourselves to be the best pays off? We *do* win wars. We *do* have the greatest economy in the world. The whole world *does* look up to us, or at least did until the Trump election and administration. Of course Trump himself was a shiny product of the entitled, exceptionalist American mindset. An "America best, America first" is exactly what most Americans, like Trump, have been taught from early childhood on. Similarly, American churches, both liberal and conservative, have taught us that Christianity is not only good but, moreover, is the best faith tradition in the world because it is the only religion that puts Jesus Christ as Lord and Savior at the center not only of the nation but moreover of the universe.

Many will ask, doesn't the Bible encourage us to become the best people we can be? Of course. Whether through the Hebrew prophets' calls for people to live as YHWH commands—to "let justice roll down like waters" (Amos 5:24 NRSV), or through Jesus's teachings in the Beatitudes—"Blessed are the merciful, for they will be shown mercy" (Matt. 5:7 New International Version), the Bible is written to evoke our best. But the Bible's admonition to the people of God is that *we do what is right*, not that we ourselves, our religion, or our nation *is* inherently best. We are called by God to *act* in certain ways—to *make justice*, to *show mercy*, to *love one another*. From a biblical perspective, being best is not about *being* any one nation, religion, race, gender, or culture. Being an American? Being a Christian? That's all well and fine, provided we love one another and all of God's creatures and creation. *Doing what is right* makes us good, sometimes even best, in any realm of our life together.

WHITE AMERICAN CHRISTIANS NEED OTHER STORIES

Those of us who are white American Christians, in thinking about what is good for us and our nation, need to know stories other than our own. This is the message of the 1619 Project, an effort to expand Americans' understandings of the some of the diverse peoples involved in founding our country.[1] We need to hear and take to heart stories and perspectives about both Christianity and the United States of America that began to be told among white people in our country and in some of our predominantly white churches during the second half of the twentieth century, following World War II. I emphasize our need as white people, because Black and other people of color have often survived by passing down their stories of their people, faith, and culture. White Americans, white Christians, especially but not only men, have needed to hear stories new to us even about ourselves, our own stories in new ways, as well as stories about other cultures and peoples. White American Christians have need to hear more stories.

We needed the stories of Rosa Parks, Martin Luther King Jr., Fannie Lou Hamer, Jonathan Daniels, Viola Liuzzo, James Baldwin, John Lewis, and so many others as the white supremacy of both Christianity and America began to be seriously challenged by the emergence of the civil rights movement in America, alongside the decline of racist European and American colonialism in Africa, Asia, and Latin America.

We needed stories of Communism's rise and fall around the world and the emergence of global capitalism as the premier way of life on the planet, not only competitive but increasingly ruthless, an economic system that historically has put the individual white male, his family, his wealth, and his power-over others at the center of all that matters. Within global capitalism, not outside of it, there have been stories of protesters—from Martin Luther King Jr. linking workers' rights to civil rights in the late 1960s to Elizabeth Warren's and Bernie Sanders's insistence in the 2020 presidential election that democratic socialism is a corrective, not a substitute, to advanced global capitalism.

We needed stories of the second wave of feminism, a movement of largely white middle-class women,[2] which emerged in the late 1960s and early 1970s, demanding testimonies that rattled the foundations of white patriarchy's misogynist stranglehold on both Christianity and most American institutions.

Soon came stories of womanists[3] in the early 1980s, angrily and honestly reflecting the particular lives, loves, and struggles of Black American women. Also sparked by the movements among white, Black, brown, Asian, and Indigenous women[4] emerged the stories of gay men, lesbians, and, by the end of the twentieth century, transgender people.[5] The queer movements embodied serious questions about rigid gender definitions, sexual categories, and the purity codes long operative in Christian America.

In the late twentieth and early twenty-first centuries, stories about the earth have been shared among many humans, stories about how we have been destroying our planet home—sometimes with malice, more often in ignorance or indifference. In contemporary America and Europe, children and young adults have insisted that we wake up before it's too late. Environmentalists[6] are urging people of faith, American Christians and all others, to wake up to what is happening to this planet and recognize our earth home as a mutually interactive organic community of life that desperately needs our love and solidarity. We are being urged not only to wake up, but also to change our ways of life so as to be more actively respectful of the earth and its astounding diversity of creatures and people.

We should not forget to seek out stories about environmental racism to learn not only what has been happening to the water, the earth, and its creatures, but also how environmental destruction is affecting human communities, especially communities of color. We might seek to learn, for example, what transpired in Flint, Michigan, when the water was being poisoned over a number of years and where most of its citizens are Black. Regarding the Flint water crisis, the Michigan Civil Rights Commission, a state-established body, determined that "the poor governmental response to the Flint crisis was a 'result of systemic racism.'"[7] We might also seek to learn what is taking place among the First Peoples of northern Minnesota and North Dakota as they struggle to prevent the Canadian oil company Enbridge from running a major pipeline through their native lands. It appears that Enbridge is knowingly putting at risk the Native peoples' resources for the sustenance of their lives. This is another example of systemic, environmental racism.[8]

SOME TOUGH QUESTIONS

Listening to other stories like these, learning of such exploitation and evils in our collective history, how on earth can American Christians boast about being the best? The best what, for God's sake?

Best at raising up white people above everyone else on the planet?

Best at heralding ever-higher profit and greater wealth above all other reasons to work?

Best at celebrating the lives, lusts, and loves of white straight men over those of everyone else?

Best at exploiting natural resources to meet the demands of economic greed? There will be more later about the deadly sins of white supremacy, misogyny and its homophobic twin, global capitalism, the destruction of our earth, and the role of violence in our life together, as each of these sins has played a role in the convergence of Christian and American cultures at their worst.

This discussion about entitlement, about not knowing our place, as a deadly sin is meant to emphasize that, from the beginning, white American Christians, especially men, have taken for granted that they are the best humans in the best nation on the earth because the Christian God, through his Son Jesus Christ, has placed not only their religion and their nation on the top of the world, but also has granted their white race and male gender a privileged status.

This set of assumptions about American and Christian entitlement began to break apart after World War II, when people other than white straight affluent men began to tell their stories and make claims for themselves, their own worth and dignity. In reaction against these rising multicultural and interfaith tides in America, especially over the past eight decades, there continues to be significant backlash from those who are determined to hold traditional white supremacist and misogynist power in place. At this particular moment in American history, the backlash is becoming a frenzy. All we have to do is look around.[9]

MANIPULATING PUBLIC EDUCATION

In 2021, the state of Texas passed a "critical race theory" bill. This piece of legislation specifies what social studies materials should be taught in public schools. Removed from previous lists of standard resources are the writings of George Washington, Thomas Jefferson, and Frederick Douglass, the Fugitive Slave Acts of 1793 and 1850, the Indian Removal Act of 1830, the history of Native Americans, the history of white supremacy, the history and importance of the civil rights movement, women's suffrage and equal rights, and the American labor movement. Expressly forbidden is anything associated with critical race theory,[10] a perfectly sound legal theory that racism has been built into our legal system during American history and therefore that American jurisprudence is systemically racist. The Texas bill and others like it throughout several dozen states also forbid the teaching of anything pertaining to the 1619 Project, as noted previously a carefully constructed series of writings by Black scholars and cultural leaders that shows how slavery continues to this day to shape contemporary American institutions in health care, banking and finance, criminal justice, voting rights, and other realms of federal and state government.[11]

The Texas law is no anomaly. Dozens of states and local communities have been rushing to set in place new standards and rules for what can, and cannot, be taught in public schools, from kindergarten through college. This is all part of an attempt by the current Republican Party, dominated by conservative white Christian men, to protect their interpretations of what matters in American history and to make sure that future generations will toe the line—like father, like son.

A brief historical journey to put this historical revisionism in place:

Most white American children of the post–World War II generation were taught that Communists far away and maybe even close to home were the chief enemy of all that is right and good. Christians believed that the worst thing about Communists was that they were atheists, and therefore totally against God and whatever is right and good. Because Communists hated God—or so Christian children were taught—American Christians were indoctrinated by church and state to fear Communism. In this anti-Communist frenzy of the 1950s and early 1960s, Billy Graham became a spokesperson not only for Christianity but also for America as a Christian country that must never let itself be overrun by godless Communists. And so it was that most white American Christian children and young people grew up in the 1950s and early 1960s believing in a God who wanted us to be wary of Communists, to remain sexually "pure" (especially if we were girls), to be obedient to our parents (especially our fathers), and to accept Jesus Christ as our personal savior (also, but secondarily, a teacher of neighbor-love). These provisions were parts of a spiritual and moral package offered by leaders of both church and state to white Christian families during the twenty relatively quiet, peaceful years—quiet and peaceful for white middle-class Americans—between World War II and the Vietnam War.

In the spiritual and political climate of the last half of the twentieth century, Christian movements among evangelists and other conservative Americans committed themselves to upholding the best of both the nation and its Christian origins. Christian leaders like James Dobson and Bill Barr were themselves products of the reactionary Christian education being promulgated among Americans in the 1950s and 1960s. First, in the name of the Christian God, the fathers and mentors of such boys as Dobson and Barr believed that good Christians had to protect white Americans from atheist Communists who wanted to rule the world. Secondly, these white Christian custodians of the American way and their ideological heirs realized they also had to protect the country from Black Americans, whose leaders like Martin Luther King (and much more, Black Muslims like Malcolm X and Muhammad Ali) were caricatured by conservatives as Communists, always as unpatriotic Americans, often as less intelligent than white people, and sometimes as violent sexual predators. As the 1960s progressed, conservative white American Christians found themselves having to protect this nation from their own children—peers of such young men at the time as Dobson and Barr—hippies and yippies and other radical sorts, like Students for a Democratic Society (SDS), who were protesting the Vietnam War and being caricatured as Communist dupes.

Throughout this turbulent period, many Americans, not just young folks, created trouble for archconservative leaders in both America and Christianity. Many American liberals and moderately conservative people seeking justice included workers and laborers who did not accept the fact that in advanced capitalism their place would always be beneath, not beside, management. These liberals and moderately conservative Americans seeking a more inclusive nation included many Christians and former Christians, millions of women and, soon, gay men and lesbians, who shared queer gender and sexual notions that their places in society should be equal under law to those of white straight men. These liberal, moderate, sometimes culturally conservative, and often nonpartisan Americans also included refugees from Vietnam and immigrants from various parts of Latin America and Africa, who imagined that they would be welcomed into America, a land of freedom and opportunity, whose great Statue of Liberty had greeted immigrants in New York's harbor for more than a hundred years.

Throughout this turbulent context—from the end of World War II until the beginning of the twenty-first century—white American Christians' fears of Communists, socialists, working-class laborers, Black and brown Americans, feminists, LGBTQ people, and immigrants generated strong resistance to accepting these people as good, patriotic Americans. Stirred by fear, American Christians created increasing numbers of Christian schools and colleges, like Jerry Falwell's Liberty University, as well as thinly disguised Republican political movements such as the Moral Majority, the Christian Coalition, Concerned Women for America, the Family Research Council, the Heritage Foundation, Focus on the Family, Well Versed Ministries, Exodus Mandate, and the Jericho March, to name a few of the organizations and movements put in place to protect and preserve the purity of white male hegemony in overlapping American and Christian cultures.

This effort to mute the telling of multicultural stories and to dim the awareness of diversity in America gained momentum under the Trump administration. Determined that only the right and best (white male) perspectives on American history and government will be taught to our young people, prominent Christians like former Attorney General William Barr have made public education a primary target of attack throughout America. They accuse public schools of promoting homosexuality, critical race theory, and other manifestations of "secular humanism," which Barr suggests is a new form of "religion." For this reason, he proposes, public schools should be ineligible for government funding.[12]

Remember that the rise of private Christian schools among Protestants did not happen on any scale until after the Supreme Court's *Brown v. Board of Education* ruling in 1954, which set the stage for racial integration of public schools, something that conservative white Christians did not want, ostensibly because they did not believe that integration was God's will. At about the same time, in the wake of the McCarthy witch hunt in 1954, Christian crusades against ungodly Communism took off in American culture. In conservative evangelical fear of both racial integration and Communism, private Christian schools became increasingly common among those evangelical Christian parents who did not want their children exposed to the dangers of race mixing or godless Communism.

Several generations later, early in the twenty-first century, these dangers and others—the demands of feminism and reproductive freedom, recognition of sexual and gender diversity, urgent concerns about climate change, and the introduction of the monumental 1619 Project—would be lumped together by conservative Christian Americans under rubrics of "secular humanism," "socialism," leftist partisanship, and anti-Americanism. This conservative Christian sentiment, among Roman Catholics as well as Protestants, is growing stronger in the twenty-first century as multiculturalism and non-Christian religions become more prominent forces in America, thereby threatening to topple the entitlement of white Christian men of economic privilege.

THE SIGNIFICANCE OF 9/11

The threat to the entitlement of white American Christian men was brought home in a most horrifying, violent way. Due to a failure of imagination and the ignoring of warnings on the parts of America's military and elected leaders, it happened one clear, bright autumn morning. On September 11, 2001, those Christians who had assumed that God would protect America from any large-scale attack by evildoers must have been not only shocked but terribly confused by what happened to the World Trade Center, the Pentagon, and in the field near Shanksville, Pennsylvania. One example of this confusion was the response by Christian evangelist Jerry Falwell who, in conversation with fellow Christian Pat Robertson, infamously remarked, "The pagans and the abortionists and the feminists and the gays and the lesbians who are actively trying to make that an alternative lifestyle, the ACLU, People for the American Way—all of them who have tried to secularize America—I point the finger in their face and say, 'you helped this happen.'"[13]

What became known as "9/11"—September 11, 2001—was not only a dreadful milestone in U.S. history but also a turning point in the so-called Christian Right's view of American history and vulnerability going forward. For the next twenty years, right up to the riot at the Capitol on January 6, 2021, many white Christian Americans—those most strongly aligned with the political Right—continued to be shaken to the core by the constant threat of the loss of their control of America to "terrorists" from outside the United States. September 11 had shown that "otherness" is dangerous, not only Muslims, but all "others" who are "different" from the white straight male-dominated heterosexual Christian majority. White Christians had once thought of America as their own, a country in which everyone had a place and everyone either knew their place or could easily enough be put in their place.

September 11, 2001, blew it all apart.

We saw our nation symbolically crumble in the Twin Towers. For some white Christian Americans, this was the fault of evil people who were most unlike them—Muslim terrorists from the Middle East, of course, but also evil people in America, people like feminists, atheists, lesbians, abortionists, and humanists. From the perspective of many conservative evangelical Christians, responsibility for the attack on America was in no way shared by true believers in Jesus Christ or truly patriotic Americans, who throughout our history had been assumed to be pretty much the same people. From the perspective of these Christian Americans, 9/11 was about people who were not good Christians attacking the good people of God, mostly white Christians, and their America.

When it was discovered that the hijackers were nineteen misguided, radicalized young Islamic men who were following the orders of Al-Qaeda leader Osama bin Laden and who believed themselves on a holy mission for Allah/ God, American Christians had a new enemy: the brown people of Islam at home and abroad.

Fifteen years after 9/11, conservative white Americans, including many evangelical Christians—those most afraid of other religions (especially Islam), cultures (especially Middle Eastern), races (especially Black and brown, and increasingly also Asian, mainly Chinese), and gender variations and ways of being sexual—would be drawn to a man promising to take care of everybody, to protect Americans from harm, to preserve our purity codes, to "make America great again." Many Christians believed that this man was speaking not only for himself, but also for God, and it appears he believed it himself. After all, throughout American history, God had always done what Trump promised to do: make America great, again—the best in God's world.

It is imperative, however, that we realize something: while the age of entitlement may be on the wane among even most white Christian Americans, the deadly sin of entitlement hangs on among us. It will continue to do so until significant numbers of us—American Christians, those who are theologically liberal and moderate as well as those who are more conservative—overcome our lingering senses of ownership and entitlement, of being God's chosen, the ones meant to be best and have most. American Christians need to accept our place as one nation and one religion among many on God's earth.

Those Christians who believe that Christianity is the best, and perhaps the only true, religion on earth need to accept the fact that there are many religions on the planet and many adherents to these other religions who believe that their religions are best. The dream of what we could be can be realized only insofar as American Christians join with people of other faith and moral traditions and begin carefully and prayerfully, strategically and wisely, to reach across our ideological divides, including our spiritual and religious diversities. Only insofar as we do this, can we begin to notice the moral complexities involved in perceiving what is good and what is evil in our life together.

As Christians, we might begin to realize how our perceptions of good and evil have always been forged by different Christian interpretations of the Bible, the Jesus story, and various components of Christian tradition as well as by very different readings of American history, depending upon our own contexts and communities and those of our ancestors. We will learn that we all have much to learn.

If we realize the complexities and diversities in interpretations of both America and Christianity, we will see that what is best among us is the very opposite of entitlement. What is best in Christianity and in America has always been our efforts, building on those of our ancestors, to come together in a spirit of mutual sharing and learning and see what we can discover and do together. Our true greatness, both as a religion and as a nation, will always reside in realms of possibility and aspiration, imagination and hope, moral visions and values that can only be shared and sustained where no one, absolutely no one of us or our race or religion or gender, is entitled, raised above others—and where everyone is empowered to pitch in and help build justice-loving communities in our nation and in our churches.

How can we help each other denounce the sin of entitlement as we begin to announce that we need not be best, nor have most, to devote ourselves to neighbor-love as the spark of our spiritualities, the lodestar of our moral choices, and the foundation of our public policies? How can we help each other see that we will be better as Christians and as Americans insofar as we can celebrate our place as one religion and one nation among many forces for good and beauty in a world in which no one race or gender, no one nation or religion, is entitled to possess and control the life of our nation, our religion, or our planet home? Later, in part 3, we will explore the liberating power of humility as a moral response to the deadly sin of entitlement.

Chapter 6

The Third Sin

White Supremacy

It is perhaps no coincidence that this section is being written on the very day that President Biden is in Tulsa, Oklahoma, to commemorate the more than three hundred African Americans who were massacred in the Greenwood section of that city in 1921. How can it be that neither I, nor many of you, were taught a word about the Tulsa massacre and the burning of "Black Wall Street," a reference to Greenwood as an economically vibrant community and, as such, a target of white resentment and murderous rage? The reason we white Christian Americans had never heard of the Tulsa massacre is because our education—as Christians and Americans—was shaped by white supremacy. It is not only Bob Jones University and other Christian schools that have failed to teach us and our children American history from inclusive, honest perspectives. Our parents and siblings and the vast majority of our white friends and neighbors were never taught about the outrageous, hideous parts of American history in addition to the honorable parts of who, and where, we have been as a nation. It is shameful, our collective failure to teach and learn the truth of our nation and our lives.

The first two sins explored in part 2—omnipotence and entitlement, the lust for power-over and not knowing our place—coalesce in the other deadly sins of white Christian nationalism. We turn now in this chapter to white supremacy as one of the most grievous sins of American Christians. Among the deadly sins of our churches and our nation, white supremacy is getting much current attention due to the convergence of three major social factors.

One factor has been the backlash against the election and presidency of a Black man, Barack Obama, a phenomenon that sparked smoldering resistance and pushback among those white people, like Donald J. Trump and other "birthers," who simply couldn't deal with having a Black person as president of the United States. There can be little doubt that Trump's election was in no small part a white supremacist reaction against the popular and widely respected President Obama. There is also no doubt that a large percentage of white evangelical Christians voted for Trump in both 2016 and 2020.[1] Either these Christians agreed with his racist views or they were willing to overlook them. From the perspective of a Christian need for moral reckoning, either possibility is troubling.

A second factor in our heightened awareness of the white supremacy in our midst is the proudly racist rhetoric and administration of Donald Trump. Recall his announcement in 2015 of his candidacy—the occasion when he famously referred to Mexicans as rapists and his pandering to the Klan and David Duke, whom he at first claimed not to know (but was later forced to admit to). Consider Trump's 2017 response to the neo-Nazis and white supremacists in Charlottesville ("There are good people on both sides") and his referencing people from "shithole" countries like Haiti. Note his welcoming the support of the Proud Boys and other white supremacists whom he asked to "stand down and stand by" in the context of Black Lives Matter protests in the summer of 2020. Think of his rabid anti-immigration policies transparently designed by his smugly racist aide Stephen Miller to keep brown and Black people out of America, to separate parents from young children, and to turn refugees back to countries in which their lives were in danger. Reflect on his administration's efforts to discredit the 1619 Project,[2] designed by scholars to teach Americans about slavery and its legacy. Trump attempted to replace the 1619 Project with his own administration's version of our nation's origins in a slim, whitewashed document titled *1776*,[3] which appeared briefly toward the end of Trump's presidency and which read a bit like the books children of my generation read in the 1950s. As this book goes to press, Trump's insurrectionist Republican Party is not even attempting to disguise its contempt for Black and brown voters, as the GOP attempts throughout the nation to roll back the voting rights that people have fought and died for.

A third factor in moving white supremacy to the foreground of public awareness is the senseless murders throughout the nation of Black and brown people by police. This pattern of state-sponsored violence culminated but did not end in the murder of George Floyd by a policeman in Minneapolis, Minnesota on May 25, 2020, for attempting to pass a twenty-dollar bill that Floyd may or may not have realized was counterfeit. As the tragedy played out, the policeman killed George Floyd by kneeling on his neck for nine minutes and twenty-nine seconds as Floyd begged for his life, said he couldn't breathe, and called for his mother. Three other cops stood by, helping pin Floyd down as a small crowd gathered. One of the observers, a seventeen-year-old girl named Darnella Frazier[4] who happened to be passing by, stopped and filmed the entire episode on her cell phone. This is how we, the American and global public, found out about the exceptionally brutal murder of George Floyd. We saw it with our own eyes. We were witnesses to a moment in American history in which white supremacy could not be denied, covered up, justified, or walked back. We saw what we saw. It was what it was: the murder by torture of a Black man by a white cop for no good reason, murder in cold blood.

And on it goes, spilling over into vigilante policing. In November 2021, a Wisconsin jury acquitted a young white man from Illinois who was seventeen when he picked up his AR-15 rifle and decided to play vigilante in Kenosha, Wisconsin. On behalf of store owners who had not invited him, Kyle Rittenhouse marched into a Black Lives Matter protest and proceeded to kill two protesters and wound a third, all who were trying to disarm him. Columnist Leonard Pitts invites a comparison of Kyle Rittenhouse's fate—acquittal, and lionization by America's Far Right white supremacist network—with the fate of another seventeen-year-old, a young Black man, Trayvon Martin—shot dead in 2012 by a white vigilante as he walked home in Sanford, Florida, carrying only a bag of Skittles and no weapon. Of these two young men, Pitts wrote:

> The killing of one teenage boy [Trayvon Martin] and the acquittal of another [Kyle Rittenhouse] reflect back to us something ugly and small and mean and true about this country. Namely that some tears matter and some don't. Some get advantages and some won't. And yes, some of us get the benefit. But others get only the doubt.[5]

AFRICAN AMERICANS, AND SO MANY OTHERS

Clearly, America's treatment of African Americans, from slavery to the present day, has been egregious. Because it has become a focus of many white Americans since the emergence of Trump and his proudly racist base, we are in danger of losing sight of this country's dreadful past—and present—in relation to other racial-ethnic minority groups, beginning with Native or Indigenous Americans, against whom the white settlers in America waged an early white Christian nationalist campaign of partially successful genocide that was followed by segregation. For four centuries, the American government, with the consent of the governed, has waged military, economic, and cultural tyranny against Native peoples and, to this day, has not considered making significant economic amends.

We ought not minimize the hatred against immigrant and refugee populations from Latin America, the Caribbean, and African nations who are usually Black or brown, and thus perceived as less worthy than European immigrants. Also often seen as brown or Black are refugees and immigrants from northern

Africa such as Libya and Egypt and such Middle Eastern countries as Syria, Jordan, and the Palestinian territories of Israel; as well as people from Iran, Iraq, Afghanistan, India, Pakistan, Bangladesh, and Myanmar. The violence against these people, often treated in America as brown and Black, is ongoing. It will continue until America crafts—and is prepared to enforce—humane, comprehensive, antiracist immigration and refugee policies. A basic part of such policies will necessarily involve some good public education about American history—how we are, in fact, a nation of immigrants, refugees, and slaves, all of us and our forebears, except those of us who are Native/Indigenous. Our leaders—government officials, clergy and religious leaders, professional educators, and certainly parents and guardians—share a moral responsibility to tell Americans the truth, to teach some real American history.

A shameful piece of American history continues to be our unwelcoming and violent treatment of large communities of Asian refugees and immigrants (e.g., from China, Japan, Korea, the Philippines); also people from South and East Asia, reaching over toward the Middle East (e.g. Cambodia, Vietnam, Myanmar); and people from Pacific Islands such as Fiji, Palau, Samoa, and Tonga, to name only a few of the many. Even today, we are witnessing a rise in violent crimes against Asians across this nation. According to a recent poll, violence against Asians and Asian Americans rose by 73 percent in 2021.[6] As this book was being edited, Michelle Alyssa Go, a forty-year-old Asian American woman from San Francisco, was pushed in front of a subway in New York.

Today we should be especially mindful of the hostility on display among some, hopefully not many, Americans toward the Afghan refugees who fled their country, which America had occupied for twenty years and then pulled out of late in 2021. Americans can—and we should—debate whether the United States should ever have invaded Afghanistan, or whether we should have pulled out after the killing of Osama bin Laden in Pakistan in 2011, or whether we should have been better prepared for the collapse of the Afghan military upon the withdrawal of our troops. Regardless of our views of our country's military presence in Afghanistan, however, surely most Americans see the moral travesty in our resistance, as a nation, or as local communities, to welcoming Afghan refugees to live among us.

We come now to the crux of the matter for American Christians: Where are our voices as Christians in response to white supremacist violence against Black Americans and other people of color? Where are our voices in relation to blatant legislative efforts to roll back gains made in the civil rights movement and by other justice workers over the last half century? Most white Christians decry racism, regardless of where we place ourselves along the liberal to conservative spectrum. Few white people intend to be racist or white supremacist in their views or behavior, and many of the white pastors, priests, and members of congregations I have known best have wanted to do whatever is right and good in relation to Black and other people of color. But the fact of the matter is this: white supremacy runs so deeply and persistently through American history that, like a fierce underground current, it tears us apart as a nation and as American Christians and it damages us all. No part of our life together has been unaffected by white supremacy, certainly not our churches, which continue to be the most segregated institution in America. White supremacy has been so pervasive, so relentless, and so cunning that it has been easier for most white justice-loving American Christians to turn away and pay attention to matters where we have felt we can make more of a difference. But what matters might these be other than our personal efforts to be kind to our neighbors? Beyond our personal, private lives, where are we— you and I—in this historical moment, in which our public efforts are needed, indeed required by the Spirit, to help bring justice-love to life in our society?

IN THE BEGINNING . . . THE WHITENESS OF ALL THAT IS GOOD

"In the beginning was the Word—and the Word was White." Throughout our history as a nation, this is how most American Christians have interpreted the prologue to the fourth Gospel. This interpretation has been largely unconscious, of course, on the parts of most people, although white Christians have for centuries pictured Jesus as a white man rather than the darker Middle Eastern man he was.[7] It is not possible to overstate the extent to which European Americans and American Christians, a largely overlapping group of citizens, have been born and educated into the assumption that whiteness—in particular, the whiteness of our so-called racial ancestry and identity—is the essence of all that is pure (clean, unpolluted, healthy) and good (the will of God, aligned with God) in and for our country.

Especially since the revitalization of the Black Lives Matter movement in the wake of George Floyd's murder, many white Americans have become more aware of the depth and power of our white supremacist history. Many of us have begun to realize what has been true from the beginning of our nation's history—that white racism, white supremacy, is in the air we breathe collectively; that all Americans, whatever our racial or ethnic identities, are infected by white supremacy; and that, therefore, we cannot simply exempt ourselves, as individuals, from this massive social problem by insisting, as most white Americans do, that "I'm not racist."

Americans may not mean to be racist, we may not want to be, but if we are alive in this country, we either benefit from being perceived as white or we are automatically liable to discrimination and violence because we are seen as

Black, brown, Asian, Indigenous, or other people of color. "Systemic racism" in America is the shaping of the nation on a deeply embedded assumption, shared by everyone in the system, regardless of what we may think about it as individuals, that being white is the best way to get ahead, and reign supreme. Whiteness is king in America.

For most white Christians, American history begins with brave white European explorers who "discovered a new and uninhabited land." This of course is a bold-faced lie from the perspective of Native—or Indigenous or First—peoples in what became known as the Americas. And for increasing numbers of white Christians, we have begun to hear a different story. We have begun to hear our history differently, as a tale of discovery, violence, domination, slavery, and the meetings of diverse religious customs—those of Native peoples and those of the first Christians to set foot on the soil of the so-called new land.

These different spiritual traditions were not necessarily incompatible or mutually inhospitable. But the religion of the European Christians made no spiritual space for other gods or ways of making sacred meaning of human life. Regardless of the welcome, or lack of hospitality, that the Europeans may have received by the Natives, the settlers' Christian God was assumed to be a jealous God, a deity with no tolerance for other gods—who Christians believe were false gods or idols. Therefore, although they themselves had fled religious persecution by other Christians, the European Christians could not allow the gods and customs of the Indigenous Americans to mingle with and pollute Christianity. And since the Europeans' chief aim was not to make peace with the Natives but rather to take control of their land and make it their own, the Christian victors raised a flag on American soil, the flag of white supremacist assumptions about their one God and the values that they had imported from Europe.

The point of this chapter is not to discuss racism or white supremacy per se. Our purpose here is to think about how American Christianity has aided and abetted in the maintenance and spread of this deadly sin. What in our theologies—our understandings of who or what God is—has given birth to white supremacy or, at the very least, allowed it to distort and damage our lives as Americans and as Christians? How have our churches fueled white supremacy in America—purposely and proudly in the nineteenth century and, often more unaware and unintentionally, into the latter part of the twentieth and early decades of the twenty-first, even among mainstream Protestant churches like those many of us have attended?

WHITE SUPREMACY IN OUR BONES

As a way into understanding the *sin* of white supremacy America—that is, white supremacy as a serious theological *problem* to be solved, in large part by Christians, mostly white Christians—I am drawing here on the brilliant insights of Isabel Wilkerson who asks that we consider "caste" rather than "race" as the structural basis, or bones, of this problem:

> America has an unseen skeleton, a caste system that is as central to its opera-
> tion as are the studs and joists that we cannot see in the physical buildings we
> call home. Caste is the infrastructure of our divisions. It is the architecture of
> human hierarchy, the subconscious code of instructions for maintaining, in our
> case, a four-hundred-year-old social order. Looking at caste is like holding the
> country's X-ray up to the light.[8]

Wilkerson continues:

> A caste system is an artificial construction, a fixed and embedded ranking of
> human value than sets the presumed supremacy of one group against the pre-
> sumed inferiority of other groups. . . . Caste and race are neither synonymous
> nor mutually exclusive. They can and do exist in the same culture and serve
> to reinforce each other. Race, in the United States, is the visible agent of the
> unseen force of caste. Caste is the bones, race the skin. . . . Race is what we
> can see. . . . Caste is the powerful infrastructure that holds each group in its
> place. . . . Caste is fixed and rigid. Race is fluid and superficial, subject to
> periodic redefinition to meet the needs of the dominant caste in what is now the
> United States.[9]

As presented by Wilkerson, caste can be considered the *theological* underpinning of race in America. Caste is "fixed and embedded," the bones, "rigid." The Christian religion first imported by white European Protestant men provided the bones and structure of what would become our American fixation on whiteness as the epitome of racial purity and goodness of white supremacy at the heart of the American way. This means that our racism as Christians cannot simply be blamed on conservative evangelical Christians. Every Christian in the United States of America, regardless of denomina-tion, shares the responsibility for carrying white supremacy forward, largely unaware, through our own spiritual traditions.

From the perspective of caste, white American Christians have been wor-shipping at the altar of a golden calf for four hundred years: the bones and structure of white supremacy. Most white Americans have done so silently—in oblivion, apathy, shame, and often pride. But it's important to recall here, with the astute Black lesbian feminist essayist, the late Audre Lorde, that "our silence will not protect us,"[10] and that if we are not struggling to topple this wretched idol, we are actively assisting in maintaining its dominance over our churches and our country.

Underscoring the religiosity of white supremacy in America, Isabel Wilkerson proceeds to discuss eight pillars of caste, the first being "divine will and the laws of nature."[11] The "curse of Ham"—as it has been referred to by white American and European Christians over the years—understands white superiority and black inferiority as the consequence of Noah's rage at his son Ham for having viewed his nude body passed out drunk.[12] For this reason, Ham's and his son Canaan's descendants were portrayed by biblically rooted white Christians as Black people, cursed by God. The sons and daughters of the archetypal Black African, Noah's Ham, would suffer oppression under the power of his brother Japheth's white European progeny. As bizarre and appalling and perhaps as irrelevant as liberal Christians of all races and cultures may find this story of origins, Wilkerson suggests that it is, in fact, the biblical story beneath the first pillar of caste in America.[13]

PURITY AT THE HEART OF WHITE CHRISTIAN NATIONALISM

Among the other seven pillars of caste in America, one in particular stands out as especially revealing of our churches' implications in perpetuating white supremacy: the fourth pillar of caste is "purity versus pollution."[14] In the course of my lifetime, white Americans have been fearful of intermarriage and sexual pollution; sharing water sources like swimming pools and drinking fountains; trying on clothes in a store if a Black person had tried them on before; shaking hands with Black people; sharing blood via transfusions with Black people; and integrating schools, theaters, restaurants, cars on trains, seats on buses, and of course, churches.

Throughout American history, politicians, eugenicists, and other social leaders have tried to determine how much "Black blood" is legally permissible for a person to be legally classified as "white." This has been necessary in order for legislators, judges, and others in authority to determine who could vote, marry a white person, be admitted to a theater, swim in a public pool, attend a certain school, eat in a particular restaurant, live in a certain neighborhood, get a mortgage, buy insurance, drive or walk in particular parts of town without risking harassment or death. Political and scientific trendsetters have also determined which ethnicities, nationalities, and religious identities have been acceptable as "white" or "pure" in America. Over decades, white Americans' perceptions have evolved, allowing some groups to achieve "white" status—the Irish come most famously to mind—while others have not. Latinx, Asians, and Middle Easterners continue to be judged irrationally, through wary eyes, as to whether they are more or less "white" and, therefore, more or less acceptable as insiders rather than as alien to white America.

We white Christians have inherited our sin of white supremacy. For white American Christians from 1619 in Jamestown, Virginia, right up to the present, racial purity has meant the preservation of the white race and its many cultural derivatives, those hallowed traditions that we normally think of as Western art, music, values, perceptions, and customs such as marriage between one (usually white) man and one (usually white) woman. None of these cultural products are necessarily good, right, pure, or anything other than cultural derivatives of our inherited racial and religious assumptions.

The civil rights movement of the 1950s and 1960s, the women's movement of the 1960s and 1970s, and the gay liberation movement of the 1970s and 1980s shook up assumptions not only about what is pure but, more basically, about whether "purity" itself ought to be honored as a moral good in realms of race, sex, and gender. Nonetheless, from a Christian theological perspective in America, the "whiteness" of God and of all that is good, and of all that we experience as deriving most wonderfully from God, continues to hold sway. Many of us continue to honor lightness over darkness, the sun and the moon over the blackness of the night sky, the brightness and beauty of life over the darkness and scariness of death, and "cleanliness being next to godliness." This is not to say that white people do not appreciate the beauty of the black sky or other images of blackness in art and fashion. Many of us do. But it seems to me that most if not all of us grant a certain "supremacy" to whiteness and lightness as ultimate sources of purity, goodness, and God-ness.

You may still protest that, of course, we gravitate toward the light, literally, to find our ways through the dark; and it should go without saying that we love the beauty of moon and stars that light up the black sky. What is the point, you might ask, of taking the "light-dark, black-white" metaphor into the realm of the ridiculous? The point was underscored emphatically by Muhammad Ali, who died in 2016. Once a pariah to white American Christians, the boxer and war resister who evolved into an American icon explained in an interview how he used to ask his mother about white representation. He said he was a curious child who noted the plethora of white objects and people, including in literature, media, and even household products and wondered why black people weren't represented in the same way.[15] The point Ali was making is that white Christian Americans have learned through our shared Euro-American heritage to associate whiteness and lightness—whether in the evening sky or among human beings—with purity and, therefore, with cleanliness, goodness, and God. In our life together as Christians and Americans, the opposite and frequent enemy of whiteness is blackness.

By association, this includes Black people and other black bearers, images, and icons of evil and death: the Black Plague, the "dead of night," Darth Vader, Voldemort, and so forth. Of course it *is* absurd. It makes no good sense, scientifically, psychologically, or artistically. But the absurdity makes it no less real—and certainly no less challenging to our sensibilities of what we perceive to be good or bad, safe or dangerous, beautiful or ugly, something to step toward or away from.

Our perceptions of whiteness and lightness as somehow better than blackness and darkness also make no sense spiritually or theologically. Yet most Christians, people of color as well as white people, continue to highlight European Christian perceptions of purity through Christian liturgies, prayers, and hymns. In America, white Christians have long since normalized these primitive, irrational assumptions about the supremacy of whiteness and lightness in all realms of our human experience, beginning with the racial identities of white people. The deadly sin of white supremacy is shrouded in whiteness.

THE 1619 PROJECT: WHITE SUPREMACY LIVES ON

"Americans need to believe that the arc of history bends toward justice. And they are rarely kind to those who question whether it does."[16] This is how Adam Serwer, staff writer for the *Atlantic*, sums up the major controversy about the 1619 Project. It is not that the motive of the project is to show that slavery lives on today in American institutions, from public education to health care to the banking and finance industry. The problem with the 1619 Project, according to Serwer, is its pessimism:

> The most radical thread in the 1619 Project is not its contention that slavery's legacy continues to shape American institutions; it's the authors' pessimism that a majority of white people will abandon racism and work with black Americans toward a more perfect union. Every essay tracing racial injustice from slavery to the present day speaks to the endurance of racial caste. And it is this profound pessimism about white America that many of the 1619 Project's critics find most galling.[17]

Serwer is right that Americans refuse to view ourselves or our country pessimistically. We adamantly need to believe, in Unitarian minister Theodore Parker's words made famous by Martin Luther King, that "the moral arc of the universe is long, but it bends toward justice."[18] But we should be clear: Nikole Hannah-Jones, the Black scholar who conceived the 1619 Project and wrote its lead essay, does not view the work as pessimistic. She sees it as an important historical corrective. The 1619 Project was written to correct the whitewashed version of American history that we all grew up with, regardless of our race.

Hannah-Jones opens her essay with these words: "Our founding ideals of liberty and equality were false when they were written. Black Americans fought to make them true. Without this struggle, America would have no democracy at all."[19] Later in her essay, she continues, "The year 1619 is as important to the American story as 1776. That Black Americans, as much as those men cast in alabaster in the nation's capital, are this nation's true 'founding fathers.' And that no people has a greater claim to [the American] flag than us."[20] The 1619 Project is a searing indictment of the white supremacy that continues to shape American society and our institutions. I found it horrifying, informative, not in the least surprising, and in some deep, precognitive way clarifying. Reading this project was cathartic to my soul as well as instructive to my historical mind. From the perspective of these reflections on the deadly sins of white Christian nationalism, the 1619 Project lays bare the real, ongoing, violent effects of a number of these interactive sins, especially white supremacy.

White Americans need to be clear. The tone and content of the 1619 Project ought not be trivialized as "pessimistic." It's simply an attempt to introduce us to our own nation, and some of the effects of our own religion if we are Christian. It invites us to get real. In response to the negative hullabaloo over the 1619 Project, someone offered an analogy along these lines: It's like we've moved into a house and then later discovered that the foundations are unstable and the waterpipes are rusted—to which we say, "Oh whatever. We didn't build this house. It's not our problem."

Slavery's ongoing legacy *is* our problem. Offering us an opportunity, the 1619 Project is a bold, sharp, piercing wake-up call to Americans of all colors, summoning people to come together to make America a more perfect union by doing everything in our power to correct the grave injustices that slavery left behind. The 1619 Project will not let us forget that our criminal justice system continues to mete out harsher punishments for Black people and that young white men do not risk death simply for "driving while white." The 1619 Project will not let us ignore the grim fact that more Black people suffer neglect and death in a health care system in which people are consumers, a system in which patients essentially have to buy their way in or prove somehow that they are entitled to get well.

White supremacy is mean spirited and out for revenge when unmasked by critics like Nikole Hannah-Jones and her fellow authors. Small wonder that, two years after the publication of the 1619 Project, the trustees of the University of North Carolina in Chapel Hill denied tenure to Professor Hannah-Jones, an esteemed professor at the university and a 2017 MacArthur

Grant recipient. Reacting to great outcry from alums, donors, and other critics of the university's abject stupidity as well as charges of racism, the trustees reversed themselves. But Nikole Hannah-Jones decided instead to cast her professional lots instead with Howard University, one of America's oldest and most prestigious historically Black universities.

The controversy surrounding the 1619 Project continues to spread in contemporary America where one of our two major political parties has staked its life on denying the presence of white supremacy in today's America. As noted by Hannah-Jones in her preface to the expanded version of *The 1619 Project* in 2021, "Some who opposed the 1619 Project treated a few scholars' disagreements with certain claims and arguments as justification to dismiss the entire work as factually inaccurate, even as other equally prominent scholars defended and confirmed our facts and interpretations."[21]

Another historian and Black studies professor, Mary Ellen Hicks, summarized helpfully much of the criticism the project has drawn from reputable scholars, Black and white. Shortly after its publication in 2019, Hicks tweeted, "The discussions about the 1619 Project . . . have made me realize that historians may have missed an opportunity to demystify the production of scholarly knowledge for the public. The unsexy answer is that we produce constantly evolving interpretations, not facts."[22]

Many white American Christians choose to deny or minimize the irrefutable historical fact of slavery as an American horror story, however varied may be its interpretations from different perspectives—economically, socially, historically, personally, psychologically. Many American Christians, especially those of us who are white, also either do not see the legacy of slavery among us today or, if we do see it, we tend to trivialize it. In this context, the deadly sin of white supremacy continues to rip and tear the moral fabric of our nation, thereby weakening our possibilities to realize more fully the American dream of liberty and justice for all.

Chapter 7

The Fourth Sin

Misogyny

In the 1970s, in the wake of major civil rights legislation and policy advancement and as the second wave of twentieth-century feminism began to break, feminists sometimes discussed whether racism or sexism was a more foundational structure of evil in American society. This question tended to be answered most satisfactorily by antisexist Black women like Audre Lorde and antiracist white women like Adrienne Rich,[1] who understood well that both of these structures of oppression, each rooted in sin, are foundational and interactive throughout American history.

Beyond a doubt, white women like me come bubble-wrapped in a cloak of white privilege that protects us from racist but not sexist violence. Whereas, Black women and other women of color have no protection from either sexist or racist violence. In that sense, Black women live in double jeopardy.[2] Black men also have nothing to protect them from racist violence and often little protection from being accused of sexual crimes and thus of being especially vulnerable to sexual as well as racial violence in America. No structure of oppression should be trivialized by comparing it to any other morally reprehensible source of human suffering, and each can be better understood when realized as interactive and mutually reinforcing. Which structure of oppression, sin, and evil is deemed worst depends on who is being harmed in particular contexts. There is no "worst" oppression in the abstract. The worst is always determined by the immediate emergency, the violence that requires our attention right now. It could be a Black man being tortured by a white policeman. It could be a woman of any color being knifed by her husband of any color.

It could be eight victims, including six Asian women, who were shot and killed in Atlanta-area spas on March 16, 2021, by a young Baptist white man who told police that his sex addiction ran contrary to his Christian faith. Which of the deadly sins was motivating the evil wrought by this young man?

Of course, violence, but how about white supremacy, or misogyny, or a lust for power-over, or a sense of entitlement as a white Christian male? Mihee Kim-Kort, a Presbyterian minister, responded to this question shortly after the killings: "[As] a scholar of religion and a child of both church culture and American culture, I have asked the same questions and can only conclude: It is all of the above. Race, gender, religion, and culture are all implicated."[3]

In this chapter, we will explore misogyny, a deadly sin that is at the root of violence against women in America and throughout the world. Misogyny and violence sometimes become synonymous, so closely intertwined are they in the psyches and lives of men who feel entitled to exercise power-over women, however violently they must, in order to control them.

WHAT IS MISOGYNY?

Like white supremacy, misogyny is a basic structure of violence in America that undercuts the possibility of our enjoying a healthy, just, and safe society. According to the *Oxford English Dictionary*, misogyny is "hatred, dislike, or prejudice toward women."[4] It is rooted in men's radical ambivalence toward women. By "ambivalence," I mean two competing, usually opposing, feelings we can have toward another being, or event, or situation. A personal example is my own love and yet fear of my own horse (I happen to love horses and have had several during my retirement). The older I get, the more I both want to go trail riding and yet am afraid to ride because I'm afraid to fall off and get hurt. I am ambivalent—and as I actually get ready to mount my dear horse, I am *radically* ambivalent—really, seriously, deeply ambivalent!

So too, men in a patriarchal social order, such as ours, as well as the gendered social order of much of the world, harbor deep, radical ambivalence toward women. Most men genuinely love women, especially those whom they know best—mothers, wives, daughters, girlfriends, lovers, good friends, and valued colleagues. At the same time, most men—especially in a strongly Christian culture like ours—grow up fearing what they have learned to experience as women's sexual lure or seductiveness as something that can spin men out of control.

All people, not just men, often project strong, challenging feelings onto other people: "They—those other people—scare me." "They make me feel this way." "They cause me to screw up." In a society in which white men learn to seek power-over others as well as the social privileges that accompany their race and gender, these men learn also to project their fears—especially their sexual fears and anxieties—onto women or onto men if they find men sexually attractive. This projection of sexual anxieties onto the very people whom they find attractive, and even may genuinely love—a beloved spouse, for instance—is a primary example of radical ambivalence. Such ambivalence provides the emotional content of misogyny.

Misogyny can turn into hatred in situations in which men really do not like certain women, or women in general; situations in which men's blaming of women for their own failures or insecurities has become emotionally overwhelming; situations in which men are consumed by wanting women sexually whom they cannot have; or ritualized situations, in which disobedient wives, girlfriends, or daughters are accused of violating family honor or community standards, such as religious purity codes or simply refusing to accept male domination. Violence against women often results from such hatred with its roots in misogyny.

One of the problems generated by misogyny is women's own self-debasement. We women learn to fear and even loathe the qualities that men project onto us. For example, women and girls often experience ourselves as seducers, because we have been told that is how our sexuality works in relation to men and boys. Men and boys may fear our seductive ways, but we imagine that they also like to be seduced. And so, women and girls are also ambivalent. On the other side of this gender tension, many men and boys in American society, thanks in no small part to traditional Christian teachings, have learned that, whereas female sexuality is impure and dirty, their own male sexuality can be played with as an instrument of pleasure and fun.

These differences between male and female sexual expectations—that boys will be boys, while girls should be good—are much less pronounced in today's America, even among most Christians, than when I was a girl in the 1950s and 1960s. However, in conversations with younger friends and relatives, as well as through observations of popular culture, it is obvious that the major difference between the male's sexual prerogative and the female's sexual subordination continues to be compelling. It is a source of tremendous anxiety and sicknesses such as anorexia among girls and boys, young women and men, in contemporary American culture.

Because misogyny teaches girls and women to disparage ourselves in relation to men, it also breeds anxiety about our bodies—our shapes and sizes, our feelings, how we move and use our bodies, what to do about our erotic longing. In this way, misogyny creates women's denials of our sexual feelings and women's repression of our sexual longing. Misogyny pictures and condemns homosexuals as being interested only in having sex, sex, and more sex. Wherever there is misogyny and sexism—which is the primary social shape of misogyny—heterosexism, homophobia, and transphobia are never far away.[5] In relation to sexism and sex phobias, both gay and straight, the Christian Church has been a basic part of the problem at least as far back as Saint Augustine's confession of his own sexual passion in the fifth century and his laying of the blame for it on humanity's original sin, our "concupis-cence" or sexual lust.[6]

Honest, thoughtful American Christians, whether more conservative or liberal, wrestle with sexual identity, sexual activity, and gender variation as challenging moral issues. No family and no community is exempt from having to deal with such questions sooner or later, often unexpectedly—in an incidence of sexual violence, the struggle of a teen to make sense of who he is, the breakup of a marriage, or a partner's turning to alcohol or another drug to cope with her erotic ambivalence. Such instances can happen in any American family regardless of what, if any, faith tradition they may practice.

Misogyny also tends to conjure up images of superpowers and superhe-roes to compensate for men's anxieties about impotence. In one dramatic display of super-manhood, a number of the white male insurrectionists at the Capitol on January 6 donned attire and carried flags and symbols denoting their ever-wishful power-over women as well as over the Congress of the United States. In this gathering of Proud Boys, Oath Keepers, 3 Percenters, Boogaloo Bois, and conservative evangelical Christians, it was not hard to detect a collective fear of a loss of manhood. Fearful to their misogynist core, the insurrectionists publicly displayed their need for a white macho man, one who calls himself a Christian, to grab power-over women, queers, socialists, Jews, Muslims, Mexicans, and all others who pose a threat to the construction of a white Christian America being led by real men.[7]

MISOGYNY IN THE EARLY CHURCH

A radical ambivalence toward women and gays as well as a hatred of inde-pendent, self-defined women has been a driving force in Christianity from early in its male-dominated history, although probably not from its origins as a devoted band of friends and followers of Jesus of Nazareth.[8] A strong case has been made by Christian scholars over the past fifty years that women were present alongside Jesus from the very beginning, but that these women were either erased entirely from the New Testament record or have been interpreted by Christian men through the lenses of misogyny: For example, Mary of Nazareth, Jesus's mother, has been lifted up, especially in Roman Catholicism, as the prototype of ideal womanhood, existing only as an impossibility: a nonsexual childbearer. By contrast, Jesus's good friend Mary Magdalene has been represented as a whore—a prototype for a bad woman.

Christian feminist theologians have labored together and separately to present Christian faith and its biblical foundations as both a source of evil and violence against women and of healing and liberation for those women who have either left the church (more than we will ever know) or who have chosen to stay in the church and keep digging our ways through and beyond the misogyny of traditional Christianity.[9] Building on each other's work as scholars, pastors, priests, teachers, mothers, grandmothers, daughters, colleagues, and friends, feminist and womanist women who have stayed in the church at least until now have found ways to celebrate the Jesus stories. We live as his sister sojourners who seek to better know and respond to one Spirit, our constant source of faith, hope, and justice-love. Christian women are called to realize the truth in Roman Catholic poet Renny Golden's declaration that "struggle is a name for hope."[10] Many women of different races and Christian cultures have taken it upon ourselves to lay bare the bones of the sin of misogyny that distorts the Jesus story and damages the whole human race as well as the integrity of the earth.

FEMINISM: FIGHTING MISOGYNY

Christian feminism is a movement against misogyny in America churches and throughout the Christianized parts of the world. Christian feminists understand that misogyny is not only a problem of conservative evangelical Protestant Christians, Roman Catholics, or Orthodox Christians, but rather of all Christians. All Christians are heirs to a profoundly misogynistic religious tradition, rooted and grounded in both Hebrew and Greek versions of misogyny, about which the Protestant Reformations (continental and English) did some but not much good. Roman Catholicism and Eastern/Greek Orthodoxy are famous for their misogyny, but all Protestants—from the most traditionalist to the most liberated—are heirs of this same problem.

Here's how it goes in American Christianity, as boys learn to be ambivalent toward girls, and girls learn how to survive: As they age, most growing boys and adult men in American Christianity are well aware that women are different—not just lacking a penis and having a vagina but also radiating a lure by which to draw boys and men to them. Like Eve, women are often seen by boys and men as wily, seductive, tempting, and dangerous. White American women are seen usually as not as physically strong or as mentally adroit in math or science as the guys. but often as better at cooking, cleaning, sewing, weaving, reading, writing, and other language arts. And of course women are great objects of sexual desire by straight and bisexual boys and men. Most men are sexually attracted to them in spite of, or maybe because of, the thrill of cozying up to and penetrating the "other," often lovingly and mutually, but sometimes coercively and violently—which is rape.

Moving along the same gendered track, women learn early on that we must survive in a man's world. This we do either by learning and playing the role of "good women"—that is, sexy and flirtatious, up to a point; and good wives, good lovers, good homemakers, good cooks, and good mothers, who love children and care for them. Some women even pretend to be less intellectually savvy than we are; and some pretend to enjoy sex when we don't. Some women reject traditional gender roles, regardless of what men may think of us or want from us. The latter—the choice to reject mandatory gender expectations—has been one of feminism's chief aims for women. Feminism is pro-choice, not anti-male.

Let's be clear. Feminism is a movement, and most feminists have not disparaged either men or heterosexual relationships. The stereotype of a "man-hating" woman is an antifeminist trope, a lie purposely concocted to thwart efforts on behalf of women's rights. Feminism has most surely encouraged women to learn to love ourselves as fiercely independent human beings. In this spirit, a favorite bumper sticker from the 1970s was "A woman without a man is like a fish without a bicycle." That slogan made me laugh back then, and it still does. A favorite T-shirt from the period, which many of us wore, declared us members of a "ladies sewing circle and terrorist society." We celebrated the radical notion that a good and fulfilled woman actually can live her own life, with or without a man. The men we wanted as friends, partners, and husbands agreed with us. If men didn't agree, we didn't need them in our lives.

Black feminist Ntozake Shange expressed this sentiment in her acclaimed 1975 choreopoem, *For Colored Girls Who Have Considered Suicide / When the Rainbow Is Enuf*, "I found God in myself, and I loved Her. I loved Her fiercely."[11] That truth reflected the basis of both feminism and "womanism"—a term coined in 1983 by African American writer Alice Walker[12] to denote "Black feminism," which took racism as seriously as sexism, something that many white feminists had not always done. Feminism and womanism became major disrupters of men's assumption of having power-over women during the latter quarter of the twentieth century and the first decades of the twenty-first.

But was feminism largely a white women's movement? Yes and no. Too many white feminists, both earlier in American history during the suffrage movement, and in the latter part of the twentieth century, acted as if white women's rights mattered more than those of Black men or Black women. Among liberals, many white women simply didn't see "color" as an issue. Liberal white women had learned not to notice race, to be "colorblind," which only white people could be, of course, since Black people have never had such a privilege. For Black people to pretend to be colorblind in America gets Black people killed, as every Black person ever pulled over by a white cop knows. White women have always had the social power, bestowed on us by white supremacy and white privilege, to ignore race as an issue if we have wished—and, therefore, to take Black men's and women's lives and voices for granted. Throughout our struggles for women's rights, too many white feminists have made this serious moral and political mistake.

Even so, there were exceptional feminist leaders of different colors and cultures in America who struggled to make sure that the most politically astute feminism reflected diverse agendas and voices. Reflecting racial, ethnic, and religious differences, Gloria Steinem, Adrienne Rich, Audre Lorde, Gloria Anzaldua, Barbara Smith, Elly Bulkin, Patsy Mink, Cherrie Moraga, and Robin Morgan were among the most outspoken feminist voices in mid-to-late-twentieth-century America. As noted earlier, Alice Walker pushed the conversations further among Black and white women with her suggestion that Black women struggling for Black women's liberation were not simply Black feminists—they were womanists. In this context, another slogan appeared on banners and T-shirts in the 1980s: "Feminism is to womanism as lavender is to purple." Womanism was presented by Walker as bolder and more radical than feminism, more aggressively antiracist as well as antisexist. Among Christian feminist and womanist theologians, any number of white, Black, Latina, and Asian women made significant contributions to the ongoing transformation of Christian liberation, postcolonial, and queer theologies. This book in your hands builds on those many contributions, some which are listed in the resources and bibliography at the end of the book. But there is no way for us to realize the extent to which our lives as women of faith are built on the work of women across cultures and around the world, women whose work we mostly do not know, yet whose impact continues to shape our lives and our world.

ANTIABORTION: A POLITICAL PLOY BY THE GOP

No issue signals justice for women of all colors, cultures, and classes as wholeheartedly as reproductive freedom, including the right to safe, legal, accessible abortion as well as the right to be safe from unwanted sterilization. There is no movement in contemporary America that reflects misogyny more brutally or seductively than the so-called right to life effort to protect the unborn fetus, often at the expense of women's lives and always at the cost of women's health and well-being. Moreover, the antiabortion movement's claim that it champions the life of the unborn is a clever distraction from what it actually champions: the Republicans' war against women. The antiabortion obsession of right-wing American Christians was designed about fifty years ago as a strategy not to protect the unborn but rather to strengthen the Republican Party's electoral chances amid an increasingly diverse and racially tolerant population who were more inclined to be Democrats.

There were two reasons abortion became a target for Republicans and conservative Protestant Christians: First was the GOP's strategy to win the presidency in 1972. To this end, candidate Richard Nixon's adviser Pat Buchanan urged Nixon, a supporter of legalizing abortion, to adopt an anti-abortion position to win over significant numbers of Roman Catholics who until then had been a reliably Democratic base. The second reason abortion became contentious was also largely a matter of strategy and not so much about principles or the value of unborn life. Until the passage of the Civil Rights Act in 1964 and the Voting Rights Act in 1965, conservative evangelical white Christians had organized politically around their efforts to hold white supremacy in its God-given place. But after the passage of the civil rights legislation of the 1960s, which white conservative Americans took as a defeat, the evangelicals needed another focus. Just as the GOP needed to increase its Roman Catholic support, the party also needed to rally its white evangelical Christian base. The new focus, which the Supreme Court's *Roe v. Wade* decision provided in 1973, became the thwarting of women's rights—in particular, the defeat of the Equal Rights Amendment and the right to reproductive freedom, including safe, accessible abortions. From the 1970s on, the Republican Party became increasingly antifeminist, managing to defeat (at least temporarily) the ERA in 1972 and putting the right of fetal life, rather than women's health and well-being, at the center of its platforms from one election cycle to the next.

And so it is that the antiabortion hysteria unleashed by the political alliance of conservative Christians and the Republican Party is only about fifty years old. Prior to this coalition of antiwoman energies in the 1970s, neither political party in America nor most evangelical Christians were opposed to women's right to choose safe, legal abortions; or if they were personally opposed, this issue was not a major political cause for them. Until the 1970s, prominent Republican leaders who were pro-choice included Richard Nixon, when he was vice president of the United States; George H. W. Bush, when he was a U.S. senator, and his wife Barbara throughout her life; Ronald Reagan, while he was governor of California, and his wife Nancy; George Romney, governor of Michigan, and father of Mitt who, as governor of Massachusetts, had advocated keeping abortions legal and safe.

We do not have to like the idea of abortion or favor abortion as a means of birth control to believe strongly that it should always be a safe, legal option—usually sad, but also usually important to a woman's health—that is accessible to all women and girls. If we do, however, genuinely respect women's capacities to exercise moral judgment and make important life choices about our own bodies, we will support women's right to choose an abortion in America. If we honestly respect women, we will be more than disgusted by the transparently misogynistic connection between immature, angry men grabbing the genitals of women and these same men often being at best indifferent as to whether women have reproductive options and choices. And if we respect all American women, not just white women, we will be as committed to protecting Black and brown women from sexual abuse and forced sterilizations as we are to protecting all women's right to choose safe, legal means of birth control, including abortion.

By the time of the 2016 and 2020 elections, almost all Republicans, in order to run for national office and for most other positions, had to be publicly antiabortion and had to speak out in favor of the Supreme Court reversing its 1973 *Roe v. Wade* decision. This was of course because, over the past fifty years, most conservative evangelical Protestants and most Roman Catholics had become adamantly antiabortion and were insistent upon their political representatives reflecting this position.

Is it coincidental that, in this fiercely antichoice context, the Republican presidential candidate's contempt for strong independent women was transparent and a matter of pride for the candidate? Because Trump's pre-dominantly white Christian voters did not make any connection between his disregard for women and his antiabortion politics, or because they shared his position, or because they did not care, or because they chose to look the other way, they elected Donald Trump as president. During his term, he was able to appoint three conservative associate justices to the Supreme Court. Because of the court's new majority, it is positioned to make life much harder and much less safe for American women and girls, as well as for LGBTQ and many other groups of American citizens and undocumented workers and families.

The final pages of this book are being written in early December 2021, as the Supreme Court considers *Dobbs v. Jackson (MS) Women's Health Organization*, the case that most observers expect the court to use to overturn *Roe v. Wade*. As the book was being edited in May 2022, a draft by the Court in which it overturns *Roe v. Wade* was leaked. Whether or not *Roe v. Wade* has been overturned so by the time you read this book, the moral work of justice-loving Christians and other Americans on behalf of women's health and freedom will continue to be urgent. This is because misogyny continues to shape the moral and spiritual foundations of American Christianity and American society.

CHRISTIAN MISOGYNY LAID BARE

Although this book is not as concerned with the Roman Catholic Church or other Christian traditions that fall outside the realms of Protestant American Christianity, no one has done a more important assessment of Christian misogyny than former Paulist James Carroll. His most recent work, *The Truth at the Heart of the Lie*,[13] directly informs my understanding of misogyny as one of the seven deadly sins in American Christianity and a tenacious root of white Christian nationalism. Keep in mind that, historically, all American Christians have deep theological roots in Roman Catholic or Eastern Orthodox traditions. Much of what is best, like festive celebrations and wonderful music, but also much of what is worstfrom these older religious cultures—most problematically, radical ambivalence toward women—lingers in American Protestantism.

In his stunning analysis of the misogyny undergirding the Roman Catholic Church and in the root system of Christianity itself, Carroll makes several illuminating connections. He connects clerical celibacy as a mandatory but arbitrary rule, the church's condemnation of artificial birth control and its fierce denunciation of abortion, its refusal to bless same-sex marriage or relationships, the ecclesial hierarchy's refusal even to talk about women's ordination to the priesthood, and the church's sexual abuse scandal that has erupted globally over the past few decades, a scandal which neither Pope Francis nor any of his less justice-minded predecessors seems even to comprehend.In other words, the men running the church don't get it; they don't see that the connecting link between all these positions is misogyny and its twins, homophobia, the fear of same-sex love and sexual expression, and transphobia or the aversion to fluid gender identities.

Indeed, Carroll contends that the church in which he once was ordained as priest shows no sign of awareness that its entire structure is built on misogyny, a contempt for women as strong, independent human beings. It's as if Roman Catholicism would collapse in its entirety if some wise and courageous pope were willing and able to dislodge and pull the thread of misogyny out of the church. As a younger man, Carroll had believed that Pope John XXIII, who convened the Second Vatican Council (1962–1965), might have begun to do just that—to unravel the misogyny and sexism of the church, which had been acknowledged by the council. But the good Pope John died in 1963, and not until the arrival of Pope Francis exactly fifty years later did Carroll have any hope that what John had begun might be resumed by Francis. Sadly, Carroll acknowledges, "I fear that I was wrong."[14] So deeply is the ambivalence toward women and sex, a contempt for strong women, and a desperate fear and denial of sexuality embedded in the world's largest Christian community.

Carroll discusses the Catholic Church's condemnation of birth control as a blatant example of its misogynistic disregard of women's moral agency as well as their health and well-being. And indeed, Roman Catholicism is famous for its treatment of women and girls as childbearers rather than as theological mentors or ethical teachers.

THE FATHER'S OMNIPOTENCE

The misogyny underlying Protestant Christianity in America usually has been less dramatic and outrageous than in Roman Catholicism, notwithstanding the Salem witch trials (1692–1693). But however subtly, Protestant Christianity in Europe and America has incorporated the misogyny inherited from the Roman Church five hundred years ago. What James Carroll describes is familiar to Protestant Christians in America—the depth of ambivalence and abiding contempt toward strong, independent women and girls that runs through Christian churches, the more liberal and moderate congregations as well as the more conservative—though not as dreadfully or transparently in contemporary liberal Protestantism as in the more conservative traditions.

Not until the mid-nineteenth century did one Christian church in America—the Congregational Church (which in 1957 would become the United Church of Christ)—open its doors to women as ordained ministers.[15] Other Protestant denominations would follow, but not for about a hundred years. Change has come, but it's been slow. We can look at the Episcopal Church's struggle to ordain women priests, which began about a century ago and, after nineteen study commissions conducted over a fifty-year period, culminated in the irregular ordinations in 1974 of eleven women in Philadelphia, prior to the church's authorization of women priests two years later.[16] We can point to similar efforts across all Protestant denominations in America, in which women and their allies have had to wage spiritual warfare to convince churchmen that women can be called by God to ordination.

In 1984, when conservatives took over the Southern Baptist Convention (SBC), the largest church community in the United States, the SBC voted against the ordination of women. This was an affront not only to Southern Baptist women in general. It was a rejection of those women who had been ordained in Southern Baptist congregations for two decades, beginning in 1964 with the ordination of Addie Davis in the Watts Street Baptist Church in Durham, North Carolina.[17] In response to the 1984 condemnation of women's ordination, the SBC lost many congregations as well as members like former President Jimmy Carter and his family. In March 2020, popular evangelist Beth Moore left the SBC due to its uncritical acceptance of President Trump, noting especially his attitudes toward women. Many "free" and "independent" Baptist churches in America, as well as some of the contemporary megachurches, either do not allow women ministers or simply prefer to have male pastors, since men are assumed to be the heads of churches and families. They are, after all, most indisputably in the gendered image of God the Father.

THE FATHER GOD'S HOLD ON
THE LIBERAL CHURCHES

Notwithstanding the Southern Baptist Convention and other more conservative Protestant churches, a number of successful movements for ordained female leadership have made a positive difference in how American Christian men view women and how we women view ourselves. And yet, in many liberal Christian churches, even those with women ministers, little has changed in how American Christians view God, the ultimate source of meaning and goodness in our life together.

How do American Christians in the more liberal and moderate Protestant traditions continue to view God? How do mainstream American Christians experience the power of God in relation to the ongoing moral and spiritual blight of misogyny in God's world? The emphasis is on liberal and moderate Christian churches in America here rather than our more conservative Christian sibling churches because so little has been said elsewhere about the ongoing challenges women and girls face in liberal churches.

In most liberal Christianity as in other Christian churches, the Fatherhood of God and his dominion with his Son Jesus over all creation is still the heartbeat of Christian misogyny. Most liberal Christian churches present themselves as gentle manifestations of power-over relationships, in which gentlemen, like God the Father, exercise polite authority over women and children, sons and daughters, servants and employees, and anyone else structured beneath them in a hierarchical chain of command. This ostensibly benign misogynist arrangement of power-over—a kindly father figure exercising his power—has been the case over the two millennia of Christian history. Some feminist historians have pointed out that this was not the case earlier in the Christian story, as told by friends and followers of Jesus, in which Jesus's disciples and companions were a band of friends, brothers and sisters, who were not structured in hierarchical chains of command.[18]

Over the next few centuries, men made themselves bishops and clergy and took over leadership of the church. By the third and fourth centuries of the common era,the Christian Church had begun to assume a rigid, hierarchical chain of command. From that point on, bishops and men in authority—professional theologians (often the bishops themselves, like Augustine of Hippo) and scholarly laymen—dictated what was true and false, good and evil, what Christians would believe, what Christians would not believe, and how Christian life would be organized around the human father's power-over his flock, much in the image of the divine Father God.

In this historical patriarchal framework of authority, the early creeds of Christianity were forged as statements of Christian unity in the midst of the church's efforts either to survive, in non-Christian territories, or to resolve differences in beliefs between competing groups of Christian believers. In its own way, each of the major Christian creeds represented a political victory of one Christian faction over another. The two creeds most commonly shared in today's Christian churches are the Nicene Creed and the simpler Apostles' Creed. Both reflect a shared affirmation of "God the Father" and of "His Son, Jesus Christ our Lord." Both bear witness to a Holy Trinity: a Father/Creator, his Son Jesus/whom Christians often revere as Christ or Savior, and the Holy Spirit. Many Christians have come to regard the Spirit as the least constricted, the freest, and most liberating member of the Trinity, sometimes imaged as a female-gendered energy "who comes sailing on the wind, her wings flashing in the sun."[19]

In churches that value honest theological questions and open-minded Christian education, a case can be made for *teaching* Christians about the credal statements. Some Christians would be interested in learning who wrote them, when, for what reasons, and why Christians have passed them down through the centuries as affirmations to unite us spiritually with those Christians who have gone before us and those who affirm these same creeds today all over the world. These and other Christian statements of belief, like the various catechisms children are taught before they are baptized or confirmed, have an important place in church history. But the language of the ancient creeds of Christendom is comparable, I submit, to Confederate statues in America. While the linguistic portrayal of a Father and Son may have an important place in history, it should not occupy the center of Christian worship or be repeated regularly as a statement of faith because people of faith know more than we did once upon a time. The Christian creeds are steeped in patriarchal theological assumptions we now know to be misleading, wrong, and harmful. God is not a Father any more than she is a Mother. The creed conveys a static shape of a Father-Son relationship as the essence of God and the spiritual root of all that is good. The creeds of the church make no mention of any woman except Jesus's mother Mary who is identified as a virgin, and the creeds are absent even a hint of Sophia, or God's Wisdom,[20] as a woman-affirming source of sacred energy.

I once asked a professional colleague, a church historian in the seminary where we both taught, how he understood the words of the Nicene Creed. "Oh, Carter, nobody cares what the words mean. We say the creed in order to be connected with Christians all over the world, not because anyone takes it literally." My response to him at the time, which is my view today, is that we should draw a line between teaching the history of the patriarchal creeds as important to the Christian story and continuing to repeat them at the center of worship. They simply do not belong there, at the center. Not only do they drive people away from the churches that elevate them in this way, but they actively harm us by underscoring the patriarchal character of our spiritual journey.

As long as the creeds are central to our worship—as they are each Sunday in the Eucharists of Roman Catholic, Orthodox, and Anglican/Episcopal Churches, and other churches as well, throughout the world—they will be making a statement, regardless of what the ministers intend, that the Fatherhood and Sonship of God continue to reign supreme in a world in which to be a woman, mother, daughter, sister, lover, friend, aunt, or other female companion is to be not as valuable as a man, and to be destined by divine decree to live forever under the controlling thumb of the omnipotent Father and his Son.

The same could be said of making the Fatherhood of God and the Sonship of Jesus central to the celebration of the Eucharist or Holy Communion in those churches that share this common meal. The celebration of patriarchal power-over women is active in every Christian church and liturgy that does not create a liturgical universe of Christian spirituality in which the sacred is celebrated as female energy, grandmother, mother, daughter, sister, aunt, woman friend, and lover. These images should be lifted up in every Christian liturgy as conduits of sacred power and as fully redemptive images of God. The celebration of femaleness and nonbinary gendered and sexual images should not be an afterthought, nor merely set aside as an alternative to traditionally shaped patriarchal worship of Father and Son. Mother and Daughter imagery, as well as a multiplicity of nonbinary reflections of the divine, should be lifted up and worshipped as central to Christian life.

It takes spiritual imagination and liturgical talent to make this happen in ways that draw from stores of Christian wisdom. But equally indispensable to the task of liturgical reform is the courage and integrity of church leadership. Until bold, brave, creative women and men step up to the task, liberal Christians will continue to collude with those churchmen who have fought for two millennia to maintain power-over women and all things sexual and who do so in the name of a God the Father and of his Son Jesus Christ.

FEAR OF SEXUAL AND GENDER IMPURITY

Through the eyes of American Christianity, the problem of a Black man touching or being touched by a little white girl, a story I recounted earlier, is at least as much about filth and pollution as about the sexual abuse of a child by a man. James Dobson's antigay obsession is at least as much about what he imagines to be a disgusting act of men putting their semen into other men as about the sacredness of his own or anyone's heterosexual marriage. Those of us who are LGBTQ identified are well acquainted with the usually unspoken, but always operative, assumption that the real problem with homosexuality and any deviancy from gender and sexual norms is pollution, filth, the very idea of people messing with other people's body parts or fluids. This is something that Christian leaders historically have treated as too shameful even to talk about. Having sex with a same-sex partner, or having an operation on one's private parts, or doing anything with one's own sexual organs for pleasure, including masturbation, is like swimming in a polluted pond, leaving scum in the soul as well as the body.

Before we move on from the deadly sin of misogyny, we must consider the profound fear of sexuality that goes hand in hand with Christian contempt for women, onto whom men's sexuality has long been projected. Adam's insistence in the book of Genesis that "the woman . . . gave me the fruit, and I ate it" (Gen. 3:12 NLT) has long been men's favorite self-justification for sexual pleasure: she made me do it! And sexual pleasure outside of marriage and childbearing has been among the gravest sins in Christianity.

Over the centuries of Christian life, the church in all its forms has invested considerable psychospiritual energy into antisexual teachings, sexual restrictions on everyone, confining sexual expression to marriage, discouraging sexual pleasure even in marriage, condemning all premarital and extramarital sex, including homosexual sex, as impure and evil, and of course denying that there is anything about homosexual sex that is natural or morally permissible. In order not to deal honestly with sexuality, all churches have participated in widespread denial of the harm done largely because repressed sexuality will eventually find a way to burst out of its artificial and dishonest containers.

Sexual denial and repression has been a major source of the sexual abuse scandals throughout Christianity in recent decades, laying bare a phenomenon that has been present in the church for most of its history —with all Christians having been encouraged to repress and hide their sexual feelings. The outrageous molestation and rape of children and of nuns by priests and pastors, and the cowardly cover-up of sexual abuse by bishops, popes, and denominational leaders in Protestant churches, testify to the depth and breadth of Christianity's sexual crisis. Until church leaders—Protestant, Roman, and Orthodox—accept the fact that this crisis is rooted in the Christian misogyny that alienates us all from our bodies as sources of pleasure and goodness, the crisis will only fester and continue to harm and sicken Christians around the world.

James Carroll is clear that, in the Roman Church, sexual abuse is directly correlated with the church's culture of denial and repression, a culture that itself is steeped in misogyny and homophobia. Our more liberal Protestant traditions also continue to deny the depths of misogyny and homophobia that still infuse Christian teachings about sex and gender. If liberal Christians want to help solve the church's sex problem, we must become more fully transparent about the universality of our sexual experiences, both good and bad, joyful and terrible. How to help each other heal from bad (coercive) sex and learn to practice good (mutual) sex should be basic to Christian education among kids as well as adults. We need to help each other move through our anxieties in realms of sex and gender so that, together, we can learn how to speak about the love we so badly want to give and receive as people on God's earth.

Until we can muster our courage to do so, Christianity will continue to contribute more to America's sexual sins than to our sexual healing. And the myriad of these problems that we share—sexism; homophobia; sexual and gendered lies and confusion; sexual repression; sexual abuse; and violence against women, children, and LGBTQ people—will continue to haunt our churches and our nation as well as our own bodies, relationships, families, and communities.

Much could still be said in discussions of misogyny about the economic consignment of women and children, girl-children in particular, to the lower rungs of food security, health care, education, and other resources basic to human well-being in Christian America (and throughout the world, whether Christian or not). But what must be emphasized here is that, whether in secular or religious realms of our common life on this planet, wherever the Christian Church and other patriarchal religious traditions wield political power, the social and economic status of women and girls is lower than that of men and boys. The misogyny that generates these conditions is a shameful and wickedly deadly sin.

Chapter 8

The Fifth Sin

Capitalist Spirituality

Along with its companion—chapter 16 in part 3—this chapter is likely to draw more resistance than any other in this book among contemporary American Christians, including liberals. This is because we are so conditioned to accept capitalism not only as the best economic system in the world but also as our only alternative to "socialism," something most Americans either equate with Communism or view as a softer version of the Soviet-style Communism, which my generation of white Americans grew up loathing. Even now, many American Christians think of Russia, China, and even our small island neighbor Cuba as dangerous boogeymen not because they don't even pretend to be political democracies but rather because we perceive their economic systems as carryovers from the Communism of the last century.

Let me say as clearly as I can before we begin the following discussion of "capitalist spirituality" that I know two things for sure in relation to this topic: First, while I do not pretend to be an economist with a deep or detailed understanding of the moving pieces of advanced global capitalism, I know enough to realize that the so-called Communist countries, like China, are major players in the global *capitalist* system, competing for *profit* with America and the rest of the world. Second, I know that American Christians need to have a conversation about capitalist spirituality because we cannot in good faith separate economic justice—matters of hunger, health care, housing, and human well-being—from what we value and believe as followers of Jesus who more than anything taught us an ethic of neighbor-love. What does love of neighbor mean if not to provide access to food security, ample clothing, livable wages, affordable housing, good public schools, and health care for all Americans, without exceptions?

In the 1990s, Christian feminist ethicist Beverly Wildung Harrison challenged all who are committed to economic justice. She contended that we need to generate holistic spiritualities for justice. Understanding that economic justice increases and strengthens democracy, Harrison believed that Christians must work for transformation of our economic system, not just practice charity. This we must do, she taught, if we intend to build a functional democracy in which all people can have meaningful lives, including voices in shaping the society in which they live.[1]

Beverly Harrison realized that her ethical vision of economic justice ran counter to the prevailing assumptions shared by most American Christians that global capitalism is the wave of the future. In contemporary American society, capitalism is simply assumed by most Christians to be not only the American way of doing business but also the will of God. Harrison knew this, but she also knew that, in the twenty-first century, most Americans do *not* have meaningful work lives, do *not* make a livable wage, *cannot* afford major health crises, have little to no disposable income, and are generally alienated from what they experience as the massive failure of their government and their country to help them live meaningful lives—that is, live without constant stress and anxiety.

Consider this vignette of life in small-town USA, as reported by Darlene O'Dell, a brilliant writer. In a recent essay on roots of white Christian nationalism in her hometown of Union, South Carolina,[2] O'Dell tells of her great-grandfather forcing his twelve-year-old daughter, a straight-A elementary school student, to leave school and work in the local mill. Several decades later, in the 1950s, wealthy textile heir Roger Milliken shut down the mill in neighboring Darlington, South Carolina, because its workers had demanded higher wages. Milliken later shut down the Monarch Mill in Union, where both of Darlene's grandmothers had worked, one at the spindles, one as a secretary. These are snapshots of working-class history in early twentieth-century America. Fast-forward a century to 2015, and we see Scott Walker, Republican governor of Wisconsin, stripping collective bargaining rights from state employees as just one instance of elected leaders, in concert with conservative business leaders and their evangelical Christian allies, attacking labor unions in America. These are snapshots of American life—and capitalist spirituality—then and now.

INNOCENT, IGNORANT, EMBARRASSED, AND ANGRY

I grew up in the last half of the twentieth century in a white Christian family that would have been categorized by sociologists as "middle class"—though, as noted in chapter 1, I learned to think of myself as "upper-middle class." Like many white children born in the prosperity boom following World War II, I was raised believing that everyone, at least all white people, had enough of whatever they needed. I always recognized the economic disparity between white and "colored" communities in the South, and this disturbed me even as a child. And yet, as far as I could tell, no one around me at home or anywhere else reflected on matters of class or discussed any of the variables that normally constitute class locations in America: race, gender, wealth, educational standing in the community, family name and heritage, cultural customs, religion, or neighborhood.

My parents, like most other white middle-class adults, had little class consciousness in a nation that preferred to deny any reality of a class system. Daddy was proud that his family tree included one of the signers of the Declaration of Independence, and he seemed to have taken it in stride that his father had been a major in the army during World War I, later had worked as a manager of a cotton mill in Pelzer, South Carolina, and as an older man had managed a motel in Myrtle Beach and had gone fishing every day from the local pier. Mama was more upwardly mobile in her dreams than Daddy and, in that sense, had a greater awareness of class, though I never heard her use that word. Both of my mother's grandfathers had been Methodist ministers, and her father had owned a wholesale tobacco company that had made him a fair amount of money for the time. He had been killed in a car accident when Mama was a teenager, and I grew up assuming that my widowed grandmother, my mother, and her younger brother been left pretty well off, without any financial worries. My maternal grandmother always seemed to be a stylish white lady who loved the finer things and who was able to afford beautiful clothes and always had "hired help," a "colored" (Black) cook and maid.

My parents also had hired help occasionally, especially when my siblings and I were still at home. Mama and Daddy enjoyed their life together in a series of small frame or brick houses as my father got transferred from one North Carolina town to another in his job as a salesman for Esso in the 1950s and 1960s. While my family didn't have a great deal of money, Mama tried to make sure that we children got a taste of what she believed were important things for kids to experience: family prayer every day and church every Sunday, music lessons, summer camp, horseback riding, membership in a swimming club, dressing up and eating out at my grandmother's club once in a while. Daddy also wanted us to have whatever educational and recreational opportunities we wanted. When I was about thirteen, however, Daddy told me how much he wished he and Mama could afford to let me keep riding horses, but they just couldn't. A few years later he said almost apologetically that if I chose to attend a private college instead of a state school, I'd have to get a scholarship or else work my way through college because he and Mama couldn't afford the tuition.

Most white American children of my generation grew up thinking of America as a nation in which social class and economic standing don't matter all that much, a country in which anyone can get ahead if they try hard enough—after all, look at Abe Lincoln and his humble beginnings. In this all-American ethos, in which socioeconomic class was a nonissue, and never an educational subject in high school, labor unions were portrayed, at least in the white middle-class South, as shadowy groups sometimes run by the Mob. Organized labor, I learned to assume, was un-American, Communist inspired. Growing up in the 1950s, most white middle-class Christian American children heard little to nothing about the ongoing struggles by workers for a living wage, unless they had parents who were union workers.

Class history in America was as deeply mystified as the history of Black people. For many white Americans, class was even more baffling than race. Little was preached or prayed in our churches about either of these major divisions in American life—and almost never was a word spoken in our mainline white churches—for the most part moderate to liberal churches—on behalf of the workers or the poorest Americans, whatever their races or ethnicities.

This failure on the part of liberal white pastors and priests may have been intentional but more likely it was rooted in the ignorance—often no doubt an *innocence* cultivated over generations—of most white middle- and upper-class Americans with regard to class. Most white American Christians, however well or poorly educated, have not known how to think about class as a moral matter. We have not known how to think about economic injustice as a serious ethical challenge, a systemic matter that transcends the quaint notion of the very Protestant, and very capitalist, "work ethic" that every white American male has been told he must embody if he wishes to succeed.

Most white middle- and upper-class American Christians have never learned spiritual or political lessons about the *system* of economic injustice that would challenge the adequacy of our spiritualities of charity in which we take turkeys to the poor at Thanksgiving. Most white lower-and working-class American Christians have never learned these lessons either. Most Americans have not been taught to think about economic injustice in ways that do not stir senses of personal shame or failure.

In the early 1980s, in my late thirties, I asked Beverly Harrison (my life partner as well as the Christian feminist social ethicist whose work we have been exploring) to come with me on a tour of the homes in Charlotte, North Carolina, where my family and I had lived since the late 1950s. Along the way, Bev said something that startled me: "You've always described yourself as 'upper-middle class,' but these houses tell a different story. Your family was just plain middle class." Bev Harrison had been studying and teaching economic ethics for years. She had been thinking and teaching about class in America, but until that moment, I had not made a conscious connection between my own class origins and what Bev had been teaching students at the Union Theological Seminary, myself among them in the 1970s.

About a year later, I was coteaching a course at Union Seminary in feminist theology with political theologian Dorothee Soelle, who was from a middle-class German Christian family, and American Christian ethicist Mary Pellauer, who was from a working-class American family. When the three of us asked students to tell us something about their class backgrounds, most balked. What business was it of ours to have such information? What difference did it make anyhow? The students refused to participate. When the dust settled, it became clear to us all—students and teachers—that the problem was that the American Christian students didn't know what to say. They knew little to nothing about their class backgrounds. It's as if we had asked them to speak a foreign language or, worse, to shed their clothes in public and tell us what they saw. They were embarrassed and angry.

ECONOMIC CRISIS AND MORAL CHALLENGE

So let us cut through this ignorance and consider for a moment the basic framework of economic theory in America within which most talk about the economy takes place on Capitol Hill as well around our kitchen tables. We need to have this conversation even though few of us (myself included) use the words or grasp the theory behind them well enough to risk even opening debate about what we do in fact know or intuit. But here we go—we take this risk because the moral urgency in this historical moment demands it.

In twenty-first-century America, ever since the so-called Reagan revolution of the 1980s, Americans have been living within a framework of a neo-classical[3] understanding of how the economy works. Long gone is any serious appreciation—by either the government or big businesses—of small-business owners, shopkeepers, and the sorts of work once upon a time referred to as "private enterprise." If small-business owners or private entrepreneurs can make it financially in corporate America, fine; but they basically are left on their own, to fend for themselves in an economic order that increasingly generates wealth in the high millions and billions, no longer in the thousands and low millions.

In this neoclassical framework of advanced capitalism, the American economy is driven by the ability of corporations to create profit for the wealthiest Americans. The neoclassical theory is that, when left alone, unbridled and uninhibited by government regulation, the profits that become wealth will trickle down—through employment, wages, housing markets, food supplies, and so forth—from the wealthiest to the poorest among us, thereby meeting everyone's basic needs.

The problem is it doesn't work. As Americans have learned over the past four decades, the wealth of rich Americans simply increases. It goes up; it

doesn't trickle down to any significant degree. There seems to be little interest in sharing among the very wealthy. We hear a lot of chatter about the
government having no business requiring "me" to share my money; a lot of
talk about what's "mine" being mine; and the constant conniving on the part
of many wealthy Americans, and their corporate interests, for tax breaks. Not
enough of the great wealth created in America ever reaches most Americans,
especially the poorest segment of our citizenry. Most of us identify somewhere in the middle of this economic scam in which the rich get richer and the
poor get poorer. For this reason, most Americans, and most Christians, find
ourselves simultaneously having to fend for our own economic well-being
and do what we can to help the poorest among us have enough food to eat
and shelter to survive.

Lots of good Americans who loved Ronald Reagan, those who say they
"loved Reagan but hate Trump," might think about the devastating economic
downward spiral that began with neoclassical's "trickle-down" scam. Ever
since Reagan's economic revolution of the rich, our country has been on a
downward spiral economically, in which the rich truly are getting superrich,
with yachts, planes, mansions, great art, and low (sometimes, no) taxes while
the poor are increasingly struggling simply to survive. Most Americans are
increasingly perplexed about what has happened to our country in recent
decades. How did this happen? If we want to know how we got Donald
Trump, we need look no further back than Ronald Reagan. Certainly we
cannot pin the blame entirely on any one president or his economic advisers,
but there is no question that Reagan's catering to the rich at the expense of
everyone else's economic security played a major role in creating the financial conditions that have produced a widespread cynicism and even despair
among many Americans who have not known where to turn, or to whom, for
help. Among these Americans, a significant number turned to the man who
promised to make America great again.

The neoclassical framework was constructed in mid-twentieth century
America by Milton Friedman and his colleagues in the Chicago school of
economics. They offered their theory of an aggressive, largely unregulated,
market-driven economy as a corrective to what they believed had been the
mistakes made earlier in the century by Keynesian[4] economists who had
advocated a closer relationship between market forces and government
regulation. The neoclassical proposals were adopted by Reagan as well as by
Margaret Thatcher in Britain and went to work increasing the divide between
American wealth and poverty.

These same proposals were embraced enthusiastically by every subsequent Republican administration and almost all Republican politicians, as
well as by most Democrats, although less enthusiastically and often with
reluctance. Although Presidents Bill Clinton and Barack Obama attempted to

be advocates of social justice and economic fairness, they did little to challenge the neoclassical basis of America's economic system. Interestingly, the Affordable Care Act (Obamacare) of 2009 began to chip away at the neoclassical system by providing government health care assistance to many Americans. Not surprisingly, Obamacare drew fierce condemnation from Republicans who railed against the federal government's intrusion into America's hallowed private halls of heath care and health insurance. The Tea Party was hatched largely among conservative evangelical Americans in protest to Obamacare. This right-wing political movement managed not only to oust Congress's Democratic majority in 2010, but it ultimately set the stage for the election of a Tea Party–type candidate for president at the end of Obama's second term. And so it was that, thirty-six years after Reagan's election, Donald Trump hitched his wagon to the same neoclassical star and took off at breakneck speed, determined to increase the wealth of rich Americans, including himself, and to do whatever he could to dismantle and destroy all regulatory functions of the federal government. Thus, neoclassicism has provided the theoretical underpinnings of America's basic economic structure for the past four decades, and it has been for the most part unchallenged except by those who identify as democratic socialists.[5]

Let's be clear that, throughout this time, not only has the American government not "owned the means of production" (historically, the gist of Communism), but the means of production—that is, corporations—increasingly own the American government.[6] Not only is America nowhere close to being socialist, we are as far away from a fair distribution of taxes, labor, and other life resources as a political economy could possibly be.

In a neoclassical economic system, there is no way to achieve any semblance of fair balance between the wages of management and labor, much less between the riches of corporate owners and the economic situations of the vast majority of Americans. Many American companies, owned and managed by genuinely caring people, good people, try to achieve some degree of fairness and to show genuine respect for workers in their businesses, but the structures of our economic system, built to increase profit and wealth, are heavily weighted against any significant mobility of those who live and work near the bottom or even the middle of the economic pyramid. Tax laws, liability laws, banking regulations, health care costs, insurance premiums, pharmaceutical expenses, and education costs are among the many variables in our society that work together to generate and secure wealth *and* poverty.

It is no wonder that so many working-class white people in America are angry. They should be able to do better economically than they do. Truthfully, the rest of us should be just as angry that we have fallen prey collectively to the corporate powers of advanced global capitalism that have taken possession of our government—especially today the Republican Party and its highly prized and packed Supreme Court. This what concerned Christians need to be aware of, speak out about, and work to change. We need to be angry, courageous, compassionate, and persistent in our pursuits of economic fairness and justice. We are facing not only an economic challenge but a major moral crisis as well.

CAPITALIST SPIRITUALITY: MAKING A CONNECTION

In the years leading up to her death in 2012, Beverly Wildung Harrison had been talking about capitalist spirituality, a subject near to her own life as the daughter of Adelia, or "Dale," Wildung. Dale had been widowed as a young mother in Luverne, a small town in southwest Minnesota. She had opened the Luverne Style Shop, a women's clothing store, to support her five children. Growing up as Presbyterians, Bev and her siblings had inherited from their mother a strong work ethic as central to their lives as both Americans and Protestant Christians. This ethic became foundational to Harrison's life as a renowned scholar and beloved teacher of feminist social ethics to several generations of progressive Christian ministers and teachers. Throughout her career, one of her academic and educational passions was economic ethics— increasingly in her later years, what she would name "capitalist spirituality." Due to physical challenges and diminished energy, Harrison was unable to pursue this topic in her waning years with as much vigor as she had wished, but she talked about it with friends and colleagues right up to the time of her unexpected death.

Harrison was clear that for much of the past two hundred years, Protestant Christianity in America had aligned itself with capitalism, to the moral discredit of both. As both Protestant Christianity and capitalism had grown stronger in American life during the nineteenth and twentieth centuries, each had contributed to the other's loss of any meaningful moral compass. In their shared fixation on the economic advancement and spiritual salvation of the individual (white male) as central to the American way of life, both American capitalism and Protestant Christianity had lost sight of the *common* good: the betterment of the *whole* society, not just its upper tiers; the advocacy of liberty and justice for *all* people, not just some; and a strong, shared concern for the *well-being of the earth as a mutual partner*, not primarily an object of economic exploitation.

Harrison laid the responsibility for these failures squarely on the shoulders of both advanced global capitalism, especially its neoclassical foundations, and Protestant Christianity, especially its idolatry of the individual white male. Like other feminist and womanist Christians, Harrison was disturbed by the individual white male's obsession with himself over others—and over any serious sense of responsibility for building human community beyond one's own personal interest. Harrison understood the building of community not only as the heart of America at its best but, moreover, as the heart of the human project itself. As a social ethicist, she often asked—what does it mean to us, to be human? What is our human responsibility on this planet? What are our opportunities to live as fully human beings?[7]

In chapter 1, I discussed the alliance between American business leaders and conservative Christian leaders in reaction against Franklin Roosevelt's New Deal in the 1930s and 1940s. Business leaders believed that Roosevelt was damaging their capitalist rights to make whatever money they could without having to give any of it away to people who didn't deserve it—poorer white and Black people who hadn't worked for it, so the capitalists charged. Conservative white Americans were frightened that the New Deal's taxation policies and regulations would empower African Americans, raising them up toward equality with white people. Thus, motivated by white supremacy and courting the political support of evangelical Christians, conservative American politicians resolved that the best ploy to win Christian votes was to link Roosevelt and the New Deal to Communism, portraying it as not only un-American but also ungodly. As discussed earlier, Billy Graham was one of the most prominent characters drawn into this drama in mid-twentieth-century American Christianity.

This American Christian antithesis to socialism, characterized by conservatives as "Communism-lite," in collusion with the corporate capitalist agenda to increase the wealth of the most affluent Americans, lives on. It steadily drives the white Christian nationalist agenda for America to this day: No to socialism is yes to God. No to collective bargaining is yes to bosses and managers. No to the distribution of wealth is yes to the individual's rights to everything that is his. No to sharing responsibility for the common good is yes to taking care of myself and those like me. And so on. The billionaire textile magnate Milliken, who bought up the mills in South Carolina, was not an anomaly but rather a representative of neoclassical economics being acted out much as Milton Friedman and his cohorts in the Chicago school proposed.

Republicans, even those most proudly antiunion and pro-business, do not have a monopoly on the fear of socialism, collective bargaining, distribution of wealth, and taxing the superrich to benefit the whole society. Most of today's Democrats, while they espouse greater economic fairness in America, are loath to be labeled "socialists" for fear that such a perception will destroy them politically. And yet most Democrats, many independents, and some Republicans realize that the reforms and regulations put in place by Franklin Roosevelt and, a generation later strengthened by Lyndon Johnson, benefited America in significant ways, especially in relation to its most economically marginalized citizens. Since the 2020 election, President Biden has emerged boldly and empathically as an advocate of poorer and more marginalized Americans of all colors and cultures. And as a white Christian man elected for his empathy, primarily to help heal wounds inflicted by his predecessor, Joe Biden has revealed his passion for economic justice and fairness to be a potent healing balm for most Americans. This is why he is so feared and loathed by Republicans.

Meanwhile those Roman Catholic prelates who are so eager to criticize the president for his support of abortion rights seem to have little if anything to say about his advocacy of fair tax policies, a federal minimum wage, labor unions, child tax credits, and other components of economic justice. These privileged Christian champions of capitalist spirituality in America seem more concerned about the "unborn" and stripping women of their rights to control their own bodies than about economic justice or even survival for the poor, including poor women and newly born infants.

If we were honest and bold, we might well ask these men of God, Protestant and Catholic leaders alike: Why is Jesus of Nazareth, an itinerant Jewish teacher from a working-class Palestinian family, lifted up so high and celebrated as a King, adorned in fancy clothes, sitting on a throne, much like so many popes, bishops, and well-to-do evangelists? Do you not realize that you have made Jesus in your image rather than conformed yourselves to his way of being in the world? Why, if you wish to follow Jesus, do you try to protect yourselves from questions like these, rather than walk alongside Jesus in spirit and humility, listening carefully to your sisters, brothers, siblings?

JANUARY 6, 2021: AN ASSAULT ON BOTH
ADAM SMITH AND JESUS OF NAZARETH

The high individualism and profit-consumed motive of advanced capitalism and its advocacy by both the Republican Party and most white Christian evangelicals was the ultimate driving force behind the January 6 riot at the U.S. Capitol. The aims of Trump and his insurrectionist party, as well as the obeisance to Trump by most other Republicans stands in stark opposition ironically not only to the teachings of Jesus but also to the teachings of Scottish economist Adam Smith (1723–1790), sometimes called the father of capitalism.[8] Both Adam Smith and Jesus denounced the horrific economic and spiritual injustices of the systemic poverty of their times. Both blasted business and political leaders' accumulation of wealth and power-over the lives and poverty of most citizens as immoral and ungodly. These two men, in whose lifework the seeds of capitalism and Christianity were planted, would likely be horrified to see what is being done by those who worship them in contemporary America.

In popular imagination, most of us probably see the Capitol riot as having been mounted by a bunch of uneducated white guys, mostly evangelical Christian at least in name or background, embodying the worst of white Christian nationalism—racism, sexism, anti-Semitism, and violence. For the record,[9] any number of these same rioters were middle-class or wealthy men and some women, mostly white with some people of color sprinkled in. Some of them were paying lip service to the Jesus or the Christianity that they believe is on their side in opposing socialism, opposing the enemies of God and Jesus, opposing feminists, queers, Democrats, and "elitist" highly educated Americans who think they're better than poor, white, hardworking American men and women.

It's ironic but not surprising that a number of economically privileged white male rioters, egged on by several highly educated U.S.senators, would denigrate their political opponents as "elitist" for being outspoken advocates of liberty and justice for all Americans. Having the moral courage to press for fair tax structures, decent jobs, living wages, health care, and high-quality public education for all Americans evidently constitutes the elitism of American leaders in the minds of Trump's insurrectionists and their GOP enablers. When Hillary Clinton spoke inelegantly of the "basket of deplorables,"[10] she might well have been forecasting the January 6 riot and the truly deplorable devolution of one of today's two major parties.

In this historical moment, where is the outrage of Christian churches, liberal, moderate, or conservative? Who are the Christians speaking publicly and unapologetically on behalf of economic justice and fairness? Where are we?

In the context of capitalist spirituality, a deadly sin of conservative evangelical Christians over time has been to side with rich, corporate America over and against poor and working-class people. Not surprisingly then, part of what we saw on display at the U.S. Capitol on January 6 was public, noisy collusion between proud capitalists and politically conservative evangelical Christians, a partnership carefully cultivated over time.

But a less visible part of what was underway in the January 6 insurrection was the creeping, silent complicity in the perpetuation of capitalist spirituality by liberal and progressive Christians, whatever our traditions. Especially over the past century, since the rise and fall of Communism as a world order, Protestant, Catholic, Orthodox, and other moderate to liberal Christians have been reluctant to critique advanced global capitalism not only as an ethical problem but as the deadly sin it is. More often than not, we have been silent, feigning indifference or pleading ignorance about such matters. Our collective failure to clearly and unequivocally denounce capitalist greed and violence continues to be our shameful part in perpetuating this deadliest of sins against the people of our nation and world, as well as against the well-being of the whole creation and its Creator.

In this moment, where is our outrage, and where are we personally and collectively, especially in our churches? With whom must Christians stand in this moral wasteland of systemic greed, poverty, and violence? How can our churches faithfully and, as effectively as possible, push against the deadly sin of capitalist spirituality and work together to reshape our nation's economy in ways that will help secure the common good? These are questions we need to answer if we wish to honor our baptismal vow to "renounce the evil powers of this world which corrupt and destroy the creatures of God."[11]

Chapter 9

The Sixth Sin

Domination of the Earth and Its Creatures

There's no debate that we are destroying our planet home and its many varied creatures, including ourselves. Unless we find ourselves immediately in harm's way, however—being overtaken by fire, floods, draught, famine, or other natural disasters—the processes of global destruction seem to most humans to be terribly slow moving and hardly an immediate priority. Whatever problems the global crisis signals will be solved further down the road—beyond us and our immediate circles of loved ones.

In America, and wherever on earth the Christian Church plays a major role in shaping cultural norms and politics, the root of planetary destruction is a bad Christian theology of domination—specifically, rulership of the earth and earth creatures—rather than of building mutual partnership with earth and animals as our way of being human. Many Christian theologians argue that this is a gross misreading of Genesis 1:26, in which God gives humankind dominion over the earth.[1] These Christians will insist that God is expecting humankind to exercise responsible care over creation, much in the image of God, and that there is no hint of violence, disregard, or cruelty in this biblical story. A problem with such a benign rendering of God's "dominion" charge to humankind is that we see so little of this tender stewardship in our society. An even more basic problem is that most people on earth, including American Christians, cannot easily imagine generating mutuality with the earth and its nonhuman creatures. Among the world's religions, the Sikhs[2] are the most notable exception to humanity's effort to dominate rather than belong to creation, a possibility we will be lifting up in part 3.

Of course, there are remarkable Christian leaders like Saints Francis (1181–1226 CE) and his companion Clare of Assisi (1194–1253 CE) in Italy, the German abbess Hildegard of Bingen (1098–1179 CE), and French theologian and Jesuit priest Teilhard de Chardin (1881–1955 CE). Each of these renowned advocates of the earth and its creatures promoted radical mutuality between humanity and creation. But these exemplary spokespeople for creation were exceptions, not the rule, in Christian life. Far and away the most common interpretation among Christians is that God has given humanity power-over creation, including the animals, to use primarily for our own benefit. Regardless of what Christians may say we believe about responsibly caring for creation, most of us continue to live as if creation is our domain to do with as we please. As with all the deadly sins, this sixth one of domination is intertwined with all the rest, including omnipotence and entitlement, white supremacy and misogyny—and especially capitalist spirituality. In today's conservative American business and political climate, buoyed by many conservative evangelical Christians, humans rule—and most Christians believe it is our God-given right to do so.

I believe we can't honestly say we've been unaware of the devastating nature of this deadly sin that is wreaking havoc on the earth and its life. Instead of total ignorance, we often plead disbelief that things are really as bad as the experts say. But the climate crisis is not only an emergency of the earth's warming. It is also a crisis of lies, cover-ups, and the carefully crafted illusion that the problem is in the future, rather than with us here and now. The lies and the illusion that "it's not that bad" are concocted by corporate and political leaders and supported by much of evangelical Christianity in America. Moreover, ours is a crisis not only of global warming, or of greenhouse gas emissions, which left unchecked and at the current rate of increase will render the earth uninhabitable by humans and most present life-forms by the end of this century.[3] Ours is a crisis steeped in the relentless greed of unbridled global capitalism driven largely by the lust for greater wealth and sustained by unspeakable cruelty to animals and the poisoning of our planet's soil, water, air, and ecosystem.

We are being undone, literally. As a planet, we are dying. We are dying collectively and individually. We can choose to acknowledge the challenge, or we can refuse to acknowledge the major problems that are infusing our societies and polluting our bodies and souls as well as the earth: global warming, the torture of animals, the toxicity of the environment—often in racially and economically marginalized communities—and the fact that we are permitting the lies or delusions of powerful men to shape our consciousness and our morality.

WAKE UP, AMERICA!

We have no excuse not to know. We've had several highly publicized opportunities to begin to open our eyes and our minds to the crisis we're in. One went right over the heads of most of us—the awarding of the Nobel Peace Prize in 2007 jointly to the Intergovernmental Panel on Climate Change (IPCC) and Al Gore Jr. "for their efforts to build up and disseminate greater knowledge about man-made climate change, and to lay the foundations for the measures that are needed to counteract such change."[4] As much an honor as the Nobel award was to Al Gore and the IPCC, the majority of Americans were unlikely to pay it any more attention than they usually do to such lofty distinctions bestowed upon intellectual leaders.

A second public warning signal was the global climate strikes in 2019, mounted in more than 150 countries by millions of children. These young people were inspired and led by teenage activist Greta Thunberg, who had taken a one-girl public stand in her native Sweden four years earlier.[5] The kids' march to save the planet had been inspired, according to Thunberg, by the youth-led protests against gun violence in 2018 at the Marjory Stoneman Douglas High School in Parkland, Florida.

A third warning—and this one is surely an alarm, a wake-up call to us all—has alerted us dramatically to the effects of climate change: the startling increase in, and intensity of, fires, floods, hurricanes, tsunamis, and other major storms that are relentlessly ravaging all parts of our planet. We have seen shocking images of Australia and California burning, parts of North America and Europe underwater, migrants fleeing droughts and starvation in East Africa, the terror of the 2011 tsunami in Japan, Hurricanes Katrina in 2005 and Sandy in 2012, and so many other devastating incidents of an out-of-control planet and the massive suffering being inflicted on humans, animals, and the earth itself.

But it is not fair or accurate to blame "nature" or the earth for its suffering and devastation. So much of the damage is our fault. In traditional Christian language, it is "our own most grievous fault" for what we have done, and left undone, in relation to the creation as well as to the Creator whose incarnate body is the earth and all creatures.

It's Personal to Us All

This sin that lives and breathes in me is gradually taking my breath away, and yours too. I ask you to consider this with me, dear reader. How does this particular deadly sin live in your life? Though we will return to this question in the last part of this book, it would be helpful now for us to ask: Where have we been all of our lives in relation to the well-being of the earth and its creatures?

Had I followed my heart and my head as a child, I'd have become a veterinarian or a forest ranger, an advocate of an endangered species or a rescuer of abandoned horses or a botanist with a special commitment to trees native to the southern Appalachian Mountains. I'd have linked the future of my passionate girl-child self with that of the creek running through the orchard in our yard and the frogs jumping around on the rocks, and I'd have taken to heart the Spirit's insistence that the water and rocks were the manger and that the frogs, as surely as the star of Bethlehem, were pointing me toward Christ.

As it was, each Sunday I went with my parents to the small ivy-covered stone Episcopal church in our mountain town and sat silently in a pew, enthralled by the reds and blues of the stained glass, and wondered what it was all about. How was my life connected to everything? What did our Father who art in heaven have to do with me? And Jesus—would he have had a dog or caught lightning bugs or played hide-and-seek with his friends too? If only a Sunday school teacher had thought it worth mentioning that God's Spirit runs through all life and is truly alive and breathing in the rocks and plants and animals and water, as well as in our human neighbors and ourselves. If only the kindly white priest had said something about why there were no "colored" people in our church and why, by the way, all the "colored" people lived far away from the white people like us. If only someone who knew more than I did had pointed out that of course Jesus would have played with his friends just like I did, because he was just like me, and that Jesus might have been asking the same questions I was asking—about what God has to do with the rocks and water and trees and dogs. If only.

I wonder about my life and yours too, and where we have been in relation to the health of our planet home. Regardless, it is time for us to take stock and move into a future that we still can play some part in shaping. Thankfully, we American Christians have some guides, theologians, and activists who have thought a lot about this. We'll be turning to a few of them for guidance in part 3. For now, they can help us examine the problems that are staring us down.

CHRISTIAN THEOLOGIANS BECOME MINDFUL

The 1990s saw a blossoming of attentiveness to the earth among Christian theologians in America. In the early 1990s, Christian feminist liberation theologian Rosemary Radford Ruether traced the dualistic raising up of humanity over creation through the early history of Christian thought and assessed it as a moral challenge.[6] Ecofeminist Sallie McFague explicitly linked our not knowing our place—what we have already named as a deadly sin—with our violation of the earth.[7] And Daniel T. Spencer, a gay ecofeminist Christian ethicist, connects our alienation from the earth with our alienation from our own bodies, our own flesh and sensuality. In a splendid study from the 1990s that gets only more relevant over time,[8] Spencer demonstrated the interactivity of the deadly sins—of misogyny and homophobia, capitalist spirituality, white supremacy, violence, our lust for power-over, and our human sense of entitlement to dominate the earth as well as everything and everyone on it.

As each of these ecotheologians note, we need the earth more than it needs us. In fact, except for the life we have domesticated, the earth doesn't need us at all. Our domination of the earth may well be not only the deadliest sin we have named but also the most all-encompassing, affecting every human and other creature on the planet and maybe even throughout the cosmos. It certainly raises some of the most urgent spiritual, ethical, and political challenges.

One of the most insightful American Christian leaders working today on environmental issues is Larry Rasmussen, a down-to-earth, good-humored, Lutheran, and retired professor of ethics. He and his wife, Nyla, a retired nurse, have settled in Santa Fe, New Mexico. I've joined them in several seminars at neighboring Ghost Ranch and in their home, where I've heard Larry discuss his passion for earth and water as wellsprings of the sacred. He is a splendid teacher and mentor, especially on our relation to the earth. In part 3, I'll ask you to consider Larry's proposal that we "belong" with and to the earth, water, sky, and animals. But first, here in this chapter, Larry Rasmussen has something to say about how our domination of the earth and its creatures functions as a deadly sin.[9] He cites five specific moral problems that face Americans, including Christians:

First is our *consumerism*,[10] an ethical problem linked directly to the sin of capitalist spirituality. Put simply, most of us want more, ask for more, purchase more, and consume more. We eat more, play with more gadgets and toys, enjoy new things, get bored with old things, waste more, and throw away more—more than we need and more than our planet can sustain. To be a middle-class American is to be a consumer. Sometimes, if I'm honest, it seems I live to produce trash—as I surround myself with plastic wrappers, useless paper, wasted food, and glass that can be recycled, but to what end? Consumerism has become a trademark sin for most Americans.

Second, Larry cites *commodification* as a major moral problem. Commodification is our use of "things" that we toss away once they are of no more use to us.[11] Chattel slavery was the most outrageous example of commodification in American history and American Christianity. White Christian nationalism has its twisted spiritual roots in this evil use of people as slaves, a racist and capitalist transaction that continues to plague our society.[12] Today we easily fall into regarding living organisms—human bodies (especially those of other races, classes, and cultures) and all animals and plants—as things, rather than as mutual partners with us in shaping our nation and world.

Third, Larry Rasmussen names our *alienation* from the earth as a source of our domination of the earth. By this, he means that we are emotionally and spiritually detached from the earth as our home. Many of us have little awareness of the environment in which we live, except insofar as we need whatever it can give us. Many of us regard the earth as just another place we happen to live. If we are city folk, we probably know very little about what it's like to live and work on the land that provides most of what we need to survive, or what goes on around us in rivers, oceans, and forests; under us in dirt and the creatures who abide there; or over us in the skies. If we are country folk, we probably have no idea how city folk survive the noise and pace of life on concrete. As for our lives on the land, we do not know our neighbors the way we once did; and we find ourselves increasingly under the control of rich corporations that have scooped up for development the land our ancestors called home. Wherever we live in relation to land and water, many Americans feel isolated and cut off from our major sources of meaning and nourishment, psychospiritually displaced from the ground on which we literally stand and walk, the land from which we receive our water and food, the source of the well-being of our bodies and our abilities to genuinely know ourselves and one another.[13] Alienation, commodification, and consumerism go hand in hand. Many American Christians have no idea how literally displaced we are from the earth and how much we take for granted—including our basic life necessities of nutritious food, clean water, safe shelter, and reliable health care.

Fourth, Larry links Christianity's disregard of the earth with *oppression and injustice*. He cites, for example, the environmental toxic waste that is dumped among poor communities of color in America far more than among poor white communities, which themselves receive more of these death-dealing poisons than affluent, largely white, communities,[14] It is almost always the poor, especially people of color but also poor white Americans, who suffer most seriously and quickly the effects of climate change.

Finally, telling it like it is, Larry Rasmussen calls us *fools*. We may be ignorant, we may be stupid, we may be indifferent, we may be confused, or we may be callous. Whatever the source of our failures to act on behalf of the earth and its creatures, we are fools[15] because we are digging our own grave and don't seem to know it.

The sins of entitlement, not knowing our place, alongside our lust for omnipotence or power-over, and our bowing to capitalist spirituality, all work together with our indifference toward the depletion of the earth's life-sustaining resources and the destruction of the earth itself as a habitable home for life as we know it. This is a challenge for Americans and a serious call to Christians to change the ways we think about God and the world, Creator and creatures, and ourselves and other participants in nature. Can we imagine being partners with, rather than rulers over, the earth? Can we imagine generating mutuality with trees and water? Is this just idealistic babble, or is there something real and actionable to which we Christians are called? It may well be not only the deadliest sin we have named but also the most all-encompassing, affecting every human and other creature on the planet. It certainly raises some of our most urgent spiritual, ethical, and political challenges.

OUR SOLIDARITY, OUR HOPE

I began to realize only about twenty years ago that I had all but omitted in my theological work a concern I have always held personally for the well-being of animals and the earth. I had never made the earth, the other-than-human animals, or our environment *central* to my work as a Christian feminist theologian of liberation. The only reason I could figure for this omission in my theological work was that my class and race identities had given me time and space—that is, privilege—not to *experience* the earth in all its wonder. My class and racial identities had also kept me from realizing that, as a human being, I needed to realize my place as a partner in our life together, not always as the central actor—even in the story of my own life. Neither my Christian faith nor my American patriotism had demanded that I wake up to what our churches have failed to teach us about knowing our place in relation to creation and, therefore, to what our nation has been allowed to get away with: blatant disregard of the earth and disrespect beyond measure toward a planet home that loans us space to live and breathe.

Moving to the mountains of North Carolina and settling among friends of various species into the woods and hills in which I had lived as a child, I began to *experience* the environment in more sustained ways than at any time in my adult life. Not that I hadn't noticed along the way both the loveliness and the danger signs—the giant oak tree at the farm and the whitewater rushing in the Nantahala River, the blue fireflies in early June and the black snake run over in the road, the bluest sky and the smog trapped between mountains, the trash tossed along the roadside and the lady slippers on the path, the dramatic sound of horses galloping through the pastures and the tiny tick on my thigh, the stunning vista from Mount Pisgah and the smoke of wildfires nearby.

Yes, I have always loved the outdoors—the beaches, woods, rivers, fields, meadows, and mountains, especially the Appalachians in which I grew up. I have long been aware of the problems we are facing, as the earth gets warmer and most people, myself included, are either apathetic or don't know what to do. And I have always had animal friends, close companions—dogs, horses, cats—that I have cherished. But not until I stopped being a professional theologian—I should say, primarily a professional theologian—and set aside academic responsibilities in favor of walking in the woods with a notepad in my pocket, did I begin to *experience* the earth again as a place of sheer wonder, alive under my feet and over my head and in my bones.

One day out walking in 1999, I noticed a solitary dark bay horse across the fence and down by a creek in the woods. The next day, and the next, and the next, I returned, and there she stood, grazing and glancing up at me. A month or two into this daily ritual, I bought that horse for almost nothing—Sugar, a twenty-eight-year-old mare that no one really wanted, except me. It turned out I couldn't ride Sugar because she'd been owned by a guy who, mistaking her for a machine, had used barbed wire as a bit—and she wouldn't tolerate anyone on her back for long. But I adored that old mare, and simply sitting beside her and grooming her day in and day out became my entry into a sustained experience of the earth and the life that is under our toes for the touching. Sugar led me eventually to my great riding horse, Red, and to Red's daughter, Feather, and to founding Free Rein, a therapeutic horseback riding center in the North Carolina mountains. Sugar also provided my introduction to a whole world of animal lovers, especially horse and dog fanatics, and into wanting to be out on trails and in as much wilderness as possible for the rest of my days. In reading and reflecting, I gravitated toward poets who loved nature and animals, sisters like Mary Oliver and Linda McCarriston; and to the mystical musings of the gentle Irishman John O'Donohue; and to the Buddhist teachings of Janet Surrey, Joanna Macy and Thich Nhat Hahn; and to the wisdom of Jane Goodall, the British primatologist and anthropologist, renowned for her work over decades with chimpanzees; and to animal rights advocates like Andrew Linzey and Jay McDaniel. All of these people, and others, have taught me much about our earth and how deeply our roots connect us as an organic whole, all of us "co-dependent arising,"[16] no one of us simply on our own.

OUR FOOD AND THE ENVIRONMENT

Over the past decade, in addition to ongoing advocacy of her beloved chimp species, Jane Goodall has become an increasingly outspoken proponent of a plant-based human diet, which she says is one thing we humans can do if we're seriously concerned about the well-being of our planet as well as its many varied creatures—about global warming (greenhouse gas emissions) as well as cruelty to animals.[17]

In her most recent book, coauthored with Douglas Abrams,[18] Goodall voices three primary concerns: First, she is appalled by human indifference to the suffering of animals being factory farmed for human consumption. Like Albert Schweitzer, Albert Einstein, Jeremy Bentham, and other ethical spokespeople, Goodall makes clear her strong opposition to how the vast majority of animals raised for human consumption are treated as things, not as the sentient beings they are.

Second, she is mindful of the increasing numbers of disease crossovers between animals—cramped in tight, unsanitary conditions and often fed contaminants, including their own waste—and humans. In 2009, without predicting the arrival of COVID-19, Goodall pointed to a number of other recent epidemics such as mad cow disease, E. coli, and salmonella, and warned of possible global pandemics in the future that would originate in crossover diseases between animals, treated with disregard in filth and neglect, and our vulnerable human species.

Third, Goodall notes the major greenhouse emissions of animal factory farming as a major source of the heat that is warming the earth and generating climate change. She insists that the connection between our food sources and the future of our planet is unmistakable and critical and, from both scientific and spiritual perspectives, demands our immediate response.[19]

Goodall's views are much like those of Michael Pollan, an American environmental journalist who links our food sources with their impact on the environment and the climate crisis.[20] Pollan also urges Americans to consider the links between what we eat, what sort of world we want to inhabit, and what sort of earth we want to bequeath to our children. Pollan and Goodall urge us to be honest about what we feel and think and believe.

What do we as Christians believe is most evil and most urgent in our environmental crisis? What is right and what is wrong about what we eat, and how? What do we believe we need to do—and what can we do—in relation to our heavy-handed treatment of the earth and the suffering of the animals? Goodall, Pollan, and Rasmussen are not idealists who view their lives and choices, or ours, through rose-tinted glasses. Their voices simply summon us to take stock of our lives and choices from moral perspectives that can help us help our planet. They urge us to think strategically. Given the shape of our lives, how we actually live in the world, what options are most doable? What can and will we do, together and individually?

These spokespeople for creation and other prophetic voices from whom we will hear later in this book are not asking American Christians, or anyone else, to model perfection. They are asking us to do whatever we can, to commit ourselves to actions that signal our awareness of the global crisis and our best efforts to contribute whatever we can to its solution—to do our parts, however small they may seem and to learn to believe that every voice matters, including our own. They are asking us to do something and, whenever possible, to do it together. They are warning us that we cannot beg off without turning our backs on the planet, our creature siblings, and ourselves.

We have a moral responsibility. Have we not known in our bones that the deadly sins are all connected? If we have not known before, then we do now if we have been paying attention. And once we know, we must confess our sin and seek the earth's forgiveness by committing ourselves to live as mindfully as possible in partnership with the earth and its creatures rather than as dominators. We cannot understand any of the sins we have named, not white supremacy, not misogyny, not capitalist spirituality, none of them, unless we make connections between them in our lives, beyond the pages of a book. Making these connections will be central to our work in part 3, when we discuss what we American Christians can do, creatively and constructively, to combat white Christian nationalism's deadly sin of domination over the earth and all earth creatures.

Chapter 10

The Seventh Sin

Violence

This sin shoots and slices its way through the other sins, giving each its ruthless, bloody shape in history. In truth, to even present violence as a deadly sin in America, one fully (if often apologetically) supported by Christianity, is redundant in the context of everything else we've been considering. No one paying attention in America or in American churches could fail to notice that our national culture centers around a pride strengthened over time by the fondness of many white Christian American men (and some women) for wars, guns, conquests, police and military readiness, and scapegoating—whether onto Jews, Muslims, or people of other nations, cultures, or religious traditions; Native Americans; Black people and other racial-ethnic populations; women (especially successful professional women and feminists); LGBTQ people; and all "others" deemed alien, unpatriotic, or dangerous to the white Christian "all-American way." American patriotism, Christian faith, and our deeply human but morally problematic inclination to scapegoat—blame someone else and punish them—have long gone hand in hand not only in lionizing those who have died in war but moreover in sanitizing the wars themselves. We are taught that American wars are fought "with God on our side,"[1] in the words of legendary songwriter and folk singer Bob Dylan.

The fact that America began losing its wars in the last half of the twentieth century no doubt has contributed to our collective sense of malaise and our loss of a reliable identity as a great nation. Today Americans are as angry and bickering among ourselves as we have been since the 1850s' buildup to the Civil War. In the wake of our withdrawal from Afghanistan and the pointless wars in Iraq, American anger is boiling over. Furious white Christian men take their fury out on their Black, brown, female, and queer neighbors as well as on Jews and Muslims, Asians and Haitians. Those American Christians who are angriest believe the Big Lie that their man had the 2020 election stolen from him. A palpable energy for violence has been ignited in our gun-packing culture in which many white Americans seem poised to fight as hundreds did on January 6, 2021, wielding American, Gadsden, and thin-blue-line flags to beat up police and others trying to protect the Capitol and its inhabitants.

There is no greater threat to the health and well-being of Americans today than the epidemic of gun violence that takes the lives of dozens of us every day. Even as I write, a fifteen-year-old boy in Michigan has been charged with killing four of his high school classmates and wounding seven others. His parents have been arrested and charged with manslaughter. They bought him the gun and taught him to shoot it and, for whatever reason, they chose to look the other way when school authorities signaled to them that the boy seemed likely to pose a real danger.

Especially since the election of Barack Hussein Obama in 2008, the attachment of many conservative American Christians to their "Second Amendment rights" has intensified—despite the fact that "through the first five months of 2021, gunfire killed more than 8,100 people in the United States, about 54 lives lost per day," according to a *Washington Post* analysis of data from the Gun Violence Archive, a nonprofit research organization. The article continues, "That's 14 more deaths per day than the average toll during the same period of the previous six years."[2]

In 2017, polls showed that 80–90 percent of Americans wanted stricter gun control. Today that number has decreased to 65 percent (with Democrats polling at 95 percent and Republicans at 35 percent).[3] This is no doubt a signal of the fear and anger that have been on the rise in America since the 2016 election and the ever-sharpening partisan divide. The National Rifle Association and other even more conservative organizations of gun owners and advocates continue to oppose the most basic gun control measures, such as requiring universal background checks to provide some oversight of who can purchase firearms in America.

Many Americans condone this violent culture in the name of the Christian God who, these American Christians are clear, is the enemy of bad people—Communists and terrorists from abroad, and those at home who embody similar un-American and non-Christian ideologies and aims. From a white Christian nationalist perspective, the bad people are Black people, brown immigrants and refugees, Native Americans, Asian Americans, feminist women, lesbians, gay men, and trans/queer people, and today's Democrats. All of these people are hated as being alien to white Christian nationalism. These groups of Americans are portrayed as seeking to overthrow the American family, the American way, America's capitalist spirituality, and America's Christian devotion to an historically white male Father God. It is no wonder that conspiracy theories like the violent QAnon fantasy that Democrats are actually satanic pedophiles, have been spawned in our nation.

According to a Daily Kos/Civiqs poll in September 2021, "some 56% of Republicans believe that QAnon . . . is mostly or partly true."[4]

We might ask, seriously: What could have been more unbelievable to Trump's true believers than the defeat at the polls of their anointed one? As far as the Trump base was concerned, the election must have been stolen. After all, the God of ultraconservative white Christian American men would not have permitted the actual election of a socialist pedophile, would he? Along this line of reasoning, there was nothing surprising about the presence of the giant cross, and a lot of Jesus talk and anti-Semitic symbols flanked by huge Trump flags at the United States Capitol on January 6, 2021. And there is nothing surprising about the ongoing threat of violence in the air being revved up by the Republican Party and its Christian base that we are on the verge of holy war or perhaps already in it. As journalist Thomas Edsall notes, "The 'big lie' is a precursor to more dangerous threats—threats that are plausible in ways that less than a decade ago seemed inconceivable. The capitulation to and appeasement of Trump by Republican leaders is actually setting up even worse possibilities than what we've lived through so far."[5]

As prelude to this situation, what could have been more threatening to these politically conservative white Christian American men of God than a Black male president? Or a well-seasoned, smart, white feminist woman candidate for president? (Remember that QAnon began in 2016, with "Pizzagate," the rumor that Hillary Clinton was running a child sex ring out of a pizzeria in the District of Columbia). Or what could be more menacing to frightened Republicans today than a charismatic Black female vice president? Or an older white male president with a remarkably common touch and a rare capacity for empathy in the political arena, a man who tries to reach out to his opponents in a spirit of hope rather than revenge or resentfulness? Notice that the targets cited above for violent rhetoric and possible violent action by white Christian nationalists are prominent, powerful people: a Black man, a Black woman, a white man, and a white woman, all progressive Democrats, and all liberal Christians.

As threatening as Barack Obama and Joe Biden have been to the white Christian nationalist agenda, as alarming is the effort by strong women, Black or white, to ascend to the highest reaches of power in the United States. The over-the-top vilification of Hillary Clinton by conservatives as soon as she decided to run for president and the ongoing attacks on the character and competence of Kamala Harris now that she sits so close to the highest office in the land both reflect the depth and breadth of the misogyny we have discussed earlier.

Indeed, violence against women is an even greater global pandemic than the coronavirus. Here in America, the trivialization of women as a group and the ongoing threats of violence against those who, like Clinton and Harris, have "too much power" constitute a challenge to all American women and girls who are paying attention to how far men—usually rich white men with the blessing of much of the Christian Church—are willing to go to keep women in our place, to show us who's boss, to do whatever it takes to hold us back. It's an all-American drama, tried and true, in the context of a global crisis that looms larger all the time. As capitalism expands and the climate worsens, women and children, especially girls, are the most vulnerable targets of violence by those men (and sometimes women) who seek not only to profit economically from capitalist exploits but moreover to survive whatever ecological disasters may be sparked. The anti-abortion movement's frenzied violence epitomizes the ongoing national and global assault on women and girls.

THEOLOGICAL JUSTIFICATIONS OF VIOLENCE

Much has been written by historians and other analysts about violence in America. Starting with European settlers' genocidal assault on Indigenous peoples and the Europeans' kidnapping and transport of Africans to the new land to work as slaves, American history has been shaped by wars, assassinations, and the glorification of weaponry and violence. Modern America has seen rises in domestic and intimate abuse in our homes, gang violence among youth in our cities, and of course ever more gun violence in our cities, schools, workplaces, places of worship and entertainment, and homes.[6] Today, our nation has become increasingly dependent upon the evil of drone warfare—planes without human pilots—which can obliterate others from a distance without putting ourselves at personal risk.

As morally reprehensible as genocide, slavery, gun violence at epidemic levels, intimate abuse, and drone warfare is, such American violence is believed by many Christians to be sanctioned by God, in what Yale historian Miroslav Volf calls a "thin," or superficial, interpretation of Christianity, which credits God for stirring violence against the ungodly, as opposed to a "thick" or more contextual and complete understanding of the faith.[7] Volf's writings on the subject of Christianity and violence shed light on Christian nationalism's quite thin rendering of God's will, such as the attack on the Capitol, being done not only on behalf of a political goal—to keep Trump in power—but moreover on behalf of God.

We are not going to belabor here what is so obvious—the ubiquitous, ongoing horror of violence in America. Rather, we are going to look at the role played by mainstream and liberal Christian justifications for the violence that is penetrating our national culture. We Christians have helped generate this all-American violence, largely through our ignorance or indifference. We can help reduce it if we so choose, but to do so we must wrestle among ourselves and think together about our spiritual and moral traditions as Christians.

Three theological threads have been woven into the lives of most American Christians from our earliest days as a nation, threads woven over time into a social fabric of our collective tolerance of violence:

1. Our enemies are God's enemies; therefore we fight them in the name of God.
2. Christians are called to practice spiritualities of charity—giving to the poor—more basically than working for systemic changes to reduce or eliminate the poverty that becomes a breeding ground for the spiral of violence: violent resistance by the oppressed and violent suppression by the state.
3. Nonviolence is too idealistic as an ethical or moral goal. Violence is simply a given in our collective life. These threads continue to shape liberal churches in America as well as Christianity's more conservative traditions and, most certainly, white Christian nationalism.

GOD'S ENEMIES

The first theological thread has been a pervasive assumption that, while God is good and kind and loves us, he (certainly a "he") is constantly under attack by his enemies—not only people who kill and steal and lie, and so forth, but also people who are perceived as hostile to God or have doubts about him and want little or nothing to do with the Christian God.

The Christian Church has long demonized Jews as enemies of whatever is most good, certainly of all that is Christian, beginning with the divinity of Christ. Because historically anti-Semitism has festered near the roots of Christian theology and is a vicious dimension of white Christian nationalism, it is the responsibility of all Christians—whether more conservative or liberal—to expunge it from our biblical interpretations, theologies, liturgies, practices, and politics. For Christians to try to justify anti-Judaism by quoting from the Gospel of John (which is indeed loaded with anti-Jewish rhetoric) is like trying to justify white supremacy and slavery as well as misogyny and violence against women by quoting scripture. Whether on the basis of faulty biblical interpretation, or wrongheadedness, the efforts by some Christians to blame God for their own wickedness are spiritually bankrupt, morally reprehensible, and unworthy of being associated in any way with our Jewish brother Jesus of Nazareth or the God whom he loved and helped bring more fully into the light of human history.

I grew up in the 1950s and 1960s, when anti-Semitism was a largely unacceptable attitude among liberal Christians, at least in public. At the same time, in the largely Protestant South of my youth, Jews—and to a lesser extent, Catholics—were almost as segregated from white Protestant Christians as Black people were. In those days, Communism was a catchall for whatever was most dangerous to America, Christianity, and God. Moreover, it was widely assumed that the very idea of racial integration, of mixed races, or mixed religions, was part of a Communist plot to infiltrate and eventually subdue America and destroy its white Christian basis.

Today, three-quarters of a century later, a fear of Communism lingers in America, an anxiety fastened in many people's mistaken ideas about socialism, notions either steeped in ignorance or intentionally fabricated. Of course, over the past several decades and certainly since 9/11, Christian America's worries about Communism have been superseded by the specter of "radical Islamic terrorism" as the most hateful and godless ideology on the planet. The readers of this book, however, should be disturbed by the fact that white Christian nationalism is a greater threat to American democracy today than either Communism or radical Islam.

In its 2021 policy statement on Christian nationalism, the National Council of Churches states:

> Theologically, Christian nationalism elevates the nation, or a particular concept of the nation, to a role closely aligned with God. In its more militant forms, Christian nationalism encourages its adherents to believe they are battling the forces of darkness on all fronts, but this combative outlook actually grows out of fealty to symbols . . . unaffiliated with historic Christianity. This mindset of embattled righteousness is applied to the perceived enemies of the state (e.g., liberals, humanists, pluralists, atheists, and various minoritized communities), and true believers are directed to employ any and all means, even undemocratic and violent ones, in order to win political contests. In this quest for political power, Christian humility is lost, as is the message of God's love for all humanity.[8]

Indeed, white Christian nationalism is a formidable enemy to our democracy, to most Americans, to most Christians, to Jews, and to people of all other spiritual or moral traditions who live in this country. For this reason, many of us believe that white Christian nationalism is a chief adversary, an archenemy, of the Spirit of Love, by whatever name or names we call this sacred power.

A Moral Challenge to Liberal Christians

The situation in which we find ourselves makes especially dangerous the theological assumption shared historically by liberal and conservative Christians that the enemies of God are our enemies. Whether we are more conservative or more liberal, American Christians need to ask ourselves what happens when our chief enemy is no longer Communists, no longer Al-Qaeda, and no longer ISIS? What do we do when the enemy of conservative white American Christians is the progressive Christian family next door, the gay kid on the playground, the transwoman behind the counter, the Black Lives Matter activist, or the Jewish city councilor? Do conservative white American Christians try to somehow get these people out of the way? Or keep them from voting? Or scare them away? Or worse? These are urgent moral questions for politically conservative Christians. How should you respond to those who you believe are threatening your deepest values, or your country, or your God?

Closer to home for most readers of this book, who are likely to be politically liberal or perhaps more moderate—what happens when the enemy of our progressive values, spiritualities, and politics are our conservative Christian neighbors? How do we respond to Donald Trump enthusiasts? Or to folks who want to cancel critical race theory and are threatening local school board members? Or to the right-wing talking heads who brand us satanic, call us nasty names, and stir violent sentiments against us? What do we do in response—anything or nothing?

We know that white Christian nationalists view liberal Christians, Black and brown people, Asians, feminists and LGBTQ people, Jews and Muslims, and Democrats as enemies of both America and God, and as fair game for hateful—sometimes even violent—behavior. And yet, when those of us who fit into any of these categories view white Christian nationalists as enemies of democracy and of God, are we not setting the stage for spiritual and political warfare, even perhaps actual violence against one another, sometimes our own neighbors?

We liberal American Christians have learned over the past hundred or more years that, in the face of evil—for example, slavery, Jim Crow, white supremacy—we may have to fight our own countrymen and women, as many Americans did in the Civil War, to put an end to the evil of slavery.

The moral challenge here—which we liberal American Christians share with our more conservative Christian neighbors—is that it requires us to view "the other side" first, and often only, as an adversary rather than more fundamentally as an errant sibling, a brother or sister who's gone wrong. Objectifying the enemies of God and country as our adversaries, rather than as siblings who are simply mistaken, or even dangerous to us and whatever we hold most dear, we can easily find ourselves wanting to destroy them, rather than making any serious effort to engage and transform them. In this way, much like our more politically and theologically conservative Christian siblings, we may be tempted to settle on quick, even violent, ways out of the social tensions, political divisions, and spiritual disagreements we experience in these stressful, divisive times.

The most important insight here, for moderate to liberal American Christians like ourselves, is to realize that we, no less than conservative evangelical Christians, indeed no less than white Christian nationalists, can fall into believing that because God is on our side, we are on the moral high ground and, thus, have a responsibility to subdue the other side by whatever means necessary. At such a moral juncture—wondering what is right and what is wrong—we need to ask ourselves a few questions, not imagining there are easy or absolutely right answers: Can we imagine ourselves as bridge builders to those whom we perceive as enemies of justice and love without compromising our values and our perceptions of good and evil? Can we struggle against evil—the consequences of the seven deadly sins—without trying to destroy the sisters and brothers who benefit from and enjoy their arrogant, racist, sexist, classist privileges at the expense of our common humanity and creatureliness?

Is violence against evildoers ever justified? Under what circumstances, if any, might it be? This is a question that might move Christians to consider the life, circumstances, and final choices of the renowned German Protestant theologian Dietrich Bonhoeffer, a lover of humanity and a teacher of God's peace, who participated in a failed plot to assassinate Hitler, and who was hanged in 1945 for his crime against the Fuhrer.[9] Was Bonhoeffer right or wrong? What do you think? Having wrestled with the question of Black self-defense as justifiable violence throughout his ministry, Martin Luther King Jr. warned in his final book that "the line of demarcation between defensive violence and aggressive violence is very thin. The minute a program of violence is enunciated, even for self-defense, the atmosphere is filled with talk of violence."[10]

Those of us on the political left or in the center can see the truth in King's warning when we look at the behavior of Kyle Rittenhouse, who killed two men and wounded a third, in Kenosha, Wisconsin, in 2020. Rittenhouse was acquitted of murder on the basis of his plea of self-defense even though he was the one who took the rifle to the rally, carried it among the crowd, and was perceived to be a threat. Martin Luther King was cautioning Black Americans and, by extension, white liberals of a morally flawed but common tendency among people of different political leanings to fall back on self-defense as a way to justify violent, or harmful, behavior toward our enemies.

There is one thing we can do as Christians—whichever side of the political or spiritual spectrum we are on. We can realize that it is usually, perhaps not always, easier to slam the door in the face of our enemies—silence them, hurt them, maybe even kill them—than to make serious, concerted efforts to transform them into partners who can work with us, in unexpected ways, toward a common good that we might be able to envision together.

Can we begin to realize, for example, that without compromising our beliefs in the personhood and dignity of women and in women's right to reproductive freedom, including abortion, we can work with the other side to forge social policies that involve some compromise, some give and take?[11] Can we affirm solutions in which no one goes home with everything they had hoped for, but everyone goes home with something valuable? Can such compromise be worth our efforts, when the stakes are high, or is this often a bridge too far for those whose values are deepest and clearest?

Readers should be aware that the 1973 *Roe v. Wade* decision of the Supreme Court, under attack for decades by those who oppose women's reproductive freedom, was itself a compromise between those who favored the legalization of all abortions and those who favored banning all abortions. And yet, abortion opponents never accepted *Roe v. Wade*'s restrictions on second- and third-trimester abortions as a compromise. If, like the most absolutist opponents to all abortion, we feel that we cannot compromise, that our values will not permit it, do we really want to insist that we, and we alone, know what is best for everyone? Do we want to insist that we know which social policies are sustainable in a society made ever more complex by diverse cultures and religions as well as by advances in medicine and corresponding ethics? From spiritual and moral perspectives, how do we square our insistence on having our own uncompromising way with the sins of omnipotence and entitlement?

Darlene O'Dell warns that, in any situation of compromise, there is a stronger and a weaker side, and that—to reach a just and fair solution—negotiators must always give the upper hand to those in the weaker position.[12] This is good liberation theology, good politics, and a good way of life. It's a perspective rooted and grounded in strong commitments to the creative power of mutuality as the movement of the Spirit of Justice and Love. In situations of open-minded, bighearted compromise, all will win something and all will lose something, and those with the most to lose will be empowered to lead the way toward the solution. This means, for instance, that in decisions involving the legality and accessibility of abortion, poor women should lead the way. In decisions regarding guns, the victims of gun violence and their families should set the basic terms. In decisions about toxic waste, the residents of the poorest communities being poisoned should have the final say. We will be returning to this moral riddle of right relation in part 3.

SPIRITUALITIES OF CHARITY

A well-known problem with liberal American Christianity is that, due to our moorings in capitalist spirituality and its emphasis on the well-being of individuals as more basic than the transformation of society, liberal Christians, like our conservative siblings, have become champions of charity—giving to the poor—rather than justice,social change to help eliminate the structures and systems of poverty. Too often we Christians, liberals and conservatives, have turned our backs on the struggles for justice as too political for Christian churches to deal with. We have not wanted our pastors, priests, or educators to say much about social justice from the pulpit. Most of us who consider ourselves liberal or progressive Christians have long realized that this is a big problem for the church, which has little credibility among those who actually struggle for social justice in contemporary America. Many of us have left the church for this very reason. Serious advocates for social justice seldom waste their time seeking active support from mainstream Protestant or Catholic churches, because they have heard for generations from Christian leaders that it's too political for churches to be involved.

Be clear that "too political" means unpopular with, and unacceptable to, those who are most invested in holding in place the seven deadly sins of American Christianity. The sin of capitalist spirituality, more than any other, is deeply invested in keeping religious leaders, especially American Christians, as far away from systemic social change as possible. This is because, if the churches were actually to take up the struggles for social justice in America, their alliances with moneyed interests and political conservatism would be scuttled in favor of newfound spiritual strength and moral power. The church would produce more prophetic voices in American culture. More Christian leaders would act and sound like Bishop William Barber and Rev. Dr. Liz Theoharis of the Poor People's Campaign. Fewer would mimic the pastors and priests of either the small politically conservative evangelical churches or the larger, so-called big steeple: heavily endowed, predominantly white, churches in which silence about most justice matters is golden.

We should bear in mind that it's not only the predominantly white Christian churches that are silent about justice matters in today's America.[13] Most of the predominantly Black churches and other churches of color are too. This was not always the case. It was most certainly not so during the height of the civil rights movement, when the Black Church and its leaders led the way. My Black colleagues in the local NAACP in which I am currently involved tell me that they perceive several reasons for Black American Christians' lack of involvement in today's justice movements: the difficulties many Black American Christians have with the presence of LGBTQ activists in the movements for justice (true also among many white Christians); the co-optation of large parts of the Black Church by the same capitalist spirituality that has defined white churches for many decades; the absence of Black youth and young adults in many Black churches (this is also true in many predominantly white churches); and the ongoing presence of systemic racism—white supremacy—in the larger community that may threaten violence or economic and social pushback against Black Christians and other racial-ethnic minority persons who become identified by their social activism in local communities.

NONVIOLENCE IS TOO IDEALISTIC

In 1971, a Brazilian Catholic Bishop, Helder Camara, wrote a small book, *Spiral of Violence*, in which he discussed how violence begets violence. He had witnessed these connections in his own culture. Systemic violence—poverty and human suffering—leads eventually to revolutionary violence, which usually quickly leads to state-sponsored repression, and this in turn generates even greater poverty and human suffering among the people, including the revolutionaries, and so forth.[14] In contemporary America, we can envision a similar scenario: the violence of hunger and racism are surely creating conditions for revolutionary violence on the parts of social justice workers and movements, which in turn spark conditions for state-sponsored police and military violence to repress these movements, and this surely generates greater suffering and oppression of all poor people and people of color in America.

Is this spiral of violence not exactly what we are witnessing today? For example, the blatantly racialized shape of our privatized prisons and the ongoing murders of Black and brown people who are driving their cars or walking home from the store have sparked the emergence of the Black Lives Matter movement, the National Institute for Criminal Justice Reform (NICJR), the Innocence Project, and other organizations working for systemic change, These movements for reform are creating tension with Republican legislators, conservative judges, private prison entrepreneurs, police unions, and others devoted wholeheartedly to the preservation of "law and order." And the conservative backlash against criminal reform, especially when harsh or dismissive, produces more passionate, and violent, protests against the power of the state. And on and on the spiral goes.

Surely it is up to spiritual and moral leaders to do whatever we can to break the spiral of violence. But this will not happen among Christians who assume that such violence is inevitable, a natural part of the human condition, or—from a premillennialist Christian view—even a necessary condition for the Second Coming of Christ. Liberal Christians are not premillennialists. We do not spend much, if any, time waiting for the Second Coming or worrying about it. However, we do often simply accept the seven deadly sins and the evils they spawn as somehow natural to the human condition. In this way, we accept the spiral of violence of which Dom Helder Camara writes, as tragic, but inevitable.

The spiral of violence is a spiral of doomsday. In this dreadful context, Christians are called by a God of hope and liberation to break the spiral of violence. At a personal and interpersonal level, there is nothing inevitable about humans violating one another as neighbors and siblings. Indeed, we hurt each other, unintentionally, sometimes maliciously, because we are human and we all experience complex mixtures of good and evil in our own lives, including our interpersonal behavior. But to violate others, to intentionally hurt, break, destroy, or kill another human being—some would say another creature of any species—is not inevitable at a personal or interpersonal level. It is a choice we make again and again. At a social level, as communities and nations, it is always more complex. Reinhold Niebuhr, a Christian ethicist in mid-twentieth-century America, made this point in *Moral Man and Immoral Society*.[15] Societies are complicated precisely because they are composed of networks of interactive systems based on many factors, including the seven deadly sins we have named and the shapes they take in our lives.

A generation after Niebuhr, one of his students, feminist Christian ethicist Beverly Wildung Harrison, whose work we have returned to often in this book, critiqued Niebuhr for his lack of transformative Christian vision on the matter of systemic social change. Harrison appreciated Niebuhr's powerful presence as a public theologian who, in the 1940s, had spoken out forcefully against fascism. Moreover, Harrison agreed with Niebuhr that America and other nations as well are badly broken societies in which injustices of many kinds permeate our collective life and seem inevitable. But Harrison did not believe Niebuhr's view of the potential power of human community was strong or hopeful enough. She did not accept his proposal that society is necessarily any more "immoral" than are its individual members. Both collectively and individually, people can do great evil. Hitler and the German people had proven that. But then for Harrison so too did capitalism prove that, both collectively and individually, human beings can be deadly sinners.

At the same time, Harrison held fervently to her belief in humanity's capacity to do good. She believed that, both collectively and individually, human beings can choose to generate justice. As a Christian and a feminist, she believed that this was precisely what Jesus had in mind and what the Jesus movement is all about. Accordingly, Harrison would ask: Are we, or are we not, put here on this earth by our Creator to help re-create the world of God? Will we, or will we not, accept that we white people must hide behind protective walls of white supremacy forever, instead of tearing them down brick by brick? What about misogyny and capitalist spirituality? Are we put here to live eternally in violent power-over maneuvers amid different genders and sexual identities, forever fixated on our private rights as individuals to increase our own capital, bank accounts, and stockpiles of weapons, regardless of the cost to others? Or are we here to participate in liberating our societies from evil? What about our disregard, and violation, of the earth and its varied creatures? Are we stuck forever in corporate-driven behavior that will eventually make the earth uninhabitable for humans and most other animals? Or are we here to take our place among the species and advocate the well-being of all of us? Honestly, Harrison would ask us, why must liberal or conservative Christians settle for life in immoral society? Harrison believed that Reinhold Niebuhr settled for too little human faith, commitment, and activism toward building a moral society.

As we move now into part 3 where we will be wrestling together with some responses to violence and the other six deadly sins, let us carry Harrison's questions with us, and let us ask these questions: What Christian stories and themes can energize us to join as partners in our moral efforts? Can we imagine living as one American community—brilliant in our multiple diversities, not without sin any of us, making mistakes as we trek on, but still moving together along a sometimes steep and rugged path of social and personal transformation?

Our journey will likely involve our pausing from time to time to share rituals of social and personal repentance and forgiveness among ourselves. Far from being humiliating, such sharing can be exhilarating, liberating, healing, as long as we are compassionate with one another, and ourselves. Let us keep in mind as we go that we need not strive for perfection. Wise people know and often remind us, as I do from time to time in these pages, that the perfect is the enemy of the good. We just have to do our best—as Sue, my life partner, suggests, just the next right thing.

PART III

A Call to Action

Chapter 11

Questions and Call

In part 2, we examined seven deadly sins of white Christian nationalism: the effort to turn our nation into a Christian theocracy, a country ruled by white affluent Christian men. We explored how each of these sins has festered in American Christianity and has contributed to the rise of the white Christian nationalism that aims to destroy our democracy. This violent and increasingly shameless movement is storming its way through our lives together as Americans. It was reflected in the rise of Donald Trump and his hate-filled administration; in his supporters who besieged the U.S. Capitol on January 6, 2021; and in the Republican Party's cynical determination to make sure that only like-minded Republicans—Trump insurrectionists and their enablers—can win future elections in the United States of America. If their plotting and scheming works, America will indeed become an authoritarian nation, a white Christian nationalist country, in which books like the one in your hands, and other resistance resources, will likely wind up in flames—and those who write and read them will be discouraged in ways proven effective in other states ruled by one man and his party. Think Russia. China. Iran. Hungary. Egypt. Turkey. The Philippines. Brazil. Myanmar. Sudan.

The rest of this book is intended to help Christians think about what we can do. How can we strengthen the moral resistance to this authoritarian movement in our midst before it's too late?[1] How can we effectively respond to our churches' collusion with the devious principalities and powers that Jesus calls us to resist? When I say that "Jesus calls us to resist," I am referring to the living Spirit of the brother from Nazareth whom most Christians identify as "Christ." For many years, I have found the image of "christic power" more helpful than the titular "Christ," which usually gets tagged onto "Jesus" as if it were his last name. As a Christian, I believe that Jesus's ongoing power-with us *is* his christic power, and that his power-with us is also the Spirit, the *Holy* Spirit. Moreover, I believe that this Spirit, this christic power—by "christic," I mean the sacred power that infused our brother Jesus—lives and breathes and works in and through us too. I believe that this is how we participate in the ongoing resurrected presence of Jesus. That tells you a little something about my faith in Jesus. I say this now so that, as you consider the questions and proposals in part 3 of this book, you'll know something about the theological assumptions I bring to these reflections. You may wish to do the same; jot down on a notepad, or on your phone or some other device, your own thoughts, feelings, and questions as you read.

Part 3 is meant to be suggestive, invitational, and provocative. I hope to spark questions and your own proposals. Nothing that I say is meant to stifle your questions, your disagreements, or your dismissal of some of my ideas. But I hope that the discussion questions which you'll find at the end of chapters 12–18 will engage and energize you and that some of what is proposed will spark your enthusiasm for changes that need to be made in our churches and our nation. More than anything, I hope that you will come up with your own ideas for how more Americans, including Christians, can be inspirations in the ongoing struggles for liberty and justice for all, and for peace on earth.

QUESTIONS FOR ALL CHRISTIANS

Drawing on biblical resources, part 3 calls Christians to help re-create our national dream of becoming a land of liberty and justice for all. To respond to this call, we must wrestle with two sets of questions. The first set is about Christian theology and the second is about American politics. We encounter them as mutually interactive in our lives as Christians and as Americans. While few, probably none, of our readers would mean to be Christian nationalists, the convergence of our spiritualities as Christians and themes in our lives as American citizens has contributed over the course of American history to the reemergence time and again of white Christian nationalism. Thus, the assumption that we are meant by God to be a Christian nation, governed largely by white Christian men on Christian principles, is in the air we breathe, much like my white South African friend Denise Ackerman once described apartheid in her country.

First are the biblically based spiritual and ethical questions for Christians, whatever our traditions. Whether we are more liberal or conservative in our theologies or spiritualities; whether we are richer or poorer; whatever our genders or sexual identities; whatever our races, ethnicities, or classes; what is God's ongoing call to Christians? How can we who identify as Christian live most faithfully in relation to Jesus, who said that the two greatest commandments are these: "'You shall love the Lord your God with all your heart, and with all your soul, and with all your mind, and with all your strength.' The second is this, 'You shall love your neighbor as yourself.' There is no other commandment greater than these" (Mark 12:30–31 NRSV)? As Jesus knew, these commandments were close in spirit to the simple but profound requirement that had been voiced eight centuries earlier by the prophet Micah. When asked by the people of Judah, in southern Israel, what God requires of us, Micah responded, "To do justice, and to love kindness, and to walk humbly with your God" (Mic. 6:8 NRSV). These are strong words, powerful charges, but how actually do we embody these values and this vision in our daily lives as Christians in America? That is the first set of questions, which pose spiritual and moral challenges for all Christians wrestling with what it means to be Christian in any culture at any time, but especially contemporary American culture.

QUESTIONS FOR ALL AMERICANS

The second set of questions meets us today with special urgency in the context of a frenzied, ongoing assault on American democracy by fellow citizens who include significant numbers of proud white Christian nationalists and far greater numbers of Christians and other Americans who simply look away, as if either nothing is the matter or there's nothing we can do about it. In this perplexing and dangerous situation, in which we are set against brother and sister Christians, as well as people of other faith traditions, what does loving God actually involve, especially here in today's America? Can we even imagine loving our neighbor in a climate and context in which we have been set so fearfully and hatefully against one another, Americans against Americans, and Christians against Christians?

What on earth does it mean—to love our neighbor as ourself—at a time when many of us honestly find ourselves wishing our hateful neighbors, political enemies, and spiritual adversaries would just drop dead? How often do we hear ourselves, or someone close to us, say things like, "I don't hate anyone, but" or "I don't really want him to die, but" or "I've never loathed anyone as much as I do him [or her, or them]"? I ask myself, and I ask you, can such strong, honest, negative feelings be transformed into energies for infusing Christianity with a passion for justice-love—and bringing justice-love more fully to life in America?

As American history is being made, how can we Christians be among the healing and liberating resources of God's transforming "justice-love," a term coined by a Presbyterian task force in the 1990s,[2] in which its authors realized that neither justice nor love is real or lasting without the other? How can we help sharpen and secure American democracy as a dream worth pursuing, a vision signaled in the Declaration of Independence by those who wrote in 1776: "We hold these truths to be self-evident, that all men are created equal, that they are endowed by their Creator with certain unalienable Rights, that among these are Life, Liberty, and the pursuit of Happiness"?

CALL

Most Americans are likely to associate "call" with Christian piety, and most Christians probably associate it with the experiences and teachings of Paul, the prolific writer of letters to early Christian communities who were trying to organize themselves in the ongoing spirit of Jesus a generation after his life. Because Paul's theology is often received as wordy, convoluted, and dogmatic, he may not be a favorite teacher for many readers of this book! But please bear with me for a moment here. In his letter to the church at Rome, Paul mentions God's "calling" to people like himself: "The gifts and the calling of God are irrevocable" (Rom. 11:29 NRSV). Christians may recall Paul's dramatic experience of his own "calling." Prior to a startling, in-person experience of one whom he accepted as the risen Jesus, Paul had been Saul of Tarsus, evidently a persecutor of the young church. But one day, walking along the road to Damascus, Saul was suddenly blinded and met by Jesus, who told him to stop persecuting him.

Whatever we may think of such a story, and whether we put much, if any, stock in the teachings of Paul, the basis of this book in your hands, especially part 3, is that we, no less than Saul of Tarsus, are being called today—summoned, beckoned, urged—by a universal moral energy, a fierce Spirit of justice-love, call it "God," call him "Father" or "Jesus Christ," call her "Mother" or "Sophia-Wisdom," call it "conscience" or our "better angels" or our "higher power." Call it or call them by whatever names, or none at all. We are being called to act on behalf of our people and our planet. We are being called to come together to help save our nation as well as to restore our collective "soul," which is the meeting place of our humanity and our divinity, the divine spark that fires us up. Our call is no less integral to the future of either our nation or the Christian faith than Paul of Tarsus's conversion was to the early church.

Faced with devastating consequences of the seven deadly sins, we will consider calls to study and to act, calls to resist these sins and to join in healing our churches and liberating our nation. It is wonderful that steps are already being taken in many Christian churches across America—especially in addressing the sin of white supremacy in our nation and our churches. Yet however involved some of our churches have become in wrestling with the problem of white supremacy in our nation's history and in our churches, we white Christians have really just begun to realize the depth and breadth of this particularly odious sin and how damaging it *continues* to be to people of all colors and cultures in America, ourselves included. The fact that Christians, both more conservative and more liberal, have been surprised by the emergence of white Christian nationalism suggests that we have much to learn about the depths of white supremacy and how we have been affected by it.

These calls are to all Christians and all churches, without exception. The prophet Micah and Jesus himself did not say the commandments are optional. They did not tell us to make justice, practice kindness, exercise humility, and love God and neighbor whenever we feel like it or if it fits into our plans. We assume that Christians will hear these calls in different ways and will struggle with them in relation to their own histories, congregations, and communities. Well-organized and well-led congregations will do whatever they can to ground significant changes in the best of their own traditions, and that is all we can hope for.

But what about those who are not in congregations? What about those who cannot find a church that is right for them, or who may no longer even be looking? Those who have left the church, as countless justice-loving people have? Those who may want nothing to do with Christianity? If you have been formed to any extent, for better or worse, by Christian culture, the questions raised here may be for you. If you are somewhat familiar with basic Christian words and symbols—like Jesus, church, baptism, sin, salvation, life, death, prayer, healing, liberation, the cross, the empty tomb—part 3 may tempt you to join up for at least awhile with some justice-loving Christians or post-Christians in your communities, and perhaps also with people of other spiritual traditions, to discuss the basic tenets of this book—the seven deadly sins. Whoever you are, I urge you to draw generously from the wellsprings of your time and talents to imagine what *your* part might be in resisting the evils being spawned by the sins of white Christian nationalism and in so doing, to help secure the democratic foundations of our nation.

This book—part 3 in particular—is written as a resource for discussions among friends and colleagues and in families, as well as for study groups in congregations, classrooms, book clubs, and neighborhood associations. The book urges you to come together to take steps against the pervasiveness of the deadly sins, to figure out together how to help heal those who have been broken and how to join in liberating those who have been oppressed by our collective sins of omnipotence, entitlement, white supremacy, misogyny, capitalist spirituality, domination of the earth and its creatures, and the violence that is tearing us apart.

Finally, you might well ask—really, how can we be so naïve as to imagine that by responding to these calls, Christians throughout America can successfully undercut and eventually disarm and defeat white Christian nationalism? I offer the following counsel, which I hope you will take to heart as we move together into part 3:

First, it will take time, more time than we personally have. We have to think beyond our personal selves. We must enlarge our spiritualities to ground us more fully on behalf of those who will inherit the earth from us. The seven deadly sins of white Christian nationalism are so tightly woven into the fabric of American Christianity that, under the best conditions, it will take several generations of Christians to make much significant headway disentangling and eliminating them. I can imagine our great-grandchildren, our great-nephews and great-nieces, their families, their spiritual communities, and their political allies continuing this struggle as they move into the latter half of this century. This being so, it is not a moment too soon for us to galvanize our efforts to do whatever we can to undercut white Christian nationalism here and now.

Second, we need to be realistic about how completely any of the deadly sins will ever be eliminated. We should not expect any of the sins to be entirely eliminated, not ever, but they can be significantly disentangled and weakened if enough of us, American Christians and others, now and later, band together in the spirits of those who have gone before—to expunge these sins wherever we can and, wherever we cannot eliminate them entirely, to blunt their effects.

Third, in the spirit of our ancestors (at their best), we must keep the faith (at its best)! We need to believe in ourselves and in the Spirit of Justice-Love that moves us forward together. As we attempt to untangle the sins of white Christian nationalism, we will be making both our churches and our nation better—not perfect, but better. Most importantly, we will be doing whatever we can to block the rise of a bleak and brutal authoritarian future. Never have the questions listed at the end of the following chapters been more urgent for us to wrestle with than today.

Chapter 12

The First Call

Empowering One Another

The goal of this chapter is to encourage Christians to think about Dorothee Soelle's belief that God cannot be both omnipotent—all-powerful—and loving unless we reconsider what we mean by "power." If, by "power," we mean power-over or control, then I believe, with Dorothee, that God cannot be, and is not, powerful. If however, we experience God as our power-with one another, our wellspring of deep mutuality, our love of neighbor, then God is indeed all-powerful—and so too are we, insofar as we generate real mutuality, or true, honest, love for one another.

Our first call is to move as far away as possible from imagining that either God or human beings at our best seek power-over others. God is love, not a coercive ruler. God is not a master of control but rather a partner in the cooperative adventure, with us, of building our families, our nation, our world. God is not a father or a mother who demands obedience except in urgent situations in which we are too ignorant to know what to do and too foolish to quiet down and listen to the One calling us to love one another and teaching us how.

In accepting the call to be open to God as source and resource of our creative power-with one another, we need to realize that Christian tradition has not often affirmed this beautifully relational spirit as divine. Christian teachings about God, though they have varied tremendously across time and space, have not often recognized and affirmed the deeply relational character of God as love. Most Christians have failed to see that God is literally, not simply metaphorically, the relational energy of love.

One of the ancient theologians who intuited the relational nature of God was Saint Augustine (354–430 CE), bishop of Hippo in northern Africa, today's Libya. Despite his seriously problematic equation of sexuality with sin and his perception of an unbridgeable gulf between the "city of man" and the "city of God,"[1] Augustine affirmed the radically relational character of God, describing the Spirit as "the love between the Father and the Son."[2]

The irony of Augustine's understanding of love as the essence of God and his condemnation of our human experiences of embodied *sexual* love put Christians in an awful bind that has made it almost impossible for most Christians to live fully, joyfully, and gratefully as sensual, sexual beings. With Augustine's emergence as probably the most influential theologian in the church's first millennium, Christians learned, through the church, to be split and, if faithful to the church's teachings, were forced to live in dreadful tension between oppositional psychospiritual pulls. We were torn between our experiences of spirit and flesh, agape and eros, grace and sin, and other dualisms, such as light and dark, white and black, life and death, which over centuries and across cultures, we learned to experience not only as dualistic but as oppositional. To be Christian became synonymous with being torn in two, according to orthodox Christian teachings: living in the sinful "city of man," we have been constantly called to aspire to rise above our embodied sensuality and take up residence in the "city of God."

Nonetheless, scattered throughout Christian history, there have been voices stressing the relational unity of God and humankind; Creator and creature; Spirit and flesh; life and death; the love of God, the love of friends, and sexual love. From Irenaeus in the second century, to Julian of Norwich in the fourteenth, to Dorothee Soelle and Thomas Merton in the twentieth, to contemporary teachers like Richard Rohr, with many others along the way, Christians have been encouraged to renounce the legacy of Christian dualism that unfortunately survived the Protestant Reformation of the sixteenth century pretty much intact.

One notable protestor against Christian dualism was the Anglican theologian and teacher Frederick Denison Maurice, who lived and taught theology in nineteenth-century England (1805–1872). Earlier in his life a Unitarian, Frederick Maurice stressed the unity of God and humankind in Christ, and the unity of all humans with Christ in God.[3] Maurice taught his students that God and humanity are not all that far apart, and that there is no great gulf between us. Indeed there is sin, and we are all sinners, but our sinfulness is not as strong or everlasting as God's love.

Maurice believed that God's love, which is God's Spirit, which is God, connects us all, making us one body in Christ. He believed that with Jesus and one another, we live eternally in a spiritual community held together by God's love. He believed strongly that the vocation of all Christians, a call we share, is to build a world fashioned by God's love into one human community marked by equality, justice, and freedom.

Even so, Maurice was a man of his time. Like the founders of the United States of America and the builders of Christian churches in America, many of them Anglicans who had come over from England several generations before his lifetime, Frederick Maurice also was shaped by white male supremacy. Moreover, he assumed that Christianity was superior to other religions of the world, although he was more tolerant of other religions, especially Islam, than were many of his Christian contemporaries. Like most Christians then and now, Maurice paid little attention to the life of the earth or to creatures-other-than-human who inhabit the planet. In these ways, Maurice's vision of "the kingdom of God" was limited, partial, and seriously wrongheaded in significant ways.

But Maurice was ahead of his peers in several regards: He deplored the excesses of mid-nineteenth-century capitalism and became an ardent "Christian socialist," a Christianized call for radical changes in the realm of economic justice, similar to the revolutionary proposals being voiced by his contemporary Karl Marx on the Continent. Maurice also was a strong proponent of education for women, especially working-class women in an increasingly industrialized London.

Maurice continues to be my primary theological mentor from an earlier time and place. His experiences of God's power-with us, rather than over us, prompted me many years ago to begin to envision community being forged across the lines that divide us, be they race, ethnicity, language, gender or sexual identity, class location, religion, ideology, or even species.

Over time, with theological mentors like Maurice, I have come to appreciate the wisdom not only in what Jesus of Nazareth said and did but, as importantly, in *how he related to those around him*. Take, for instance, Jesus's telling the parable of the Good Samaritan, which may well be the most beloved of his parables:

> Just then a lawyer stood up to test Jesus. "Teacher," he said, "what must I do to inherit eternal life?" He said to him, "What is written in the law? What do you read there?" He answered, "You shall love the Lord your God with all your heart, and with all your soul, and with all your strength, and with all your mind; and your neighbor as yourself." And he said to him, "You have given the right answer; do this, and you will live." But wanting to justify himself, he asked Jesus, "And who is my neighbor?" Jesus replied, "A man was going down from Jerusalem to Jericho, and fell into the hands of robbers, who stripped him, beat him, and went away, leaving him half dead. Now by chance a priest was going down that road; and when he saw him, he passed by on the other side. So likewise a Levite, when he came to the place and saw him, passed by on the other side. But a Samaritan while traveling came near him; and when he saw him, he was moved with pity. He went to him and bandaged his wounds, having poured oil and wine on them. Then he put him on his own animal, brought him to an inn, and took care of him. The next day he took out two denarii, gave them to the innkeeper, and said, 'Take care of him; and when I come back, I will

repay you whatever more you spend.' Which of these three, do you think, was a neighbor to the man who fell into the hands of the robbers?" He said, "The one who showed him mercy." Jesus said to him, "Go and do likewise." (Luke 10:25–37 NRSV)

WHAT IS JESUS DOING HERE?

Immediately prior to this parable, Jesus is in conversation with a lawyer about what he must do to inherit eternal life. Jesus's response is that the man must love God and his neighbor as himself. But the lawyer, to "test" him, we are told, presses on: "And who is my neighbor?" Jesus then tells the story of the Good Samaritan. Most Christians know the story well. As the parable ends, the lawyer acknowledges to Jesus that the person who showed mercy, the one who stopped by the side of the road and tended the wounded man, the Samaritan, is the person in this story who loves God. Not the religious leaders who passed by on the other side but rather a religious outsider and social pariah, a Samaritan, is the person whose action reflects God's love being given by one human to another.

Jesus's telling this story in his time and place was bold and would have raised some brows. It would be like a Jewish rabbi telling Jews a story today in which a Palestinian whose home has been bulldozed by the Israelis stops to help a poor Jew who has been mugged on his way home. Or a mom telling her kids about a conservative Christian minister stopping to care for a transgender neighbor who has been robbed and beaten up on his way home. Or a Union soldier after the Civil War telling his Northern friends an odd story about a Confederate soldier who had stopped along the way to tend the wounds of a Union man lying by the road. Who is my neighbor indeed? The Confederate. The Christian minister. The Palestinian. The Samaritan. Because to love one another—loving even those whom we may fear or despise, as historically Jews and Samaritans had hated each other—is to love God. In so doing, we embody God's love in the world, bringing the Spirit and power of love to life again and again.

But let's keep going here, because it's not just the content of the parable that is engaging. One of the great things about Jesus is that he used parables to teach his peers—short, cryptic stories that usually end in questions, like "Which of these three do you think was a neighbor to the man who had been robbed?" Jesus asks the lawyer to answer the question and solve the ethical puzzle. Implicit in the story, and in the lawyer's response, is that, no it's not always the folks we'd expect to stop and do the right thing. It's often the very people we most dislike, people we don't trust, people we've learned to fear and hate. So that's one thing we learn from the parable of the Good

Samaritan. This is a rather universal interpretation, though not one that many of us take to heart, especially when we are as badly divided as we are right now in America.

We come away from this parable assuming that both Jesus, as the teller of the story, and the Samaritan, as its hero, are reflecting God's love—and that maybe we can too. Jesus is reflecting God's wisdom in telling this parable and God's love in connecting respectfully with the lawyer who is interrogating him, goading him. The Samaritan is reflecting God's love in stopping to care for his enemy. So we are given glimpses of God's activity through human beings—through Jesus and also, in the parable, through God's love manifested in a social and religious outcast, a Samaritan.

Can we believe that someone who despises everything we stand for, or everything we are, might actually stop to save us if we were in serious trouble? Can we imagine that we ourselves might do what the Samaritan did in a similar situation, thereby bringing God to life in a most unexpected time and place? Does this story throw us a little off balance when we think about it, and leave us a bit unsure what we would do in a similar situation? It probably should.

POWER-WITH AS GOD'S LOVE AND GOD'S POWER

But another lesson—and perhaps the most elusive learning for many Christians who are thinking about the parable of the Good Samaritan—is that the primary images of God's love in this story are not about anyone, including God, reflecting "power-over" others. Rather, the parable reflects a sharing of power—power-with—which we can assume is an image of God that Jesus is trying to convey to his listeners.

Think about what Jesus is doing, and how. Jesus and the lawyer are talking, two people in conversation. Each is taking the other seriously, at least by the end of the story, when the lawyer—who has been "testing" Jesus—basically says, okay, yes, it's the one who shows mercy who loves his neighbor. In their exchange, Jesus is not treating the lawyer as a lesser person. He is not gloating, not acting like a big shot, a know-it-all, or a teacher with a store of knowledge that the other man doesn't have. Jesus is inviting the lawyer into the same realization of God's love, and of what constitutes eternal life, that he himself has. He is sharing his power-with this man. In this way, Jesus is loving his interrogator, empowering him to experience God with, and through, the mutuality that Jesus has generated with him. *The "how" of Jesus's teaching is through sharing power-with, not power-over, the lawyer.*

Meanwhile, inside the parable, those who are accorded a great deal of "power-over" in the world—authority in organized religion, the priest and the

Levite—are those without any power at all in this story. They walk on by and disappear into their important business of being religious authorities. Whereas the Samaritan, who has absolutely no religious authority, no power-over any-one in Judaism, emerges as the bearer of power-with—in this story, shown to be the love of God, sacred power, healing power. Of all the characters in this story, the Samaritan emerges as the bearer of the power of God.

The parable of the Good Samaritan becomes a window into witnessing the healing power of God's love as a power we share with one another whenever we love—and especially whenever we love those who are most difficult for us to love and care for: the strangers, the foreigners, the immigrants, the people not like us, those who may frighten us because they don't speak like us or dress like us or worship like us or think like us. And yet—it is in sharing our power-with these others, in loving them, that we are sharing God. Our power-with them is our sacred power, and it becomes theirs as well, because love is a contagious power, an energy passed on among us.

As noted earlier, this is not what most Christians have learned to believe about God's power. Historically, Christians have believed that God is "omnipotent," all-powerful, the exercise of power-over others. This has been a primary Christian image of God: an almighty deity with power-over us and ultimately power-over everything. For much of Christian history, our churches, whether Catholic, Orthodox, or Protestant, and whether more or less liberal or conservative, have shaped our theologies and liturgies in an assumption that God epitomizes power-over and that, at least in the end, he will reign over all creation.

Refuting this traditional Christian assumption, the great German theologian Dorothee Soelle, whose life centered around helping God's love be realized in peacemaking and justice building, believed that God cannot be both good and powerful. If God is powerful, God is not good, she taught. And if God is good, God is not powerful. From her earliest works on, Soelle's theology was a protest against an omnipotent God, understood to be a God who wields power over humanity and creation. I was introduced to Dorothee's work in the late 1970s through our mutual friend Beverly Harrison, who loaned me a copy of *Christ the Representative: An Essay in Theology after the Death of God*,[4] written in the mid-1960s, in which Soelle presents "Christ" as repre-senting God to humanity and humanity to God, as if introducing one friend to another. The only sacred power in the story is the mutual (or "christic"—my word) energy generated by Jesus toward both God and humanity, speaking to each on behalf of the other. Soelle was writing on behalf of a down-to-earth God, a Spirit of Justice-Love who infuses our lives, not a pie-in-the-sky or far-off deity who governs, rewards, and punishes humankind. She was drawing heavily in her own theology from her fellow countryman, Dietrich Bonhoeffer, who had been martyred two decades earlier.

Dorothee Soelle and I had any number of conversations over the years in which, through writing, teaching, and traveling together, we helped each other realize increasingly that God truly can be—and is—both good and powerful, but only inasmuch we radically reimage "power" as "power-with," or "mutuality," rather than as "power-over," which is how God's "omnipotence" is traditionally understood. Whether in base communities outside Managua, Nicaragua, or looking at the tiny flowers growing where the Neuengamme death camp outside Hamburg had once been, we realized that *God's love is God's power.* I believe that both Dorothee and I experienced an ongoing deepening of a shared belief that the resurrection, whether literally or not a physical phenomenon, is a sign that God's love, which *is* God's power, has the last word and lives forever in every act and even aspiration of justice-love, compassion, and courage.

Soelle herself and I too had been strongly influenced by the later writings and life of Dietrich Bonhoeffer, a German theologian who was martyred by the Nazis in 1945. In his *Letters and Papers from Prison*, which he wrote from his cell as he awaited execution, Bonhoeffer famously declared that only a God who is powerless can help us.[5] That is to say, only a God who does not have "power-over" us can help us. Such a God helps us by teaching us how to love one another—by sharing whatever we have: our possessions, and also our faith and hope and especially our love. God loves through us as we care for one another in darkness and grief as well as in bright and joyful times. Through many sources, including each other and probably, for most of us, through spiritual energies we cannot fully understand, God is with us through dark times as well as times of celebration.

Another important influence on my learning to experience God as our sacred power in mutuality, or our "power-with," was Martin Buber, a Jewish mystical social philosopher, whose *I and Thou* changed my life when I read it in college in 1965. First published in English in 1958, this book was immediately misunderstood by most American Christians as a spiritual tract largely about the individual's relational journey instead of the strong critique Buber intended it to be of a consumer society in which people were being conditioned spiritually as well as politically to experience one another as "it" rather than "thou." The Austrian Buber lamented that, in the aftermath of World War II, the European and American victors as well as his own vanquished people had learned to objectify and use each other to transact business and make deals. His fear was that they, and we as their children and grandchildren, would not learn well how to regard each other as "thou" rather than as "it"— in Jesus's words, we would not learn how to love one another.

Buber understood that only insofar as we can imagine ourselves as sister and brothers, cosubjects, each a sacred "thou" to the other, each in the image of God, can we imagine ourselves forming "beloved community" as a basis of American society. Buber believed that if we can imagine ourselves connected mutually in this way, then we can perhaps experience God—by whatever names or none at all—as the source of our power-with one another, the root of our love for one another, the wellspring of our ability to care for each other, friend and foe alike, and the confidence that we can do it because we are not alone. We are not alone because we have power-with each other and with God. God truly can and often does bless America—but only insofar as we love one another.

DISCUSSION QUESTIONS

1. Discuss Dorothee Soelle's belief that God cannot be both omnipotent (have power-over us) and loving. What did she mean? Do you agree with her? Why or why not? Discuss the contradiction between omnipotence and love as you experience, or witness, it.
2. English priest and theologian F. D. Maurice believed strongly that the vocation of all Christians, a call we share, is to build a world fashioned by God's love into one human community marked by equality, justice, and freedom. How might our churches help shape our nation at this time if we took this moral commitment seriously? Discuss what your roles could be in this prophetic activity.
3. When have you been the one lying in the ditch? The priest who passes on by? The Samaritan who stops to help? Where is God in this story? What kind of God do you see in this story? How would you describe God's power in the parable of the Good Samaritan?
4. Martin Buber lamented that, after World War II, the European and American victors as well as his own vanquished (Austrian) people had learned to objectify and use each other to transact business and make deals. He feared that they—and we, their children and grandchildren and our heirs—would not know how to regard each other as "thou" rather than as "it." How do you respond to Buber's fear? To what extent was he correct? How can we respond to this moral challenge in our church and our nation today? Think of some steps we might take.

Chapter 13

The Second Call

Embodying Humility

The goal of this chapter is to empower us to accept our true selves, and to help us know our place in creation, which is neither better nor worse than the rest of humankind and no more or less valuable than the rest of creature-kind.

Humility may be the most misunderstood psychospiritual gift of all. The second of the deadly sins is entitlement, assuming the right to be hailed as best, to have most, and to be exceptional. In response, the second of these calls is to humility, a deep sense of being grounded with others, neither above nor below our neighbors.

As a recovering alcoholic who has learned much from friends and colleagues in Alcoholics Anonymous, I can testify to how deeply and utterly human it is to fall into imagining that we are either better than others ("I never acted like *that* poor fool when I was drunk") or worse ("Why am I such a loser who can't seem to get with the program. What's wrong with me?"). To be entitled—to think too highly of ourselves—is obviously a moral problem and at the root of much evil in history. But just as problematic, spiritually and morally, is to think so little of ourselves that we try not to get in the way of all the important business in the world around us, including the work of justice making. To play down our strengths, or even deny that we have them, creates major psychospiritual challenges—especially for white Christian women in America. Not only do we fall easily into playing down our own worth—and that of our daughters—but our lives are less effective in the larger world. Imagining ourselves to be of little use to anyone—except, if we are lucky to be part of a functional family, church, or other local community—we cannot imagine ourselves as helping build a more justice-loving world beyond ourselves and the people we are most at home with, people like us.

NOT ERASING OURSELVES

Humility as erasure is exactly what the church has taught us, especially if we are women. Christianity traditionally has taught faithful Christians to think of humility as a self-effacing attitude, in which people, mostly women and "soft" men (think of the stereotypes of monks and priests) are trained to lower their eyes and ask to be excused for even being noticed. The less seen, the better. The less space we take up in the world, the closer to God we can be in this world and the next. This is nonsense, both theologically and psychologically. Even worse, such spiritual folly breeds dishonesty, depression, and dysfunctional Christian families, churches, and communities. Often the healthiest, most genuinely humble human beings are so put off by this dehumanizing expectation that they leave Christianity behind to seek healthier communities of meaning and worship, in which they can be themselves—and love themselves.

Self-effacement is not an attitude to be associated with Jesus of Nazareth, in neither his personal style nor his teachings. We can imagine that, with nothing to hide, Jesus engaged people. He probably looked them in the eye, which is a sign of respect. He touched them and was touched by them, and he spoke in parables, which was a way of drawing listeners into solving ethical and pastoral problems for themselves. The Christian Bible presents a Jesus who was direct, honest, and forthright in his conversations with friends and enemies alike—a bold and humble man, teacher, rabbi, friend.

NOT PRETENTIOUS

"Humility" (from Latin *humilis*, meaning "low") is about being low to the ground, down to earth, common rather than exceptional, modest not arrogant, meek as opposed to pretentious. Jesus was humble insofar as he shared his power-with others, walked beside them, and encouraged them to feed the hungry and serve the poor just as he did. Here's a passage from Mark, in which Jesus is empowering his disciples:

> He called the twelve and began to send them out two by two, and gave them authority over the unclean spirits. He ordered them to take nothing for their journey except a staff; no bread, no bag, no money in their belts; but to wear sandals and not to put on two tunics. He said to them, "Wherever you enter a house, stay there until you leave the place. If any place will not welcome you and they refuse to hear you, as you leave, shake off the dust that is on your feet as a testimony against them." So they went out and proclaimed that all should

repent. They cast out many demons, and anointed with oil many who were sick and cured them. (Mark 6:7–13 NRSV)

Mark is describing a band of humble folk, following Jesus's example. Don't take food and money (remember that Jesus and his disciples moved mainly among those who would not have had much food and money). Don't wear more than you need to wear (don't show off). Do your best and don't get bent out of shape if people refuse to hear you. Just leave and "shake the dust that is on your feet as a testimony against them." Jesus is not suggesting that his followers allow themselves to be humiliated. To the contrary. He tells them: Do what you can. Then leave. Don't worry about it if you fail. This happens sometimes. Shake the dust from your feet and keep moving along; doing your best. You can't reach everyone,

HUMILITY AS BLESSING

Such humility is amplified by Jesus's teachings in the Sermon on the Mount, better known to most Christians as the Beatitudes:

When Jesus saw the crowds, he went up the mountain; and after he sat down, his disciples came to him. Then he began to speak, and taught them, saying:

Blessed are the poor in spirit, for theirs is the kingdom of heaven.

Blessed are those who mourn, for they will be comforted.

Blessed are the meek, for they will inherit the earth.

Blessed are those who hunger and thirst for righteousness, for they will be filled.

Blessed are the merciful, for they will receive mercy.

Blessed are the pure in heart, for they will see God.

Blessed are the peacemakers, for they will be called children of God.

Blessed are those who are persecuted for righteousness' sake, for theirs is the kingdom of heaven. (Matt. 5:1–10 NRSV)

Later in this sermon, Jesus teaches his followers to pray "thy kingdom come" in the prayer we know as "The Lord's Prayer." Spiritual teacher Richard Rohr has written about this prayer:

It is incredible dishonesty in the human heart to pray daily that this kingdom should come, that God's will be done on earth as in heaven, and at the same time to deny that Jesus wants this kingdom to be put into practice on earth. Whoever asks for the rulership of God to come down on earth must believe in it and be wholeheartedly resolved to carry it out. Those who emphasize that the Sermon on the Mount is impractical in order to weaken its moral obligations should remember the concluding words, "Not all who say 'Lord' to me shall reach the kingdom of heaven, but only those who do the will of my Father in heaven" (Matthew 7:21).[1]

In the Sermon on the Mount, which includes the Lord's Prayer, Jesus is telling people that life in this world—creating insofar as we can God's "kingdom" here on earth—is what we need to be concerned about, and that we are called to live in a spirit of humility here and now. In a word, Jesus calls those who do live this way "blessed." They are favored by God not because they are best, smartest, most, or the center of any religion or community, including Jesus's own circle of friends. They are blessed because they embody qualities associated with humility:

They are meek—alive with a sense of their own spiritual size, neither too large nor too small. They are merciful, not hasty to judge or condemn, and certainly not vengeful. They are pure in heart, vulnerable to giving and receiving love. They hunger and thirst for righteousness, or justice-love. And, if they are following Jesus, they probably have been, or will be, persecuted for righteousness' sake, like Jesus himself would be. They are peacemakers, not motivated by the desire to stir things up and get people at each other's throats.

They may even be "poor in spirit," which seems an odd image for the friends and followers of Jesus. Perhaps this refers to those who are sick at heart—because, like Jesus, they *do* love their neighbors and have suffered because of it, a sad consequence of neighbor-love in badly divided societies like ours today. Interestingly, the abbreviated version of the Beatitudes in Luke's account of this sermon does not say "poor in spirit" but rather simply "Blessed are you who are poor" (Luke 6:20 NRSV). This may reflect Luke's special concern for those who are physically in need or in harm's way. The author of Luke (who was also the author of the Acts of the Apostles) is, after all, said to have been a physician. A concern for people's health and well-being seems to have been one of his special concerns.

> Then [Jesus] looked up at his disciples and said: "Blessed are you who are poor, for yours is the kingdom of God. Blessed are you who are hungry now, for you will be filled. Blessed are you who weep now, for you will laugh." (Luke 6:20–21 NRSV)

In both Matthew's and Luke's versions of the sermon, Jesus is exhorting his friends and followers to be humble.

WE CAN BE PROUD OF OURSELVES

Being humble does not mean we can't be proud of our accomplishments or appreciate awards for our achievements, or refuse affirmations for the quality of our lives, relationships, and work. God, the energy of love working among us, encompasses our delight in ourselves, and gratitude, for what we can do well and enjoy and share. The God whom Jesus loved, and whose love Jesus and the rest of us are called to embody, surely absorbs our joy and the pleasure we take in our accomplishments, provided it is all unfolding in a spirit of the love we are sharing with one another morning by morning and day by day.

The pride that "goeth before destruction, and an haughty spirit before a fall" (Prov. 16:18 King James Version) has to do with the attitude we explored in part 2—the arrogance of assuming that we are the best, and that our way of life, our religion, our nation, or our culture is superior to others. That is the pride that goes before a fall. And it is to combat such boastful and hateful pride, the pitiful arrogance so evident in high seats of American power today, that we have encountered entitlement as one of the sinful tangles in the ugly tapestry of white Christian nationalism.

We need to step beyond the big spiritual lie—that we are the best—and more fully realize our place in the world, as one among many. Such humility would make all the difference in how we live together as Americans and as Christians.

But we need to be clear here. Not only is genuine humility not a self-effacing attitude, it is often manifest in bold speech and action. If we understand ourselves as grounded together on this earth, sharing the same soil, none of us are entitled to greater respect as human beings, none more entitled than others to nutritious food, adequate health care, protection from harm, or other basic human rights. Believing this as the way of Jesus, our humility often will become a shout-out for justice.

THE BOLDNESS OF HUMILITY

We can turn to a modern-day prophet to bring home this point about humility as bold and empowering. In September 1955, when he was only twenty-six years old, Martin Luther King Jr. preached a sermon in Montgomery, Alabama, on the parable of the pharisee and the publican (better understood as the tax collector):

> [Jesus] told this parable to some who trusted in themselves that they were righteous and regarded others with contempt: "Two men went up to the temple to pray, one a Pharisee and the other a tax collector. The Pharisee, standing by himself, was praying thus, 'God, I thank you that I am not like other people: thieves, rogues, adulterers, or even like this tax collector. I fast twice a week; I give a tenth of all my income.' But the tax collector, standing far off, would not even look up to heaven, but was beating his breast and saying, 'God, be merciful to me, a sinner!' I tell you, this man went down to his home justified rather than the other; for all who exalt themselves will be humbled, but all who humble themselves will be exalted." (Luke 18:9–14 NRSV)

Martin Luther King is comparing the Pharisee to religious leaders who assume that they are best and right and should exercise control over everyone and, moreover, who take satisfaction from boasting, lauding themselves over others. King compares the tax collector, by contrast, to those who are down on their luck ("blessed are the poor in spirit") and need not condemnation but rather encouragement. King praises the tax collector for "having a soul open to God while the Pharisee was locked in himself."[2] "Having a soul open to God." This is how a very young Martin Luther King Jr. described humility early in his public ministry.

But King goes on to say something bold and tough, something that surely would have rankled many white Christians had they been privy to what he was preaching to other African American Christians: "That jury in Mississippi, which a few days ago in the Emmett Till case, freed two white men from what might be considered one of the most brutal and inhuman crimes of the twentieth century, worships Christ. The perpetrators of many of the greatest evils in our society worship Christ." And he continues: "To those who would follow such a religion, we can hear God saying through the prophets: 'Get out of my face. When you make your loud prayer, I will not hear. Your hands are full of blood.'"[3]

In keeping with prophets before him, King is describing the opposite of humility—the loud prayers, the arrogant spiritual boasting, and the contempt for others that spawns evil and violence. King is daring to use the case of fourteen-year-old Emmett Till's horrific murder and to condemn the unrepentant hatred and relentless violence of the white supremacist Christian men who killed Emmett Till as well as those who exonerated them. King singles out the all-white, doubtlessly Christian, jury for special condemnation. Back in 1955, he denounces in the strongest possible terms white Christian Americans' perpetration of the deadly sin of the white Christian nationalism that continues to plague our nation almost three-quarters of a century later.

This same holy rage, voiced by Martin Luther King Jr., is in the air today, especially in the wake of George Floyd's murder in 2020 and scores of other killings of Black and brown people by police, as the United States Senate, a bastion of white entitlement, continues to block the passage of a police reform bill.

We white Christian Americans need to be clear that, to the extent that we and our churches reflect even a shadow of such contempt for Black Americas who are intent upon exercising their constitutional right to vote; for brown people who are seeking refuge in America; for Asian, Pacific Islanders, Native Americans, and other Americans of color who have to cope with the entitlement they encounter among white Americans; God's response to white American Christians is "Get out of my face! Your hands are full of blood."

God, the wellspring of our hope, is clear, angry, and unequivocal. So then, where are we in this moment? Where is our voice? Can we speak honestly, lovingly, angrily to each other and, truthfully, to ourselves?

How dare we condemn Black Americans for protesting police violence against them, when we say not a word about the systemic forces of entitlement that hold in place white supremacy and entitlement throughout America's criminal justice system?

How dare we turn our entitled backs on brown refugees and immigrants from Latin America and other parts of the world who come seeking shelter and safety and a chance to build community in America, just as our ancestors did a few chapters earlier in the history of this country!

How dare we trivialize and ignore Indigenous peoples, Asian Americans, and Pacific Islanders as if they have no right to the same quality of life that we and our European ancestors imagine we deserve.

Imagine God saying to us, "Get out of my face and get moving in the work of justice!"

Discussion Questions

1. In what circumstances does God say to us today, "Get out of my face! Your hands are full of blood!" Let's talk about this. This is not about partisan politics in America. It is about ways in which we all are implicated in perpetrating the seven deadly sins, especially in this instance the sins of entitlement and white supremacy. What is God saying to you personally? What is God's message to white Christians in general?

2. Why do U.S. senators and congresspeople refuse to pass a police reform bill? Why are they hesitant to protect their white siblings from legal accountability and not their Black and brown siblings from violent death? Discuss your views on this. What can be learned in this discussion about humility?

3. What specific connections can you make between righteous anger and the boldness of humility? Can you give examples from your own life or from the lives of others?

4. "Having a soul open to God": this is how a young Martin Luther King Jr. described humility. What does this mean to you? In what ways are our souls, collectively and individually, open to God? In what ways are they not? How can our churches help feed our souls in ways that will open us more to God?

Chapter 14

The Third Call

Approaching the Blackness of God

The goal of this chapter is to encourage white Christians to imagine and approach the Blackness, or darkness, of God and the power and goodness of Blackness—Black culture, Black history, and Black people, as well as the power and goodness of other cultures, histories, and people perceived as "colored" in America.

In part 2, we examined the deadly sin of white supremacy as a foundation of white Christian nationalism and as an ongoing moral challenge for Christians and all Americans. Here we are called—and challenged—to embrace the Blackness of God. As noted earlier, the image of Blackness is not only a racial reference to African Americans but also is intended to reference people and cultures whose "colors" are deemed "darker" than "white." I have put these words in quotes to indicate how imprecisely they signal the color of the skin pigment of human beings and the cultures associated with these colors. How many Caucasians actually have white skin, like white snow or white hair? Nonetheless, in the United States, most Caucasians are legally considered white. We often are granted social privileges such as memberships to private clubs and associations, even to churches of our choice, as well as easier access to housing, banking, legal advocacy, and voting than if we were Black or otherwise "colored."

In this same American context, Africans and African Americans historically have been perceived, categorized, and punished as Black; Latin Americans as well as Middle Eastern people are often seen and treated as brown, lesser than white; Asians and Asian Americans are commonly caricatured as yellow and treated like brown and Black Americans; and Native or Indigenous Americans have long been designated as red by white people and segregated from white society. Each of these colored designations is held to be darker than the whiteness of European and European Americans, who call ourselves white and, simply on that single designation, believe ourselves entitled to various social privileges not accorded to darker, or "colored," people in America. In this book, Blackness—like whiteness—is assumed to be a historical construct built around white people's use and abuse of power-over Black people. Neither whiteness nor Blackness is accepted as a fixed biological category but rather as a social designation of a group's proximity to, or distance from, social, economic, cultural, and political power.

These pages invite readers, who are mostly white Americans, to begin to experience Blackness as a resource for our continuing education, personal transformation, and social change. White readers may feel strange and a bit cautious since we have been shaped so foundationally by white supremacy—what I am naming here "a theology of normalized whiteness," including a usually unconscious, or barely conscious, attraction to the whiteness, lightness, and brightness of the sacred. If you are Black or another person of color—Asian, brown, Native, bi- or multiracial—a spiritual foray into the Blackness of God may not be strange at all—except insofar as your spiritualities, like those of white Christians, have been formed by white supremacist assumptions about God.

To think about how our churches might address a problem that has haunted American culture, including American Christianity, since the early days of the seventeenth century, let's try to wrap our heads around the question of why it has disturbed so many contemporary white Christians to hear that "God is Black" or that "Black is beautiful" or that "Black Lives Matter." Why do we hear Black people's anger about white supremacy as personal attacks on us rather than as invitations to share Black anger at white supremacy and to join in Black celebrations of the value and goodness of Black lives? What angers so many of us? What frightens us? Why do our hearts hear these affirmations of Blackness, Black lives, and Black people as personally threatening to those of us who are white? Why is it so hard for us to see the moral depravity in white supremacy?

A THEOLOGY OF NORMALIZED WHITENESS

Here is an answer: white American Christians have been shaped by a theology that seeks to normalize white European American culture and white American Christian power. To make something "normal" is to render it unexceptional, just the way it is, a settled matter. To have normalized the Caucasian racial-ethnic identity in America is not primarily about the pallor of white skin, the tint of pastel eyes, the texture of light straight hair, or body structures adapted to mid-northern European shores and soil. The physical traits of "white people" are symbols of the social (including economic) power we hold over others—and of the cultural (including religious) entitlement we have assumed, whereby we set the norms of what it means to be fully human and worthy of economic power and social privileges, including the love of God.

In a theology of normalized whiteness, it is simply expected that white people of European origins will lead the American nation that they founded, or imagine that they did. It is normal for good Americans to be grateful for the blessing of this headship as the will of our Father God, of his Son our Lord Jesus Christ, and of the hardworking white Christian men who protect and defend American land, American families, American prosperity, and American values from America's enemies—from without and within.

The God of Christians in this story is omnipotent and entitled and, in his image, so too are American Christians, especially white men. This is why they have to fight hard not to let themselves, their nation, their churches, or their God be overcome by those who would challenge their theology, their view of God and the world, and their lives in relation to both.

This theology is not just about normalizing white American Christian men in general but, most of all, the power and privileges of successful Christian businessmen who, in the twenty-first century, have become the quintessential Americans. They have become the archetypical Protestant capitalist icons— whether or not they are, in fact, Protestant or Christian. Although quite a few are not, most of these people are Christians, at least nominally, and all are either wealthy or aspire to be. They are independent, successful in wielding power-over others, nearly always white and male, and always assuming themselves entitled whatever they most need or want.

But here are some important questions for all American Christians, including white men of privilege: Who, in this story of normal American aspirations, do we Christians imagine are "the least of these" that Jesus refers to in Matthew 25:40? Who are the people in exile, and how did they get there? Who pushed them to the margins and when and why? Why are they kept down and out today, marginalized from those with social and economic power? Where are we in this story?

Most humans identify "up"—we want to be on, or near, the top. We do not want to fall to the bottom or be pushed to the margins of our families, communities, or societies. This naturalization of upward aspiration makes the normalization of whiteness understandable in a nation built on white supremacy. Of course we want to be white; doesn't everyone? Don't even Black Americans have to contend with "colorism,"[1] in which lighter skin is prized, especially for Black women? Our tendency to identify "up" presents a moral challenge to Christians, since aligning ourselves with those on the bottom social rungs of our society does not come natural to many of us. We are just not comfortable when we are too close to the poor.

In American Christianity, we need to help each other *learn how to love*, which involves learning how to love ourselves as well as how to love those who are positioned beneath us in American society as well as those positioned above us. We need to help each other move beyond a theology of normalized whiteness so that we can begin to see ourselves and others in right, mutually empowering—loving—relation to one another, regardless of our race, our class, our religion, or our sexual or gender identity. We have so much to learn together.

In a theology of normalized whiteness, white American Christians normally see our own white bodies as imaging the body of God—hence our attachments to visual fantasies of an old man with a white beard in the sky and a light-skinned European-looking man with blue eyes as his Son Jesus. In the history of American Christianity, our God is portrayed as an old king, a powerful white man, robed in finery, sitting on a throne.

A theology of normalized whiteness holds our gaze on the old white king and conceals from us images of Black suffering. Seldom if ever is God imaged as the slave woman being raped by her white master. A theology of normalized whiteness depends on our identifying upward—with those who have succeeded, those at the top, those whose God and Jesus are white men of privilege, gods constructed historically in the image of a white king and his prince. This identification with, and wanting to be like, those who rule, whether human or divine, pulls fiercely against the empathic lure of the God of justice-love for us to stand with those at the bottom of the social ladder and economic rungs and participate in the ongoing struggles for justice.

One of the most seductive and softest ploys of a theology of normalized whiteness is to draw our gaze away from the outer world and fix our attention upon our inner lives and feelings. The spiritual message of a theology of normalized whiteness is that it is more important to be aligned internally with God and Jesus than to do anything else, whether working, playing, or participating in the ongoing struggles for justice. In a theology of normalized whiteness, good Christians pay more attention to how we *feel* about ourselves and our spiritualities than to how much good we could *do* in the world if we would. Often, we assuage our consciences by assuring ourselves that we cannot do much about the nation or world anyhow, but we can take care of our own spiritual nourishment.

Not that self-care, spiritually as well as in other realms, isn't important, because it is. But, dear people, we are expected within the sanctuary of most American Christianity to attend *primarily* to our private spiritual yearnings and, only if we have time and energy and special interest in social justice, to get involved in some sort of social action. In this way, a theology of normalized whiteness spiritually shrinks us. It diminishes our moral sensibilities, which lead us to small personal token acts of sacrifice and service rather than to actually organizing and acting with others toward transforming the structures of oppression that loom large around us in America.

Because we have been conditioned by this inadequate Christian moral theology, we assume that, if our whiteness is not normalized, if our white male–dominated power structures and culture are not central to the American story, something is the matter with us and our story. In moments of this fear-based confusion, we white American Christians do not know who we are in our society or in the larger world. We are afraid and confused because, throughout our lives, we have learned that there can be only one people, one culture, one history, one language central to the American story and to Christian faith. Only Euro-Americans—specifically, *white* Euro-Americans—can matter most in America and only *Christians* can matter most to God. That is the essence of a theology of normalized whiteness. Most of us white American Christians don't know how to transcend it—that is, how to cross over from a theology of normalized whiteness toward a theology of the Blackness, the darkness, of God without losing ourselves and all that is actually good about our lives as both Americans and Christians.

For all the harm the theology of normalized whiteness has done to people of other colors and cultures, it has also badly damaged white American Christians. It generates our fear and our confusion, and it causes us to wall ourselves off from all that we do not see or accept about God or the world, other people or ourselves. We embody a deep and abiding fear that somehow Blackness—Black people—will overcome us, our power, our culture, our Christian faith. To the extent that Black people invoke the presence of a Black God in our midst, white Christians are likely to be dumbfounded, even terrified.

Several deadly sins quite obviously converge in the theology of normalized whiteness and in our resistance to the power and beauty of Blackness and darkness:

First, we worship a God who normalizes the omnipotence—the power and privileges—of white Christian men.

Second, we practice a religion of entitlement, in which we assume that our white ways of worshipping God are normal, best, and often the only ways to honor our God, our church, our nation—and our race. In our religion of entitlement, genuine humility—being grounded with others on common soil—is easily caricatured as weakness.

Third, we pay homage to the idol of our own white racial identity, our Euro-American whiteness, our stories as white people, the tales and images and memories constructed by our white ancestors as somehow testifying to our superiority.

Fourth, we aspire to generate, and possess, ever more capital—money and the power it produces—and we hold this aspiration as more essential to our lives than the struggles for justice for all. This aspiration is at the heart of capitalist spirituality, and it provides the economic basis of an American Christian theology of normalized whiteness.

The other deadly sins—misogyny, domination of creation, and violence—are also interwoven into the theology of normalized whiteness and especially into how it is actually embodied and practiced in the daily lives of Americans and Christians. As a matter of fact, moving through these chapters on how we can address each of the deadly sins, we are likely to realize that, if we are truly paying attention to any of the sins, we wind up having to deal with them all.

Though American Christians may slough off or protest the hold that the theology of normalized whiteness has on us, our churches have aided and abetted in perpetuating this morally indefensible and politically dangerous theology. Historically, the liberal to moderate mainline Protestant churches, with their often highly educated clergy, have been as much at fault as the more theologically conservative evangelical and fundamentalist churches and the popular megachurches today that are filled with enthusiastic Christians. The fact that all American Christians have celebrated, to some extent, American Christianity's historical normalization of a white Lord of all and the special entitlement of a wealthy few white men and their families should be a matter of shame and sorrow for all of us, whether we are Episcopalians, Southern Baptists, Congregationalists, or Pentecostals.

All of us share in the perpetuation of a theology of normalized whiteness that has secured white supremacy as a bedrock of American history and of Christian churches in America. So how then might we move beyond this dreadful theology toward an affirmation of the God whom Jesus loved, the one true God of all creation and humankind? There is only one path here, and it leads us toward the Blackness of God as a source of grace and redemption.

Let me say here, before we go further, that there really needs also to be a moral reckoning between white Americans with Indigenous Americans, Asian Americans, Latinx, and other Brown Americans. God knows there needs to be some moral accounting between American Christians and people of other faith traditions and none at all. And, in the Wisdom/Sophia of God, there needs to be serious confessional and reparative work between American Christian men and women, and between heteronormative and genderqueer American Christians and others.

So much wrong is done constantly, and we recognize so little of it. But that we are able to recognize and are willing to confess our failures and wrongdoings is a spiritual step as great and hopeful as any we will ever take. In this spirit, American Christians must take these significant moral steps as we get to them. It is never soon enough, and it is never too late. And the step we take here is toward realizing and appreciating the Blackness of God.

APPROACHING THE BLACKNESS OF GOD

If we were living in a time-space in which Caucasians had been enslaved, tortured, murdered, and kept in bondages of many sorts for more than four hundred years by Black, brown, Indigenous, or Asian people, our moral task today might well be to meet, and learn to love, the whiteness of God. But that is not our time-space. Today, in the real world we share in which our whiteness has been normalized, our spiritual journey and moral challenge is to approach the Blackness of God and see what awaits us.

We can begin by taking a look at the Black theological tradition in America that reaches back to 1619.[2] While there are some interesting points of contention about how the 1619 Project was constructed—how the authors were selected, how topics were chosen, who and what was left out, how it was funded, and whether it did what it intended—these academic debates are not what has driven white resistance to the 1619 Project. The very mention of this project is upsetting to many white people, as if looking closely at the beginnings of slavery and how its legacy lives among us is either too upsetting or too dangerous for white Americans to risk learning about, or even debating.

But honest learning and open-minded debate are skills that white American Christians, like people of other colors and cultures, need to develop if we are going to learn as much as we can about ourselves, one another, the world around us, and our Creator God. If our churches have not already (and many have) done this, we should form study groups, or call together other groups of friends, neighbors, and colleagues, to get to know the history of white supremacy in America, including the racial histories of our own churches. This will help us better understand who and where we have been and therefore see more clearly where we can go from here—as Christians and as Americans. We need to urge each other beyond defensiveness toward sharing in openhearted, open-minded ways whatever we can about where we and our people—ancestors and progeny—have been in the past and where we now can go together into a present-future that is ours to help build.

One of the many things we will learn is about the Black embodiment of Christianity that first took shape in the colonies through African and early African American life and culture. This Black Christianity was the life force of many slaves and the salvation of generations of Black Americans through slavery, Reconstruction, the so-called redemption movement of white supremacists in reaction to Reconstruction, and the Jim Crow of the late nineteenth and twentieth centuries.

This historical religious foundation became a renewed spiritual resource among Black Christians, and some other Americans, in the 1950s, 1960s, and 1970s. In addition to community leaders, preachers, teachers, and scholars like Howard Thurman, Thurgood Marshall, Pauli Murray, Rosa Parks, Ella Baker, Martin Luther King Jr., John Lewis, and countless others, perhaps the most widely published scholar-teacher of the era was James H. Cone, who taught for almost fifty years, until his death in 2018, at the Union Theological Seminary in New York City. Cone's early work centered on the Blackness of God and on the necessity of our becoming Black in order to join in the work of liberation.[3] Cone's assertion of the "Blackness of God" was shocking at the time among the liberal white scholars, teachers, and students with whom he worked at Union Seminary. I was among them. In the late 1960s and early 1970s, I was frightened by the idea of a Black God.

Like the majority of white Christians, including those of us who were theologically and politically liberal, I first heard Cone's declaration as a put-down of white people rather than as a rejection of white supremacy, which is basically how Cone and other African American teachers, preachers, and activists intended it. They did, however, intend to equate the oppressive history of whiteness with evil, the very opposite of the Blackness and goodness of God. The distinction between the basically good essence of white (like all) people and the moral evil of what we had perpetuated against Black people was quite difficult for white people to comprehend. It was almost impossible for white people to understand what liberation theologians like James Cone meant when they said that, in the context of white supremacy, we all have to be Black to be either liberated or liberators; that the goodness of all humanity is its Blackness; and that God is Black.

If there is one key learning in this chapter it is that Black and Blackness, like white and whiteness, are not primarily about skin color. These terms and images are about moral choices in the context of American history and Christian culture in which "white" has long been associated with whatever is good, pure, and safe; and in which "Black" or "dark" has been almost synonymous with whatever is evil, dirty, and dangerous.

Therefore, it is imperative that we keep in mind the real historical context of Black liberation theology. Over centuries, white people had done great evil to Black people—and almost always in the name of a white God and a white Jesus. Then as now, in a color-coded moral universe, in which white supremacy is a prevailing power, white is evil from a moral perspective. In this same color-coded moral universe, Black and Blackness is liberating and healing. Goodness and kindness and joy are Black. People—all antiracist people, Caucasians as well as Black people—can be Black, regardless of our ethnographic identities.

It was (and still is) confounding to most people of all races how white Americans could be Black! Like most contemporary white American Christian progressives, I was confused and frightened, but I was also drawn by the spirit of liberation that had met me through particular Black teachers and colleagues, starting in late 1960s. Several stand out as mentors who touched and changed my life in lasting ways: One was C. Eric Lincoln, my first Black professor, who also led students at Union Seminary to join in the protests against Columbia University's racist treatment of its Harlem neighbors in the spring of 1968. Dr. Lincoln showed us that boldness is basic to theological wisdom. My sister student and later colleague Delores S. Williams's courage and creativity as a womanist theologian and poet inspires me to this day. Delores embodied theological creativity of behalf of justice for women in general, Black women in particular. Paul Washington and Charles Willie were feisty, outspoken Black leader-participants in the Philadelphia ordination of eleven white women priests in 1974. Their liberation ethics required them to stretch the boundaries of justice-ministry into the realm of gender. Barbara C. Harris and Pauli Murray were pioneering Black women whose tenacious spirits led them not only to be ordained in the Episcopal Church but, moreover, into lifetime advocacy for justice in all forms. Over time, I would come to realize that, through the witness of such Black women and men, the Blackness of God had been luring me, encouraging and empowering me to come along for many years.[4]

Like many other white liberal Christian women, a factor that helped me begin to hear and heed Black liberation theology was having been marginalized myself, as a woman and, in my case, as a lesbian and bisexual woman. This is by no means to equate my experience of gender and sexual oppression with that of any Black person or other person of color in America. Sexual, gender, and racial oppressions take different shapes and damage humans in different ways. In American history, there is no oppression—except arguably that of Native Americans—that comes anywhere close to the Black experience of slavery and its ongoing violent legacy.

The shapes of misogyny, sexism, and heterosexism, which we will be responding to in the next chapter, have their own insidious and damaging character, which cuts across lines of race and class, and can be every bit as destructive of women and queer people as race-based violence and oppression. But during most of American history, because white Christian men have prized their women and daughters, white women as a group have legally lived under the control—though by no means always, the protection—of white men. To compare most white men's treatment of most white women to slavery, bondage, or servitude is ridiculous, grossly inaccurate, and racist.

Those of us who are white—women and LGBTQ folks as well as white straight men—need to be clear that, regardless of what we may think about it, white supremacy is a deadly sin that we have benefited from in a myriad of ways. In fact, it is probably how many economically marginalized or physically abused white women, gay men, lesbians, transwomen, and transmen have escaped violent assaults with their lives. Being white may well have given their violent assailants only one good reason not to finish them off.

Of course, many Black people, including James Cone, were enraged at white people, women as well as men—but who can seriously wonder why? Can we not see today what many of us could not seem to realize fifty years ago—that anger at white supremacy, even rage, then and now, can become a deeply ethical, even loving, response?[5] This realization was what had sparked the young Martin Luther King Jr. to suggest, in 1955, that God's response to white racists was, "Get out of my face! Your hands are full of blood." An angry, loving young Black man was speaking on behalf of an angry loving God who wanted no part of this white violence.

Approaching the Blackness of an angry, loving God, we begin to notice the fullness of God's embodiment in the lives and deaths of those brought to American shores on slave ships; those Black men, women, and children chained, whipped, mutilated, and tossed in heaps on American soil. To see God's Blackness is to view her body as that of the slave woman raped by her master and as the body of her Black child sold to the highest bidder. To approach the Blackness of the God is to hear and see the historical righteousness—the moral imperative—of the Black cry for freedom and the Black struggles for liberation; the nobility of John Brown and Nat Turner as well as the heroism of not only Rosa Parks and Martin Luther King Jr., but also of those Black leaders whose anger and rage terrified most white people in mid-twentieth-century America—people like Bobby Seale, Huey Newton, and the Black Panthers; Elijah Muhammad and the Black Muslims; Angela Davis, and Malcolm X.

I well remember the intense outcry among Episcopalians in North Carolina when it became known that the national Episcopal Church had made a grant in 1970 to the newly founded Malcolm X Liberation University, which had opened in Durham in October 1969, in response to protests by students at Duke University over the lack of an African American studies program there.[6] At the time, I was working in as a lay seminarian assistant in an Episcopal parish in Charlotte. I have vivid memories of the fury of many parishioners about this money being given to anything associated with Malcolm X. Virtually no one, including the liberal white priest of the parish who was sympathetic to the students' desire for a Black studies program, knew how to defend the church's gift to a program named after Malcolm X, a hero to Duke's Black students but a touchstone of fear and revulsion among many, if not most, white Christians, certainly most members of my entirely white Southern parish.

Thinking back over these fifty years, I'm aware that the ranting today about critical race theory is much like the outcry in the 1960s and 1970s against those Black leaders most associated with movements for Black power and Black liberation—even Martin Luther King Jr. Though he is lionized today as a great figure by all but the most proudly white supremacists, many Americans forget that Dr. King was a subject of fear and hatred by large numbers of white Christians during his lifetime.

Today, as always, the Black God indicts the whiteness of our omnipotence, entitlement, and the violence that continues to shape major institutions in American society, such as health care, public education, and criminal justice. The Black God condemns white Christians to the extent that our idolatry of whiteness continues to undercut the possibilities of there ever being liberty and justice for all Americans. But there is a better way, and that is why we are wrestling in these pages with the challenge—to do something.

LEAVE GUILT AND SHAME AT THE DOOR

Most Americans and most Christians have a fresh chance if we really want to participate in transforming our churches and our nation into more justice-loving communities. It may be in the smallest ways, but we have a chance to make a difference if we are able to keep our eyes on the Blackness of God and be guided by her energies. However, we may imagine the power and energies of God's Blackness, they are coming to us, inviting us not to dwell upon our guilt, not to sink in shame, but rather to "stand up, take [our] mat and walk" (John 5:8 NRSV). The Spirit—our Black life force—calls us to get up and get moving, to join in "let[ting] justice roll down like waters, and righteousness like an ever-flowing stream" (Amos 5:24 NRSV).

In the Gospel of John—the last written of the four Gospels and the most mystical and symbolic—Jesus tells the afflicted man to get up and get going rather than sitting there fretting about how unfortunate he is. In the fourth Gospel, Jesus is talking to someone with a disability. How much more so the Spirit of a Black God confronts those of us today who are whining about feeling guilty, ashamed, and helpless to do much if anything about the deadly sin of white supremacy! How much more vigorously God in her Blackness confronts those of us white people who react defensively when we are called racist!

Imagine what this Black Spirit is saying to us today: "Look, people! White supremacy is in the air you breathe, the air every one of you breathes constantly. Yes, you are racist. All Americans of all creeds, colors, and classes are infected by the glorification of whiteness. Don't waste time or energy denying this truth, or fretting about how it makes you feel; just pick up your beds and walk! Get up and do something, and do it together!"

The God of Jesus—his Black Mother and Father—wants no part of our being held back by feelings of guilt or shame of what we, or our ancestors, may have done or left undone, in the words of the Episcopal Prayer Book. Later in John, Jesus tells a woman taken in adultery to "go, and sin no more" (John 8:11 KJV). Period. The message is clear: Whatever your ancestors did, whatever you and your churches have done or failed to do, your work in today's church and today's America is to do whatever you can on behalf of racial justice and racial equity. Do what is just, love what is kind, practice what is merciful—and your sins are forgiven. Go, and sin no more. In the realm of white supremacy, this spiritual challenge puts three urgent tasks before American Christian congregations and individuals today.

TIME FOR ACTION

Secure Voting Rights

At the top of the Christian moral agenda right now must be to secure and guarantee voting rights for all Americans, especially Black and brown people whose right to vote is under fierce and transparent attack today by the Republican Party, much as it was 150 years ago by the Democratic Party—and for the exact same reason: to keep America in the hands of white privileged Christian men. This is idolatry. This is sin. It ought to be illegal, and hopefully it will be illegal, by congressional statute, before this book is published. Regardless, it is morally indefensible for Christians in America. We cannot be silent in this moment. There is no compromise on this urgent moral mandate. Not now, not ever.

Concerns about "states' rights" (a different conversation) or "voter fraud" (a sham) have no spiritual value or ethical meaning in the urgent effort to secure the vote of all Americans, regardless of where we live. "States' rights" and "voter fraud" are bogus excuses being used now, as they were in the late nineteenth century, to deny Black people and other people of color the right to vote.

Whatever our politics or ideologies, if we have any desire to follow Jesus, American Christians must speak up and do whatever we can, collectively and individually, on behalf of a voting system that makes it possible for the voices of all Americans to be heard and encourages the votes of all Americans to be cast, counted, and determinative of who wins and loses in every election. Every Christian preacher in America, in the name of Jesus, should be raising the roof about this.

Repentance and Conversion

To repent the sin of white supremacy is essential, because—if honest—our repentance signals a taking of responsibility for helping shape the future. In fact, repentance is a key to a just and compassionate future. And honest repentance will lead to conversion, a turning around to go the other way. It means not getting stuck, bogged down in guilt or shame, but rather encouraging one another to do the next right thing—to work and struggle for liberty and justice for all, not just some. That is what Jesus means when he says to those who are immobilized by guilt, shame, confusion, despair, or any form of inaction—get up and move on. We cannot, in good faith, stay stuck, resigned to the status quo or willing to let others do the right thing while we stand on the sidelines and quietly applaud. We, all of us, must take up our mats, and walk.

This will take us and our churches to any number of possible social justice endeavors in realms of health care, mental health, addiction, immigration reform and refugee support, criminal justice reform (including law enforcement, prisons, rehabilitation, elimination of the death penalty and the "three strike law" for minors, gun safety laws, etc.). Honest repentance and true conversion will also lead us to the moral matter of reparations.

REPARATIONS

As we join ongoing conversations about reparations, we ought not let ourselves be confused or distracted by questions of how it would work, whether it's feasible, and how it could be fair—questions often intended to deflate the serious moral call to white Americans to collectively offer some "repair," however inadequate it will always be, to our Black sisters and brothers.

It will work fine. Ways will be found to make reparations feasible and fair. Rep. Sheila Jackson Lee (D-TX) is heading up the congressional effort to pass H.R.40—Commission to Study and Develop Reparation Proposals for African Americans Act. Congressional Democrats will struggle to bring this bill to the floor, and sooner or later it will become law. Meanwhile, over the past few years, many American church bodies, Roman Catholic and Protestant, are urging reparations, and groups like the Jesuits are offering them; American cities like Evanston, Illinois, and Asheville, North Carolina, are taking steps toward bringing reparations to life in forms of housing assistance and community development; and schools like Brown University, Georgetown University, the Virginia Theological Seminary of the Episcopal Church, and Princeton Theological Seminary plan to offer reparations via student debt cancellation and scholarships.

That white Americans are not personally—individually—responsible for what our ancestors did to slaves is beside the point and rings pitifully hollow in discussions of reparations. Of course, we are not personally responsible for what our ancestors did or did not do. But we most certainly are responsible, collectively, for helping clean up their mess, much like the men and women who work in the wreckage of collapsed buildings. People of good faith, people who love a Black God who calls us to pick up our mats and walk, cannot simply walk away from the damages left by those who preceded us. We must get into the wreckage, assess the damages, salvage whatever we find that may be usable, and do whatever we can to help rebuild a stronger future. Only in this way, working as faithfully as we can and empowered by the Spirit of a Black God, can we turn back the tide of the white Christian nationalism that threatens to engulf our nation and overpower our efforts to walk with Jesus.

This is one sure way we can begin to dismantle the theology of normalized whiteness—by turning away from concerns about our own entitlement and turning instead to who we are graced to recognize as we catch a glimpse of ourselves in the fullness of who we are, reflected collectively in the translucent Blackness of God.

DISCUSSION QUESTIONS

1. Why do we hear Black people's anger about white supremacy as personal attacks on us rather than as invitations to share Black anger at white supremacy and to join in Black celebrations of the value and goodness of Black lives? Let's discuss this.

2. Talk about ways in which "a theology of normalized whiteness" does, and does not, ring true to your experiences as white American Christians or as people of other religions or national cultures.

3. Can you relate to the author's recollection of the outcry in 1970 against the Episcopal Church's funding of the Malcolm X Liberation University in Durham, North Carolina? Discuss any memories you may have of this sort of resistance to Black liberation movements in America, in the past or present.

4. The Black God indicts the whiteness of our omnipotence, entitlement, and the violence that continues to shape major institutions in American society, such as health care, education, and criminal justice. The Black God condemns white Christians to the extent that our idolatry of whiteness continues to undercut the possibilities of there ever being liberty and justice for all Americans. How might your church respond to this through its budget, outreach, education, and liturgical life?

5. Leave your guilt at the door, leave your shame behind, and do something. Discuss this spiritual call. What does it mean to you?
6. How will you help energize your church and/or community to struggle for voting rights (an unending struggle in American history) and also to think hard about what forms of reparations your church could offer to help repair the lingering damages of slavery and Jim Crow?
7. What hope do you carry as you approach the Blackness of God? Please share this with each other.

Chapter 15

The Fourth Call

Empowering Women, Celebrating Sexuality, Affirming Gender Diversity

*The goal of this chapter is to demonstrate that empowering women, cel-
ebrating sexuality, and affirming gender diversity is not only an urgent, long
overdue, call to Christians but also that honoring these moral commitments
would strengthen the fabric of American Christianity and transform its character. This chapter invites us to imagine churches that are genuinely woman
affirming, sexually liberating, and genderqueer.*

The fourth deadly sin is misogyny with its attendant homophobia. In
response, this fourth call to us rises up from within Sophia, the Wisdom of
God, she whose divinity is seldom acknowledged, much less celebrated,
by most American Christians. A primary way for the Christian churches
to empower women is to tell stories of strong women, to tell these tales as
sacred stories, through which we meet women whose lives reflect God and
her saints.

Holding misogyny and homophobia in place, American Christianity's
ongoing war against women and LGBTQ persons continues to explicitly
embolden Christian nationalism by preaching and teaching oppression and
trivialization of women and of gender and sexual minorities. Most mainstream Protestant churches continue to sideline gender and sexual justice as
matters to be dealt with later, after more urgent matters have been resolved.

Our churches' collusion in the perpetuation of injustice against women and
against gender and sexual minorities is not because there actually are more
urgent issues like racism, the environment, world hunger—issues that are
indeed as important and sometimes more urgent. But the point is, those who
resist dealing with misogyny and homophobia are seldom losing sleep over
other major injustices and structures of oppression. They usually are trying to

change the subject to anything but women's rights and LGBTQ justice mat-
ters.Other justice matters easily provide an empty excuse not to take women
or queer people seriously.

"Changing the subject" is how most liberal men resist examining their own
lives and privileges as white males who at least pass for straight. Changing
the subject is how they avoid confronting the political and moral traditions
that allow them to remain ignorant and unchanged. Of course white women,
women of color, and men of color, can share in this resistance to change, and
American churches are full of such people. But the problem is rooted in the
determination of white privileged men—self-defined as "real men"—to relin-
quish their power-over women as well as over men who are not "real men."

As a way of raising, rather than changing, the subject of women's invisibility, marginalization, and oppression in Christianity, we will look at the
lives of two women about whom you probably haven't heard much in your
church. Whether or not you know who they are, if you are white Christians,
we doubt you've come to know either of these women as the bold, creative
characters they were. Whether historical or legendary figures, both Hagar the
slave woman and Mary Magdalene, Jesus's beloved friend, were compelling
figures. Hagar is seldom mentioned and is largely unknown among American
Christians. Mary of Magdala, better known as Mary Magdalene, usually
has been caricatured as a whore and dismissed by Christian leaders. Neither
woman has been taken seriously by most white Christians. Their invisibility
or trivialization reinforces the misogynist foundations of the church.

HAGAR

Womanist ethicist Katie Geneva Cannon points out that 1993 was a banner year for Black American women: Toni Morrison won the Nobel Prize
in Literature for *Beloved*; Maya Angelou read her poem "On the Pulse of
the Morning" at the inauguration of President Bill Clinton, and Delores
S. Williams published her groundbreaking *Sisters in the Wilderness: The
Challenge of Womanist God-Talk*. In her foreword to the twentieth anniversary edition of Williams's book, Cannon calls it "a revealing window that
encourages us to look to the margins, rather than the central spaces for the
divine presence in women's real-world liberation struggles."[1]

What makes Williams's work so important to the theological questions
being raised in this book is that, in introducing her readers to Hagar's story,
Delores Williams invites Black Christian women (and all wise women and
men) to look for God in places most white American Christians, men or
women, wouldn't think of looking, because so many of us don't have to
look in places that many Black people routinely look—"in the struggles for

survival and quality of life."[2] We are challenged by the story of Hagar the slave woman to look for God not so much in church, in what we usually think of as "spirituality" or "personal growth," in the Bible, or even in liberation movements, but in struggling to stay alive and "make a way out of no way."[3]

Keep in mind that Hagar was a slave, subjected to the desires of her master Sarah, the wife of Abraham, who would become the patriarchal figurehead of Judaism, Christianity, and Islam. This fact alone puts Hagar, a slave woman from Egypt, in a very lowly position in relation to the man who would become a chief symbol of power-over everyone associated with Western monotheism. The house of David, which eventually would produce Jesus, stands in this lineage of power-over being passed on from one man to another for centuries, right down to the present day for Christians. Next to these powerful men of God, a poor dark woman from Egypt was not worth much, certainly not worthy of being celebrated as a role model or sacred figure for Christian women, much less men, to remember.

But Christian womanist theologian Delores S. Williams challenges the nonremembering and disregard of Hagar, whom we meet in Genesis 16:1–16. It is important to read this story in its entirety, especially since many of us are unfamiliar with Hagar's story:

> Now Sarai, Abram's wife, bore him no children. She had an Egyptian slave-girl whose name was Hagar, and Sarai said to Abram, "You see that the Lord has prevented me from bearing children; go into my slave-girl; it may be that I shall obtain children by her." And Abram listened to the voice of Sarai. So, after Abram had lived ten years in the land of Canaan, Sarai, Abram's wife, took Hagar the Egyptian, her slave-girl, and gave her to her husband Abram as a wife. He went into Hagar, and she conceived; and when she saw that she had conceived, she looked with contempt on her mistress. Then Sarai said to Abram, "May the wrong done to me be on you! I gave my slave-girl to your embrace, and when she saw that she had conceived, she looked on me with contempt. May the Lord judge between you and me!" But Abram said to Sarai, "Your slave-girl is in your power; do to her as you please." Then Sarai dealt harshly with her, and she ran away from her.

> The angel of the Lord found her by a spring of water in the wilderness, the spring on the way to Shur. And he said, "Hagar, slave-girl of Sarai, where have you come from and where are you going?" She said, "I am running away from my mistress Sarai." The angel of the Lord said to her, "Return to your mistress, and submit to her." The angel of the Lord also said to her, "I will so greatly multiply your offspring that they cannot be counted for multitude." And the angel of the Lord said to her,

> "Now you have conceived and shall bear a son; you shall call him Ishmael, for the Lord has given heed to your affliction. He shall be a wild ass of a man, with

his hand against everyone, and everyone's hand against him; and he shall live
at odds with all his kin."

So she named the Lord who spoke to her, "You are El-roi"; for she said, "Have
I really seen God and remained alive after seeing him?" Therefore the well was
called Beer-lahai-roi; it lies between Kadesh and Bered.

Hagar bore Abram a son; and Abram named his son, whom Hagar bore,
Ishmael. Abram was eighty-six years old when Hagar bore him Ishmael. (Gen.
16:1–16 NRSV)

Because Sarah has not conceived, she tells her husband to "go in to" her slave
girl, Hagar, so that she might bear a child, which Sarah would then raise as
her own. When Hagar conceives, she and Sarah have some sort of falling-out,
Sarah treats her harshly, and Hagar runs away into the wilderness, where an
angel comes to her and tells her to return to Sarah, which she does. Speaking
for God, the angel also tells Hagar that she will bear a son whom she will
name Ishmael, who "shall be a wild ass of a man." Hagar then names God
"El-roi"—the one who sees—and returns to Sarah and Abraham where she
gives birth to Ishmael.

The point of this story is that Hagar, a slave woman from Egypt in northern
Africa, is assumed by Sarah and Abraham to have no life of her own and to
be entirely at their disposal. She belongs to them. She is their property. She is
a slave. Because they want a child, it is perfectly acceptable for Abraham to
rape and impregnate Hagar. As American Christians in the twenty-first century, this story strikes us as beyond the pale. But Delores Williams presents
Hagar as an image of womanhood not so far removed from the experiences
of contemporary Black American women:

Once upon a time in America, slave women were used and abused by both
women and men of the ruling race and class, including being raped and used
as surrogate sexual objects by men and as surrogate mothers by men (and
women). Contemporary Black women bear this legacy. Even now, many
Black women are relegated to servitude of one form or another according
to the privileged whims of white people and, in many cases, the sexism of
Black men as well. Margaret Atwood's *The Handmaid's Tale* is not all that far
fetched from the perspective of Black women in America.

And the story of Hagar continues in Genesis 21:1–21 (NRSV):

The Lord dealt with Sarah as he had said, and the Lord did for Sarah as he had
promised. Sarah conceived and bore Abraham a son in his old age, at the time of
which God had spoken to him. Abraham gave the name Isaac to his son whom
Sarah bore him. And Abraham circumcised his son Isaac when he was eight
days old, as God had commanded him. Abraham was a hundred years old when

his son Isaac was born to him. Now Sarah said, "God has brought laughter for me; everyone who hears will laugh with me." And she said, "Who would ever have said to Abraham that Sarah would nurse children? Yet I have borne him a son in his old age."

The child grew, and was weaned; and Abraham made a great feast on the day that Isaac was weaned. But Sarah saw the son of Hagar the Egyptian, whom she had borne to Abraham, playing with her son Isaac. So she said to Abraham, "Cast out this slave woman with her son; for the son of this slave woman shall not inherit along with my son Isaac." The matter was very distressing to Abraham on account of his son. But God said to Abraham, "Do not be distressed because of the boy and because of your slave woman; whatever Sarah says to you, do as she tells you, for it is through Isaac that offspring shall be named for you. As for the son of the slave woman, I will make a nation of him also, because he is your offspring." So Abraham rose early in the morning, and took bread and a skin of water, and gave it to Hagar, putting it on her shoulder, along with the child, and sent her away. And she departed, and wandered about in the wilderness of Beer-sheba.

When the water in the skin was gone, she cast the child under one of the bushes. Then she went and sat down opposite him a good way off, about the distance of a bowshot; for she said, "Do not let me look on the death of the child." And as she sat opposite him, she lifted up her voice and wept. And God heard the voice of the boy; and the angel of God called to Hagar from heaven, and said to her, "What troubles you, Hagar? Do not be afraid; for God has heard the voice of the boy where he is. Come, lift up the boy and hold him fast with your hand, for I will make a great nation of him." Then God opened her eyes and she saw a well of water. She went, and filled the skin with water, and gave the boy a drink.

God was with the boy, and he grew up; he lived in the wilderness, and became an expert with the bow. He lived in the wilderness of Paran; and his mother got a wife for him from the land of Egypt.

The Lord has promised Sarah and Abraham their own son. With the birth of Isaac to Sarah, this promise is kept. "But Sarah saw the son of Hagar the Egyptian, whom she had borne to Abraham, playing with her son Isaac. So she said to Abraham, 'Cast out this slave woman with her son; for the son of this slave woman shall not inherit along with my son Isaac'" (vv. 9–10).

At this point, Sarah drives Hagar and Ishmael into the wilderness, where both boy and mother are protected by God. They survive and make for themselves some quality of life. Hagar is a good mother and Ishmael becomes an archer, able to procure food for himself and his mother, and to provide protection for them both.

Hagar and Ishmael become key figures in the history of Islam but are largely dismissed or denigrated within both Judaism and Christianity. Can we imagine telling Hagar's story as one of Judaism's and Christianity's most important narratives, central to our understanding of many women's lives in a patriarchal religious culture? Hagar stands for marginalized women—slaves, Black women, poor women, and often mothers and children regardless of social class. How appropriate would it be for Hagar to be canonized—by churchwomen, white as well as Black—as a representative of marginalized and oppressed women, whose historical call has been to "make a way out of no way," one of Katie Geneva Cannon's favorite descriptions of Black women's work?

MARY MAGDALENE

Most Christians know the name of Mary Magdalene, a beloved companion and intimate friend of Jesus and, according to John 20:1, the first witness to the resurrection, a most esteemed place in Christianity. How is it that this woman is so often caricatured as a prostitute and, in any case, is so seldom celebrated as one of, if not *the*, most revered woman in the early Christian story? Although venerated not only in the Roman and Eastern churches but also in the more catholic of the Protestant churches—the Anglican and Lutheran denominations—Mary Magdalene tends to be played down and minimized even though officially designated as a saint. Why is this?

French theologian Jean-Yves Leloup, who translated *The Gospel of Mary Magdalene* from the original Coptic, may offer a clue. Leloup believes that Mary Magdalene's special relationship with Jesus, whatever its nature, was marked by their meeting in the "nous" (the French pronoun for "us"), an "intermediate realm between the purely sensory and the purely spiritual."[4] Many would call this a "mystical" relationship; others, simply a profoundly empathic, friendship, which carried a special "charge," perhaps even an erotic energy. Defying reason or logical explanation, Jesus and Mary's relationship was and is difficult for the rational mind to grasp, and thus could be suspect: Was something not told to us by the ancient authorities? Is something being hidden from us even today, things we might resist knowing about the relationship between Jesus and Mary? Things the church does not want us to think about?

There is no doubt that Mary Magdalene was one of Jesus's best friends. Alongside Leloup's perception of the "nous" between Jesus and Magdalene, Karen L. King raises the possibility that members of Jesus's inner circle of friends were jealous of this relationship. King, a historian of religion and author of *Mary of Magdala*, writes that what mattered in the early church was not whether you were at the crucifixion or the resurrection, or whether you were a woman or a man. What counted was your firmness of character and how well you understood Jesus's teachings.[5] That a woman knew Jesus as well as, or better than, any of his male disciples would not have been an easy pill for early churchmen to swallow. It's one thing to have women milling around Jesus, paying him respect as friends and fellow workers, but what if Mary was Jesus's closest companion, his best friend? Jealousy-induced assaults on the character of Mary Magdalene might have begun quite early in the life of the young church.

Still another, and perhaps the simplest, reason for Mary Magdalene to have been downplayed or caricaturized negatively by Christian leaders over the two millennia of church history is summarized by Christian theologian and teacher Cynthia Bourgeault in the preface to her book *The Meaning of Mary Magdalene*. "The shadow side of Christianity's notoriously undealt-with issues around human sexuality and the feminine get projected directly onto her."[6] And that is where we find ourselves today, we women in Christian churches—still embodying "notoriously undealt-with issues around human sexuality and the feminine." Throughout the history of Christianity, Mary Magdalene has carried the burden of female sexuality as constructed and fixated upon by Christian men, including celibate clergy.

On March 16, 2021, in a section of Atlanta, six Asian women and two other people[7] were murdered by an evangelical Christian man who said he felt tempted by women and tormented in his mind. Korean American Angie Hong, formerly a student at Duke Divinity School, reminds American Christians that women other than white and Black women are subjected to the same "purity culture," including the traditional Christian expectation that all good women, of all races and classes, should be chaste until marriage and, once married, should submit to their husbands, sexually and otherwise.[8] Hong points out that Asian women often bear the burden of being more highly sexualized and prized in the fantasies of Western men.

"As I followed my calling into the evangelical ministry world," she writes, "I felt vulnerable in the midst of powerful white male domination. I blamed myself for feeling uneasy when a Christian social-justice leader planted a wet kiss on my cheek and held on to me while saying I was the Asian American voice of racial reconciliation. . . . In every uncomfortable situation, I figured that I was the common denominator—the great whore—and I absorbed the shame of feeling impure and far from God."[9]

WOMEN'S BODIES, WOMEN'S CHOICES

The stories of men's sexual abuse of women and of impurity being blamed on women—Hagar's experience, Mary Magdalene's caricature as whore, and accounts from contemporary women like Angie Hong—coalesce in American Christianity around issues of women's bodily integrity, women's moral agency, and women's freedom to choose how we experience and use our own sexuality. These empowering attributes of womanhood were denied entirely to both Hagar and Mary Magdalene. Today women's strength is assumed by white American Christians—often by white women as well as men—to be diminutive and passive in Asian and Asian American women. In modern American society, Asian women, even more than Black and white women, are objectified and trivialized as sensual and sweet to the eye, "China dolls."

Like Black and white American women seeking control over our own bodies and sexualities, Hagar and Mary Magdalene have been maligned historically. According to the legendary stories told about them, the father of Western religious monotheism abused one of them sexually and cast her out to fend for herself; and Christian men long ago concluded that the other woman was a sexual sinner redeemed by Christ.

The Black woman in the wilderness with her son, the brown whore that Jesus befriended, and the "China doll" are all archetypes of women whose sexuality has been defined and locked in place by religious men in authority. Questions about who women might actually be—sexually and in other ways—are irrelevant to men who themselves have been shaped and educated by misogyny. Neither Jewish nor Christian (nor Islamic) men have been trained or encouraged by their religious traditions to care about the integrity—wholeness—of women's sexuality, women's bodies, and women's choices about their bodies, sexuality, and relationships. In this same mindset, questions about women's bodies, integrity, morality, and choices continue to be contested today around the matter of women's contraceptive freedom, including the easy availability of birth control and access to safe, legal abortion.

ABORTION, AGAIN, WORTH THE STRUGGLE

In today's churches and American culture and politics there is no more contentious a political issue than abortion. We need to remember that abortion and birth control had never been of serious concern to most American Protestants, including conservative evangelicals, until the early 1970s—following the passage of the major civil rights legislation of the mid-1960s. Only after these civil rights victories did the Republican Party realize it needed to come up with a new issue to unite white conservatives in America and to serve as a wedge to divide white people in America, liberals from conservatives.

Prior to the civil rights movement, most Republicans—mainly white conservatives—had been united around opposition to busing and other means or manifestations of legally coerced integration (Black teachers in previously white schools, more Black students than white in some previously all-white schools, heralding of the civil rights movement as a positive development in American history and of Martin Luther King as an American hero, etc.). After the civil rights movement's legal victories (including the Civil Rights Bill in 1964 and Voting Rights Bill in 1965), the Republicans seized on the women's liberation or feminist movement as a new issue to frighten as many white people as possible and, therefore, by which to strengthen a new, white, antifeminist base of voters.

This strategy worked, up to a point. In the increasingly antifeminist climate being whipped up by conservative Americans in alliance with conservative evangelical Christians, the Equal Rights Amendment (ERA) failed to pass in the 1970s.[10] However, against this antifeminist trend, the U.S. Supreme Court, in its landmark 1973 *Roe v. Wade* decision, ruled that women have a constitutional right to have an abortion without excessive governmental interference.[11] From that point in time on, women's "right to choose" became a target of political and Christian conservatives, working in tandem to persuade Americans to vote for "life"—the life of the embryo, not the integrity or quality of the woman's life or the life of the child once born. Moreover, as Representative Barney Frank (D-MA) quipped at the time: "Apparently these anti-abortion politicians believe that 'life begins at conception and ends at birth.'"[12] Like the majority of American women then and now, Barney Frank understood that those who opposed women having access to safe, legal abortions tended to be less worried about the "unborn" and more concerned with keeping control over women's lives, bodies, sexualities, and choices.

Thus, starting in the late 1970s and early 1980s, any Republican running for national office had to toe the party line and become pro–fetal life and anti–women's choice. This is why, for example, Ronald Reagan, who as governor of California had championed one of the most liberal abortion laws in the nation, suddenly became antichoice when he ran for president in 1980. It is happening today with even greater misogynistic enthusiasm. No Republican can support a woman's right to choose and expect to win nomination, much less election, in the third decade of the twenty-first century.

Moreover, as this book is being finalized, the U.S. Supreme Court is heading toward either a reversal, or gutting, of *Roe v. Wade*, which—when this happens—will toss the issue of abortion and its legality back to the states. Where will this leave women and girls faced with unwanted pregnancies in states where abortion is illegal? As women and girls realize their limited choices, those with resources will probably find their ways across state lines, or out of the United States altogether. But those who feel most powerless might go back down those infamous alleys in which, once upon a time, desperate women and girls got illegal abortions at the hands of men and women who sometimes were skillful and compassionate but sometimes were butchers who left bleeding female bodies mangled or even dead on the floor.

Blessedly, we are almost fifty years beyond the 1973 *Roe v. Wade* decision and much has happened in intersecting realms of women's reproductive health; feminists' and womanists' absolute moral commitment to reproductive choice for women and girls; and the likely irrepressibility of the general public's advocacy for women's right to reproductive freedom, including the freedom to choose whether to bear a child. Indeed, not to be undone by misogyny, women across America will always make a way out of no way. Whether or not they are legal, medical solutions—pills (abortifacients) to end pregnancy, rather than surgical abortion—will become more widely available to American women and girls. While this will not likely quell rancorous political debate among die-hard opponents to women's reproductive health, and while (until the political winds shift) it will generate an illicit market much like Prohibition did in the 1920s, abortifacients will make life simpler and more compassionate for millions of women and girls.

SEXUAL IDENTITIES AND GENDER BENDING

Beverly Wildung Harrison's prophetic presence looms large in this book because, as a white Christian feminist ethicist, her work touched upon all of the seven deadly sins, including misogyny, which she contended was the root of not only sexism but also heterosexism.[13] For Harrison and other Christian feminists and womanists, misogyny was steeped in Christianity's spirit-body dualism, in which the human body had lesser value than the spirit. For almost two millennia, Christianity had taught that the human spirit—in right relation to God—was informed and animated by God, the divine Spirit. In this theological schema, the human body could be redeemed by the divine Spirit, saved—that is, brought into God's realm—but only insofar as the body renounced the sins of the flesh, especially sexuality.

The way that early Christian theologians and church leaders, who were often the same men, understood this dualism was to imagine that they—living as close to God as possible, and seeing themselves in his image—were motivated by God's Spirit to exercise control over, and denial of, their bodies' natural yearnings. These churchmen, including the influential Italian Dominican philosopher Thomas Aquinas (1225–1274), contended that women were body driven, animated by the sensuality of their female flesh, and even more in need of redemption than men. The only paths of redemption for women were either to be celibate virgins, or to be faithful wives and mothers. In the Roman Church, the Virgin Mary was lifted up as the exemplary woman—totally unreal, but the ideal female, sexually pure, a perpetual virgin, entirely non-sexual throughout her life (although there are several references in the New Testament to Jesus's brother, including one named James).[14] That women and men have to copulate to bear children was considered by Augustine a flaw in God's creation. It was an unfortunate sin for which all humans would forever need to repent, especially women who, represented by Eve's seductive lure, generated the sins of the world.

This was all in the minds of early church fathers. It was a sex-denying fantasy created by men like Augustine to make sense of their embodied sexual tensions and behavior. If you can't deny your own sexual lust, then blame it on the woman. Beverly Harrison is among many feminist and womanist Christians, men as well as women—white, Black, and other people of color—who have flatly rejected this projection by Christian men of their sexual lust onto women, and their subsequent labeling of sexual lust as the root of all sin, ungodliness, and evil.

This anti-body and antisexual obsession of the Christian fathers is the basis of Christian teachings not only against women's leadership in the community but also against all sexual experience outside the narrow confines of Christian marriage, where even there it must be redeemed by childbearing. Through such an anti-body, antisexual perspective, homosexuality is not surprisingly viewed as morally depraved, intrinsically evil in Roman Catholic teachings. And misogyny—the hatred of women—is entirely justified as a component of what it means for pious Christian men "to love the Lord their God with all their heart, and with all their soul, and with all their mind" (Matt. 22:37, adapted).

This is why Episcopal women in the ordination struggle of the 1970s realized that the struggle for gay rights was waiting in the wings and was theologically and morally closely connected to the controversy over women priests. We understood that the problem that some of our fellow Christians had with both women priests and openly gay male priests was that both challenged the misogynist power that white men were determined to maintain over women—and other men, literally and figuratively. The first women priests in America understood that LGBTQ persons of whatever sexual or gender identity, to be healed and liberated, would have to break free of misogynist assumptions about their own powerlessness in relation to both God and ostensibly straight men. Like all women, gay men, lesbians, and other queer Christians in America were sure to provoke wrath, rejection, and even violence from brother and sister Christians.

The more recent acknowledgment of transgenderism reflects theological and spiritual underpinnings that challenge the assumption that either gender or sexuality is a fixed or static category of human identity. Earlier, in the 1960s and 1970s, the term "bisexual" had begun to be used by men and women whose primary erotic energies were not limited to either homo- or heterosexual attractions but rather extended to both. At the time, bisexuality was largely rejected by gay and lesbian activists as being a cop-out, perceived as a person's way of not accepting being gay in an intensely homophobic world and church. Today's sexual and gender culture—especially in urban centers—is a different matter. Many women and men are bisexual, not simply gay or straight; others identify simply as queer in a further affirmation of gender fluidity. It is interesting that Freud himself believed that all humans are bisexual, that our particular sexual identities take shape as we mature.[15]

Although sex and gender matters are discussed more openly and often in blue America, we would be fooling ourselves to imagine that LGBTQ people live solely or even mainly in American cities, rather than in small towns, suburbs, and the countryside, or that most queer Americans are either highly educated white people or folks outside Christian churches. Sex and gender questions are ubiquitous. They are not confined to the people who study or advocate for sexual justice and gender equality. In the fluid realm of gender, increasing numbers of people in America, including Christians, identify as "trans."Even more recently, some American Christians and others have begun to define themselves as "non-binary," meaning they are neither male nor female. Like trans people, non-binary folks are not "cisgender" (identifying themselves by the gender assigned at birth).

Many American Christians who are over fifty find ourselves baffled by what seems to us an eccentric use of personal pronouns by nonbinary people. For an individual to say that "they" identify as "they" rather than as "he" or "she," for example, can be disarming to those of us wed to the rules of English grammar in which we were schooled. Plus, most people still think of gender as a binary concept: "normal" humans are either male or female. But we need to realize that many of the younger people in our families and among our friends have no trouble thinking about gender in ways that are shattering the old binary boundaries. Red America may think of this as elitist babble by liberals, but it would behoove conservative Christians to try to prepare themselves for the arrival of queer, trans, nonbinary, and yet-to-be-named discoveries about sex and gender among the very people they care about in their own families and communities.

For American Christians, the push beyond misogyny into fluid experiences of gender and nondualistic images of our bodies and experiences of our sexualities may be opening us up spiritually. We may be called into Christian spiritualities known previously largely to mystics like Julian of Norwich, who called Jesus her Mother.[16] We may find ourselves called into the common mystical experience of being united with God as well as another human being, whether in acts of enthusiastic lovemaking or simply in the delights of deepening friendship.

DISCUSSION QUESTIONS

On Building a Church That Affirms and Emboldens Women and LGBTQ Christians

1. What would it mean for American Christianity if the lessons offered in this chapter were taken to heart? What would our churches look like if women of all colors and cultures, and queer people, were honored as fully human beings with the same moral challenges—to love our neighbors as ourselves—as every other Christian? Discuss what difference such a transformation would make in our liturgies and theologies, and in other realms of our life together as Christians in America. Would we even recognize a nonmisogynistic church? Would it be Christian any longer? What do you think?

2. If "quality of life" were associated by American Christians less with how much we own, control, or can purchase, and more with the qualities of our relationships, how might this affect the shape of our families, our churches, as well as the larger society?

3. Imagine what might happen if we put Hagar's story at the center of our worship once a year, or more often, as we do other spiritual giants? What would it signal if we named our baby daughters for Hagar as often as we do Sarah? Let's discuss this.

4. What if we were to experience God as "El-roi"—the one who sees us as we really are, not in our productions of self that we present in public and eventually even to ourselves? What would El-roi see, looking at us, collectively and individually?

5. Discuss Angie Hong's experience of being sexually objectified as an Asian American woman. How can our churches respond to this "China doll" theology?

On Women's Reproductive Freedom, Including Abortion

1. How might Christian churches emboldened by Hagar and Mary Magdalene respond to questions about birth control and abortion as a moral and a political challenge in contemporary America? What should our churches say about women's health care, including the right to safe,

accessible birth control and abortion? A question for our conservative Christian siblings, whether Protestant, Catholic, or Orthodox, is
whether we can find some common ground on the important questions
about women's reproductive freedom, options, and choices.

2. Discuss the ethics not simply of abortion but also of reproductive
freedom and, even more broadly, of women's moral abilities to make
decisions about our bodies, our pregnancies, our families, our health,
our happiness, our capacities to be good mothers, and other matters
pertaining to the fullness of our humanity and the full range of our
moral choices.

3. Can we consider the value of fetal life and the "rights of the unborn" in
relation to the value and quality of women's lives, health, bodily integrity, and ability to make moral decisions, and women's rights not only
as Americans but also as people of God?

On Sexual and Gender Identity

1. Although many today view Freud as an almost quaint, long since for-
gotten, crusader against Victorian standards, especially in the realm
of sexuality, Freud had some important hunches about the ubiquitous
character of our sexual energies. How do you respond to Freud's suggestion that we are all bisexual? What difference would this make to
you if we were?

2. If you identify as a lesbian, gay, or bisexual Christian, talk about how
you have experienced the church's regard for your sexuality, for good
or ill. Please tell a story that illustrates your experience. If you are a
straight, or heterosexual, Christian, how have you begun to come to
terms with the presence of gay, lesbian, and bisexual people in your
life? What role has the church played in helping you?

3. What can we learn from trans and nonbinary people about their experiences of gender? If we ourselves are trans, or if we are nonbinary, what
do we want our friends and families to know about our experiences?
What do those who identify as cisgender need to know about how to be
good allies to those who are not cisgender?

Chapter 16

The Fifth Call

Transforming Capitalism

The goal of this chapter is to help Christians and others imagine a constructive path beyond capitalist spirituality. To encourage us to wrestle with how we might actually build and secure foundations of economic justice in America that not only would be compatible with Christian values but moreover would be advocated by Christian leaders and affirmed by Christians of both more liberal and more conservative traditions.

> Then Jesus said to his disciples . . . "Again I tell you, it is easier for a camel to go through the eye of a needle than for someone who is rich to enter the kingdom of God." (Matt. 19:23–24 NRSV)

Of the seven deadly sins we have named in this book, the one most difficult for most of us even to discuss is capitalist spirituality. This is because we have been so conditioned, as American Christians, to be terrified of "socialism." As an economic aim, not a political philosophy, socialism refers to structures of shared, mutual responsibility for one another's well-being over capitalism's emphasis on the individual person (historically a white male) and his family, making his own way and depending largely on himself for access to basic life resources. American Christians have learned to confuse self-esteem and an enterprising spirit with a deference to the operations of advanced capitalism and, for three-quarters of a century, we have confused capitalism with God's will for America and for all good Christians.

OUR FEAR OF SOCIALISM

America's abiding fear of socialism is largely a holdover from the anti-Communist preoccupation of the McCarthy era in the early 1950s. During this post–World War II period, when the Soviet Union was emerging as America's potential economic competitor and military foe, American political leaders called upon the rhetorical talents of such Christian leaders as the Protestant evangelist Billy Graham and the Catholic bishop Fulton Sheen to stress a devotion to capitalism—and its attendant emphasis on the individual white male's freedom—as the only path for faithful Christians and patriotic Americans, pretty much the same group of citizens.

It is difficult to overstate the importance today of American Christians trying to understand the roots of our fears of what we think of as "socialism." Let me say clearly that I am not blindly committed to socialism as our path forward. In fact, I am not committed to socialism as an ideology[1] but rather to a more equitable and fairer distribution of wealth and basic resources for human well-being in America than is possible under our present, highly deregulated and dehumanizing, system of economic control through which the rich are getting richer and the poor, poorer.

I have included a brief glossary of terms related to "socialism" in the notes following this chapter rather than including them here in the body of the text.[2] For the purpose of helping us better understand our fear of socialism, I believe we ought to acknowledge the failure of most Communist nations in the twentieth century to respect, honor, and care for their people. Though most Americans have a hard time believing this, because our own leaders have for so long equated "Communism" and "socialism," Soviet-style Communism had little to do with the socialist vision of Karl Marx and much to do with the greed of the Communist leadership. As a matter of fact, the Communism that rose and fell in the Soviet Union between 1917 and 1989 has now morphed into a corrupt oligarchy that functions much like a collectivized capitalism on steroids, yet is happy enough to be caricatured as "socialist" by its adversaries like America and some of Western Europe. From the outset, Soviet and now-Russian-style Communism has had little to do with feeding hungry people or empowering workers to collectively own their businesses. Like advanced global capitalism, Communism has served mainly to line the pockets of the superrich. For Russians like Putin to trumpet their system as "socialist" is to mock both the integrity and intelligence of Karl Marx and the ignorance of most of Americans and other capitalists who, for whatever reasons, cling to our antiquated view of capitalism as a just, fair, and almost quaint system, the opposite of what we have learned to call "socialist"—like Putin's Russia and Xi's China.

Let me say here that I have great respect for friends and others who have experienced firsthand the horrors of regimes that have practiced what they have called "Communism" or "socialism"—nations in Europe, Latin America, Africa, and Asia. The economic systems and authoritarian politics of the Soviet Union and Cambodia have little to commend them in terms of human well-being. China and Cuba are more mixed in what they have achieved economically as well as morally for their people, in contrast to previous oppressive governments. But overall, "socialism in Communist garb," as we might call it, has little to commend it to American Christians as a way of organizing an economy, and nothing whatsoever to commend it as a political system.

LESSONS NOT LEARNED

We might or might not have noticed something happening to the south of our border during the past six decades. We might have caught fleeting shadows of several nations trying to do something new. Their experiments might have flashed before our eyes, and we might have caught brief glimpses of some new possibilities. We might have gathered some hints of what might have been helpful to America had we not been too frightened to engage in a spirit of mutuality the ideals of revolutionary efforts among a few of our neighbors to the south. Three examples of socialism that were attempted in the Western Hemisphere in the last half of the twentieth century stand out in this regard.

In Cuba, the young Fidel Castro, for example, led a successful struggle culminating in 1959 to overcome the oppressive rule of Fulgencio Batista. A decade later, in 1970, Salvador Allende was elected as the socialist president of Chile, only to be overthrown three years later by the fascist Augusto Pinochet. In 1969, just six years after Allende was ousted by Pinochet, Nicaragua's socialist Sandinistas, led by a young Daniel Ortega, overthrew the ruthless rule of Anastasio Somoza. These decades in the mid- to late twentieth century were brimming over with revolutionary energies in Latin America. The young revolutionaries were not determined to become "Communist." Like anticolonial fighters in Africa a decade or two earlier, those seeking social change and economic justice had no attachment to "Communism" or "socialism" or "capitalism" or any other particular economic system in the world. They simply were determined to build nations in which the hungry would eat, the sick would be nursed, the homeless would be sheltered, and prisoners would be treated with compassion. They believed, and hoped, that justice would at last prevail.

Not all, or even most, of the Latin American revolutionaries were Christian, but those who were, like Fr. Ernesto Cardenal, Nicaragua's Sandinista minister of culture, would have been inspired by Jesus, who—quoting from the prophet Isaiah—had spoken to people who undoubtedly knew his parents and had known him as a boy:

> When he came to Nazareth, where he had been brought up, he went to the synagogue on the sabbath day, as was his custom. He stood up to read, and the scroll of the prophet Isaiah was given to him. He unrolled the scroll and found the place where it was written:

> "The Spirit of the Lord is upon me, because he has anointed me to bring good news to the poor. He has sent me to proclaim release to the captives and recovery of sight to the blind, to let the oppressed go free, to proclaim the year of the Lord's favor." (Luke 4:16–19 NRSV)

While history has shown that Castro, and more recently and probably ruthlessly Ortega, became authoritarian dictators whose regimes have bridged no opposition, that was not how it began. In the beginning, these were idealistic young men fighting for economic justice in lands that they loved. Cuba and Nicaragua are excellent examples of what happens when basically good dreams—of shared, mutual responsibility for one another's well-being—are not encouraged by stronger neighbors who could have helped them grow. In the cases of Cuba and Nicaragua, the United States of America, their huge neighbor to the north, would not permit their economic dreams even to begin to take shape. This was because America did not want socialism in the Western Hemisphere, period—and would not tolerate even tiny Nicaragua's stated desire for a mixed socialist-capitalist economy.[3]

This had been why, under President John Kennedy, America had tried to overthrow Castro's barely two-year-old government. In collusion with a small group of antirevolutionary Cuban exiles in 1961, the United States had failed miserably at the Bay of Pigs. What we did accomplish was to drive Cuba into the Soviet Union's orbit for economic support and strategic friendship, thereby helping create "Communist Cuba" as an enemy just ninety miles to the south of Florida, an adversarial relationship that persists to this day.

Twenty years later, an American-supported "contra"—Nicaraguan counter-revolutionaries—fought throughout the 1980s to undermine the Sandinistas' efforts to begin building the new nation. The contra and their allies, primarily Nicaragua's wealthy business communities, succeeded in electing the opposition candidate to the Nicaraguan presidency in 1990. Over the next couple of decades, an increasingly determined Daniel Ortega would rise back to power through democratic elections. Today this very same Ortega is sometimes compared by Nicaraguans on the left as well as the right to the dictator Somoza whom his own Sandinistas overthrew in 1979. Authoritarian, prone to violence, and unwilling to tolerate opposition, President Ortega rules Nicaragua with an iron fist. He seems to have become the sort of leader he once despised. Interestingly, while the young revolutionary Daniel Ortega had been an atheist, the older dictator has been converted to Christianity. What do we make of this?

Was this inevitable? Why did most Americans not notice, or connect with, the aspirations of the young revolutionaries? How could America have helped Ortega steer a different course in Nicaragua or, twenty years earlier, have prevented Cuba from turning to the Soviet Union for economic help and friendship? Instead of putting our energies into fighting the socialist dreams of such young people as Ortega and Castro, could we have noticed the goodness of the dream being seeded in Latin America? Could we have reached out in friendship to Cuba, Chile, and Nicaragua—to the advantage of everyone in each of these countries, everyone that is except some of those superwealthy individuals who were aspiring capitalists and who would always need the poor to provide cheap labor?

In all three instances—Cuba, Chile, Nicaragua—America was bound and determined to force adherence to our capitalist economic framework. Even more shocking than what happened in Cuba and Nicaragua, America had staged its own coup in Chile. In 1973, Salvador Allende, an older, democratically elected, well-established, and much admired socialist leader had been ousted by the fascist general, Augusto Pinochet, in a coup supported by the United States of America, thereby launching two decades of "disappearances" and violence against those Chileans who dared question him, write about him, or oppose his rule.

Sadly, we Americans have never been able to see what might be able to happen if some of socialism's best features were mixed with some of capitalism's most important contributions to the world. Imagine combining what we call "private enterprise" with a single-payer, government-sponsored, health care system. Imagine stirring much of what we most value about local businesses and creative entrepreneurial efforts by young people with reliable retirement benefits for all workers. Imagine paying a larger portion of our wages and wealth as taxes—and having to pay nothing out of our pockets or savings for medical care, education, childcare, elder care, pre-K, or retirement.

Some readers might recoil at some or all of these notions. But imagine our talking about such possibilities even if they are, or seem to us, unimaginable. My point here is that, as American Christians, we simply must find ways to humanize our society, its economic system and basic institutions such as our health care system. If we are serious about loving the God of Jesus, and Jesus himself, who told us to love our neighbors, we must transform capitalism into an economic system that is rooted and grounded not primarily in profit, but rather in neighbor-love. That is what this chapter invites us to consider and act on.

F. D. Maurice on "Christian Socialism"

In discussing God's love as our "power-with" one another, as we have been doing in this book, we have looked at contributions of Frederick Denison Maurice, an Anglican theologian in nineteenth-century London. Among his various notable offerings to human well-being in his own time and place was his founding of a Christian socialist movement in England.[4] Unlike his contemporary Karl Marx, who was working on a similar project on the European continent, Maurice's view of socialism was mediated by what Marx and his followers would have critiqued as Maurice's "idealism," an irrepressible faith in God's love for all humankind and, consequently, Maurice's and our Christian duty, as lovers of God, to make sure that no humans are denied life-sustaining resources such as food, shelter, work, medical care, and education. For Christians, this not optional in our society. It is a moral imperative, driven by our faith.

As one of the founders of the Christian socialist movement, Maurice was indeed an idealist, writing and teaching to inspire his fellow Christians to share with the poor whatever they had, whereas Marx was a materialist calling workers to revolt against the wretched conditions in which they labored. Maurice was no less appalled than Marx by these conditions of working men and women. However, rather than urging workers to unite and take over the businesses that kept them in chains, *Maurice urged Christians to put in place a government that would establish an economically just and fair social order*. That's what his dream was, because he was a Christian. He knew better than to imagine that the English Parliament could build a perfect society, but he believed that its leaders—all white Christian men of economic privilege, of course—could move the social order in such a direction. By contrast, Marx, himself an atheist, had no such illusions about the goodness of religious leaders. Since his lifetime, many religious and nonreligious workers for economic justice have been inspired by Marx. But his interest was less in "inspiring" anyone—a spiritual effort he would probably would have dismissed as idealist—and more with attempting to rally workers to organize on behalf of their own interests. Frederick Maurice was not opposed to Marx's proposal for an economic revolution. In fact, he probably shared its goal—that workers would work for themselves and not for bosses who towered over them. But Maurice's motive and primary concern was to persuade English rulers—white entitled gentlemen (with the exception of Queen Victoria)—to take up for the working people and insist via legislation that economic justice be established throughout the land.

An interesting question meets us here: Was Maurice's vision for his country a Christian *nationalist* vision in the sense that he assumed that the best goals of the Christian Church and the English government not only could, but should, merge in a Christian socialist vision of society, in which there would be little if any distinction between church and state? We could argue that, if Maurice's vision of a just and loving society had actually blossomed into reality and had become the cornerstone of economic well-being for English people, the English nation would have become, at least in the economic realm, a partial and imperfect image of "the kingdom of God" on earth.

But other problems, including those that Maurice never saw or acknowledged, would have quickly dimmed the moral brightness of England. For example, Maurice didn't see or make much of the presence of anti-Semitism, English colonialism, Christian imperialism, or the British and Christian "exceptionalism" that was being exported around the British Commonwealth and laid on people of other cultures and religions. Despite his more egalitarian teachings about our power-with one another in this world, Maurice didn't name the prevalence of a power-over view of God as implicit in each of these social ills—colonialism, imperialism, anti-Semitism—and surely represented by the monarchy. Maurice also held a decidedly exceptional view of both Christianity and England as the best religion and nation in the world. He seemed to accept white supremacy as simply a given. Similarly, he seemed to accept the cultural pervasiveness of misogyny and its attendant homophobia despite his strong advocacy of economic justice for working women in industrialized England. Maurice never raised questions about how the industrialization of the West might affect the environment; in that way, he was a person of his time who cannot be judged fairly by people today. Finally, Maurice had little to say about violence as a way of life for the English.

Maurice might himself be called a "Christian nationalist" in that he was committed to Christianity and England merging in the work of economic justice in mid-nineteenth-century England. But there is a major and huge distinction: Maurice's view of both Christianity and England was polar opposite to the Christian nationalism that threatens American democracy today. Maurice's vision was inclusive and expansive of those who were marginalized in England—especially the working class and poor people—whereas the white Christian nationalist vision for today's America taunts an exclusively white male capitalist view of what will make America great.

Maurice's vision was limited and partial and, for that reason, could not have been wholistic or fully inclusive of all that he did not see—for example, the horror of anti-Semitism and its implicit presence in Christian teachings, the value and fragility of the earth, women's full personhood, the presence of gay men and lesbians in English society, or the full truth in various religious traditions. We can well imagine, however, that given his actual life, values, and quality of moral presence in the world of his time, Frederick Maurice would have grown and changed over time and, were he living today, would be a chief advocate of various groups of marginalized and oppressed peoples, a champion of the earth, and an activist especially on behalf of those who had been victimized by the practices or teachings of the Christian Church. We can assume this because, from beginning to end, Frederick Denison Maurice promoted the opening up of society and the Christian Church's welcoming of diverse perspectives.

Much to the contrary, white Christian nationalists in contemporary America work to shut out all whom they think do not belong here and to narrow the definition of what it means to be either Christian or American. Given what we know today about the violence and dangers of white Christian nationalism, especially in America but also in England and elsewhere in the world, Maurice would have been a passionate opponent of white Christian nationalism. There should be no false equivalence drawn between the Christian idealism of F. D. Maurice and the Christofascism of white Christian nationalists, two totally different understandings of how Christians can help shape our societies.

Can we incorporate the moral basis of Maurice's passion for economic justice without sharing the necessarily "Christian" character of Maurice's life or his views? Can we affirm his commitment, as a Christian, to economic justice as a national imperative for all? Can we also reject, emphatically, any notion whatsoever that America should be a Christian nation in order to fulfill this economic dream? I think F. D. Maurice, were he with us, would ask these kinds of questions. It is clear to me that he would totally reject, and urge us to struggle against, white Christian nationalism.

THE EARLY CHURCH SPEAKS

The Acts of the Apostles was written several generations after Jesus's death by an author usually identified as "Luke the physician," who also wrote the Gospel of Luke. "Acts," as it is often called, recounts the life and ministries of a young church reaching beyond Jesus's Jewish followers and moving into the Gentile (non-Jewish) world. In a passage sometimes used to support Christian socialism, the author of Acts writes:

> Now the whole group of those who believed were of one heart and soul, and no one claimed private ownership of any possessions, but everything they owned was held in common. With great power the apostles gave their testimony to the resurrection of the Lord Jesus, and great grace was upon them all. There was not a needy person among them, for as many as owned lands or houses sold them

and brought the proceeds of what was sold. They laid it at the apostles' feet, and it was distributed to each as any had need. (Acts 4:32–35 NRSV)

This passage has always struck me as charismatic and compelling, surely a call to take socialism to heart as a Christian way. This may be exactly what we should do, but this particular passage probably refers to how Christians should treat each other and was not intended to be a commentary on how the entire society should be organized. We could argue, agreeing with Maurice, that the entire nation ought to follow this teaching, and it may be more historically accurate to admit that this is not what Luke the physician had in mind. Or it may not be. As my friend, retired pastor Earle Rabb, recently said to me, it may be exactly what Luke and early Christians had in mind, eventually for the whole society. But however the early Christian communities may have organized their life together and shared their resources, there is not a hint of ambiguity in what Jesus himself called us to do.

JESUS'S TEACHINGS ON THE SUBJECT

Let's examine Jesus's own take on personal wealth as he encounters a rich young man in the Gospel of Matthew:

> Then someone came to him and said, "Teacher, what good deed must I do to have eternal life?" And he said to him, "Why do you ask me about what is good? There is only one who is good. If you wish to enter into life, keep the commandments." He said to him, "Which ones?" And Jesus said, "You shall not murder; You shall not commit adultery; You shall not steal; You shall not bear false witness; Honor your father and mother; also, You shall love your neighbor as yourself." The young man said to him, "I have kept all these; what do I still lack?" Jesus said to him, "If you wish to be perfect, go, sell your possessions, and give the money to the poor, and you will have treasure in heaven; then come, follow me." When the young man heard this word, he went away grieving, for he had many possessions. (Matt. 19:16–22 NRSV)

Not surprisingly, this particular encounter between Jesus and the rich young man usually gets minimized ("This is not one of Jesus's most important teachings") or equivocated ("possessions" do not refer literally to material wealth but rather to things that mean too much to us). But it takes a lot of dismissive distortion for Christians *not* to hear Jesus's challenge to the rich young man as a requirement that, if he wishes to follow Jesus, he must "go, sell [his] possessions, and give the money to the poor, and [only then will he] have treasure in heaven"; moreover, "[only] then [can the young man] come, follow [Jesus]." Like many good Christians in our own time and place, men and women who attempt to live faithful lives and obey the commandments, the rich young man "went away grieving, for he had many possessions."

There seems to me no question that, in this challenging story, Jesus is telling the man that, regardless of the quality of his discipleship, he must shed his wealth if he wishes to follow Jesus. Even if he has kept all the laws and commandments of Judaism, he must give away his possessions and discard his economic power and privilege to follow Jesus. This young man is not a religious leader. He is simply an observant Jew, like Jesus himself, a good religious practitioner. But there is just one thing: he is also wealthy and, according to Jesus, must share his wealth to follow Jesus, something the man apparently cannot or will not do.

Immediately following this exchange, Jesus says to his disciples something that most of us learned in Sunday school when we were kids, passages that few of us want to talk about: "Truly I tell you, it will be hard for a rich person to enter the kingdom of heaven. Again I tell you, it is easier for a camel to go through the eye of a needle than for someone who is rich to enter the kingdom of God" (Matt. 19:23–24 NRSV).

Now I learned in seminary that the image of the camel going through the eye of a needle *may* have referred to a particular geographic passage—the "eye of a needle" being a gate in Jerusalem through which real camels had to pass, often with difficulty. This interpretation has been debated among Christians for centuries. Most Christian teachers[5] agree, however, that Jesus clearly expects his followers to share their wealth and possessions—and that he recognizes how unlikely it is that the very rich will do this.

THE IDOLATRY OF INDIVIDUALISM

Earlier,we encountered Beverly Harrison's indictment of capitalist spirituality as the convergence of global capitalism's obsession with wealth and the reverencing of the individual's salvation and freedom over community well-being, a spiritual prioritizing put in place by the Protestant reformers. Harrison's moral concern, as a Christian ethicist, is that America has been immeasurably weakened as a morally vibrant, just, and caring nation by this unholy alliance of capitalism's relentless pursuit of wealth and the individual (usually white male's) insistence upon his own freedom to make money without having to share it or account for it via taxes or regulations.

This American attachment to freedom as an individual's right amounts to idolatry in the biblical sense. God's response to idolatry is rage—fury against those who turn to graven images, be they golden calves (Exodus 32) or the lust for power-over. As Jesus says to the devil who promises him power over the world, "Away with you, Satan! for it is written, 'Worship the Lord your God, and serve only him'" (Matt. 4:10 NRSV; see also Luke 4:8).

In American Christianity, keep in mind that the idolatry of individual rights typically applies *only* to white men: their property, their women, their families, their bodies (and the bodies of their women and children), their guns, their speech, their interpretations of their religion, their rights to swing their fists at whomever they please, their rights to sex, all of these rights apply to them and them alone. Imagine, for example, that large numbers of Black men in America were in the streets marching on behalf of their Second Amendment rights. Imagine that the majority of American women of all classes, cultures, and colors took to the streets demanding our rights to safe, legal access to reproductive options, including the right to abortion. Imagine that vast numbers of LGBTQ Americans and our allies were in the streets demanding our rights to freedom of gender expression throughout this nation. Imagine that Black, brown, Indigenous, and Asian Americans and their allies were demanding in great numbers that all schoolchildren be taught American history that includes the real stories of slavery, the Trail of Tears, immigration and the Alamo, Japanese incarceration during World War II, and other tales of horror, real American horror. Imagine, that is, an America in which our collective rights were honored and celebrated—our rights as straight white men of course, but also as people of color, women, LGBTQ people, kids, seniors, sick persons, communities of disability, and others historically marginalized by the rights of white men to their so-called freedom.

RETHINKING SOME HISTORY

There are particular figures and movements in American history with much to teach us about what might be possible in America on the basis of what has already happened:

One individual worth raising up and studying as one of America's boldest economic visionaries was Frances Perkins, President Franklin Roosevelt's secretary of labor and one of the chief architects of the New Deal's retirement policy that would become known as Social Security.[6]

Another noteworthy connection is between President Lyndon Johnson's "Great Society" program and the beginnings of Medicare and Medicaid, as special insurance programs for older or poorer Americans.

A related ongoing movement has been the drive toward universal health care insurance, first imagined by President Theodore Roosevelt, articulated and called for a half century later by President Harry Truman, and advocated to some degree by every American president—with only tepid support from President Ronald Reagan—until finally the passage of the Affordable Care

Act in the administration of President Barack Obama in 2009. Today, many Americans are in favor of at least a "public option" for all Americans to choose as their health care insurance, and many Americans would prefer a single-payer system, denoting government-administered health care insurance for everyone.

At the other end of the political spectrum, about a dozen states continue to hold out against Medicaid expansion that would cover millions of poor Americans who make too much money (by their state's standards) but too little (by national standards) to qualify for Medicaid assistance as it is currently structured. This is a stunning example of state and federal laws being followed absurdly to the detriment of the people they were intended to serve. Moreover, in refusing to expand Medicaid, Republican legislators callously turn their backs on those whose lives literally hang in the balance.

TRANSFORMING CAPITALISM: THE LEAST WE CAN DO

Not to end on an angry note—we should try not to end honest talk in anger—let's go back to the critical question of how we can transform the capitalist structures in which we live and breathe as American Christians. Liberals, conservatives, moderates all, can we Christians share our visions of what a truly justice-loving nation would look like? What is most important to each of us? How could we make it happen? What should our churches be teaching our children?

Let's not get sidetracked arguing about whether or not we are capitalists. Of course we are capitalists. Like white supremacy and misogyny, capitalism is in the air we breathe. We simply take it for granted. Unlike racism and sexism, however, we have come to imagine that capitalism is an unambiguously great global invention. Let's not try to prove or disprove that possibility. Can we agree that even the best things change over time? In this spirit, how can we help transform capitalism in even small ways whereby we really do "bring good news to the poor . . . proclaim release to the captives . . . recovery of sight to the blind . . . and let the oppressed go free" (Luke 4:18 NRSV)?

Sisters, brothers, siblings, if we take Jesus seriously, it's the least we can do.

DISCUSSION QUESTIONS

1. What economic idols are most evident in America? How could our churches help bring these idols down?

2. Discuss ongoing tensions that you experience between our personal freedoms and our collective well-being. Think of examples where they clash. How can we help each other navigate these tensions?

3. What are we to make of Jesus's call for us to move beyond our attachments to possessions and wealth to follow him? Do we take him seriously but not literally, as liberal Christians often interpret scripture? Or do we imagine, in this case, precisely because we are left so defensive by these passages, that we might need to wrestle with what really is required of us if we take Jesus's call to heart? How would our lives change?

ABOUT SOCIALISM

1. "Then Jesus said to his disciples, 'Truly I tell you, it will be hard for a rich person to enter the kingdom of heaven. Again I tell you, it is easier for a camel to go through the eye of a needle than for someone who is rich to enter the kingdom of God'" (Matt. 19:23–24 NRSV). Let's discuss this passage, which is attributed to Jesus. Few Christians and probably fewer Americans want to think about this—which is why we need to discuss it.

2. Discuss America's refusal to affirm anything good in the early efforts among the socialist revolutionaries in Latin America during the last half of the twentieth century. What did America's refusal to affirm the dreams of these young reformers do to *America*? What can we learn from this that might help us even now, as Americans and Christians, create a more fully justice-loving society?

3. Try to imagine a social and economic order that is not stymied by a fear of socialism that is steeped in ignorance. Can we make good-faith efforts to take the best lessons we can from Jesus and the early disciples and try to relate them to our actual experiences as twenty-first-century American Christians? What would such efforts look like?

4. How do Jesus's words to the rich young man speak to the prevailing anti-socialism anxieties in America, especially among white Christians?

5. Unlike his contemporary Karl Marx, who was working on the European continent, F. D. Maurice's view of socialism was mediated by his irrepressible faith in God's love for all humankind and, consequently, our Christian duty, as lovers of God, to make sure that no humans are denied life-sustaining resources such as food, shelter, work, medical care, and education. Discuss Maurice's vision of Christian socialism. Can you imagine such a vision for America? If not, why not? If so, to what extent?

Chapter 17

The Sixth Call

Belonging with Earth and Animals

The goal of this chapter is to encourage our senses of belonging. Drawing from Christian ethicist Larry Rasmussen and other teachers, to make a case for our kinship not only with other humans but also with the earth and other earth creatures; to invite us to build moral cases in our church communities and elsewhere for ethical practices that will strengthen our belonging to one another on this planet.

For many of us, the earth's other creatures are an afterthought. Those we call "animals," as if we are speaking of lesser species than ourselves, are here on earth for our pleasure, our use, or for whatever other reasons that don't much concern us unless we happen to have special animals that we love as family, value as transportation, or enjoy as food. The Genesis creation story says that God has given us dominion over them:

> Then God said, "Let us make humankind in our image, according to our likeness; and let them have dominion over [Hebrew: *radah* = rule over] the fish of the sea, and over the birds of the air, and over the cattle, and over all the wild animals of the earth, and over every creeping thing that creeps upon the earth." (Gen. 1:26 NRSV)

No question that humanity's rulership, or dominion, over animals has been assumed from the beginning of human history. In this context, Christian assumptions about a human-centered creation with animals and other parts of creation as our subjects and at our disposal have been rooted in our belief that God created human beings alone in his image—and that at least part of what it means to be in the image of God is to be rulers of creation. The theological assumption shared by most believers in monotheism, including Christians, has long been that humans rule—specifically, as we have seen throughout this book, that the male human rules creation. This domination theology is the basis of the sixth deadly sin of white Christianity nationalism: the disregard of the earth and other earth creatures.

Some of the best Christian preaching is *against* whatever scripture is used to promote injustice or violence. The "Adam's rib" interpretation of Genesis 2 is a famous example of texts that many Christians, especially liberal, feminists, and liberationists, have become accustomed to preaching *against*. Similarly, Ephesians 6:5, in which Paul admonishes slaves to be obedient to their masters, is worthy only of being preached vigorously *against*. Some of the long-standing anti-Jewish readings of the Gospel of John must be preached *against* if we are to be faithful to a God of all people and not just some. In other words, Christians cannot be wed uncritically to literal readings of scripture. We have to consider the actual conditions of our lives in our world, our nations, our communities in order to make good moral sense of the Bible.

As a means of illuminating the call sometimes to preach *against* the Bible, let me recount a brief story about the authority of scripture, as I've come to understand it over the years. Back in 1973, shortly before I was scheduled to be ordained an Episcopal deacon, I was struggling with the oath that must be taken by all ordinands prior to their ordination as deacons or priests in the Episcopal Church. The part I had the most trouble with was this: "I believe the Old and New Testaments to be the Word of God and to contain all things necessary to salvation." I was unsure I could take such a pledge or go through with the ordination.

Living in New York City at the time, I phoned Bob DeWitt, bishop of the Diocese of Pennsylvania at the time and a friend I had made when we both worked on the board of *The Witness* magazine. I told him about my struggle of conscience. He said he'd meet me the following morning in the coffee shop at Pennsylvania Station in New York City, and he did. After telling him that I could not, honestly, say that I believe the Bible to be either the Word of God or to contain all things necessary to salvation, his response was unforgettable. It makes me smile and sustains me to this day: "Carter, to say that the Bible is the Word of God doesn't mean it's the only Word of God; and to say that it contains everything necessary to salvation doesn't mean that everything it contains is necessary to salvation." I was ordained a deacon several days later and, the following summer, a priest—by Bishop DeWitt who, with my sister deacon and beloved friend Sue Hiatt, had organized the ordination of the first eleven women priests in Philadelphia on July 29, 1974.

I tell this story to underscore not only the urgency and importance but also the faithfulness and wisdom in preaching *against a theology of human domination, rulership, control, or power-over creation and other creatures*. We do not have to obey laws that are unjust, take spiritual paths that lead nowhere good, or accept highly individualistic moral values or business practices that ensure not only the depletion of our souls but also the demise of our planet. We should teach, preach, and act against everything and everybody who dares to mock, trivialize, and disregard the life of the earth as a living, breathing organism. Other creatures, indeed the whole of creation, are called to be our partners in belonging together on planet Earth. To learn to honor this partnership is our life's work. It involves the best science, religion, spirituality, imagination, and—more than anything—the widest and deepest love we can bring to our life together as siblings/earth creatures.

Everything that follows should be read with the other creatures in mind and heart. Keep in mind not only the trees and rivers but also the crawfish and cattle as you read. I am writing on their behalf and urge you to read on their behalf as well.

BELONGING

"How [can] we sing the Lord's song in a foreign land?" (Ps. 137:4 NRSV).

Christian ethicist Larry L. Rasmussen writes, "We are far too many and many of us are far too rich, with far too much stuff, and the wrong kind of economy, for the planet to bear, on our terms. So we find ourselves awkwardly astride a turning time when we must learn to sing a new song in a strange land. Only this time the strange land is not Babylon, and we are not Israel but all humankind."[1] In his major ethical work, Larry Rasmussen draws on earth sciences as well as on the best from religious teachings, not limited to Christian resources, to make a case for our "belonging": "All that is, is kin and born to belonging. All is relational. Humankind and other-kind live into one another's lives and die into one another's deaths in relationships that either sustain or subvert creatures and the land."[2]

It is in this radically relational context, a world of belonging, that we must learn to sing a new song. But how can we sing with our whole heart about the beauty of the earth when, for centuries, we have learned to regard it with unapologetic disrespect and in such remarkable ignorance? Larry Rasmussen is one of many American Christians urging us to realize that, as humans, it is way past time for us to seek God's guidance in even knowing how to love the earth and its creatures. Here we are today, in the midst of floods, fires, famine, the displacement of humans and creatures of all kinds, and a brazenly ignorant disregard for the earth's well-being. A friend of mine, a longtime lover of birds and nature, said to me back in the 1990s that she believes humankind is beyond hope and that, if the earth and animals have a future, it will be without us. This friend, who happens to be a psychiatrist and psychotherapist, believes that humanity is lost. She would agree wholeheartedly with Christian theologian Sallie McFague who has noted that while we humans need the earth, the earth does not need us.[3]

It has certainly mattered to some notable Christian teachers—German Benedictine abbess, mystic, and musician Hildegard of Bingen (1098–1179) and Italian Catholic friar and renowned friend to animals, Francis of Assisi (1182–1226), spring immediately to mind. So too does the great French Jesuit paleontologist and theologian Pierre Teilhard de Chardin (1871–1955), who taught that all creation is an evolutionary process moving toward an "Omega point," which Teilhard believed to be "Christ."[4] Though Hildegard and Francis have been designated as saints, Teilhard continues to be controversial in more orthodox Catholic circles where he is sometimes dismissed both by religious critics for denying, or minimizing, the supernatural and by scientists for his mystical approach to scientific theories of creation and evolution. Nonetheless, Teilhard's standing today among most liberal Christian theologians and teachers, as well as among scientists who are not averse to religious-scientific interaction, is strong and appreciative.

The point here is that a love for the earth and its creatures has precedence in Christian history. A passion for creation and for animals is not new, but it has never been mainstream as foundational to Christian spirituality or Christian ethics. To the contrary, Christians on the whole have been inclined to take creation and other-than-human animals for granted. We have valued them largely insofar as we have been able to use them for profit or pleasure. This "utilitarianism"—things being valued according to their usefulness—has been the basis of how, over the centuries, most Christians have regarded the earth and earth creatures.

THICH NHAT HANH AND JOANNA MACY

Over the past thirty years, a number of public religious figures have been outspoken on the subject of the earth and environment, including the animals,[5] calling us beyond a utilitarian view of creation into a deeper sense of belonging. The great Buddhist monk Thich Nhat Hanh, knowing deeply the wholeness, the oneness, and the belonging of all creation, connects earth-care with peace itself. "If we take the hand of a child and look at the small flowers that grow among the grasses, if we sit with him or her and breathe deeply and smile, listening to the birds and also to the sounds of the other children playing together . . . we will know that our future depends on both. Looking deeply into the present moment, we know what to do and what not to do to save our precious planet, and each other. This is real peace education."[6]

For more than a half century, another esteemed Buddhist teacher, Joanna Macy, has been one of America's most commanding and compassionate voices on behalf of the earth's well-being and of our belonging. Granddaughter of a Presbyterian minister, Macy was one of those Christians who, as early as sixteen, took the life and teachings of Jesus seriously. Following a weeklong youth conference and a conversation with the chaplain about the risen Christ, Joanna returned home and declared to her mother, "Oh, Mama, What happened with Jesus and the disciples is happening right now!"[7] She had become aware of the urgency and presence of Jesus's life with, among, and through us all—an experience of Christ or Jesus's christic power-with us. Over the next two decades, this awareness of the deepest meaning of Christianity led Joanna Macy into Tibetan Buddhism as the spiritual foundation of her life's work as an activist and scholar on behalf of the planet and our belonging together in it.

Renowned for her workshops focusing on the grief and despair being experienced by lovers of the earth and its creatures, Joanna Macy's compassionate teachings have encouraged people to speak honestly and boldly about their grief and their despair. Experiencing themselves as belonging together and as mutually empowering one another, hope and determination take root. And a resilient activism is born, again and again, generation upon generation, around the world.

Thich Nhat Hanh, Joanna Macy, and Larry Rasmussen join a long line of sages, both ancient and modern, who understand that learning to belong, truly caring for creation, living as if we are the siblings that we actually are to one another and other creatures, requires spiritual discipline. We need a *way* to follow. We need a *practice* of some sort to attend. We need a *call* from those whom we trust. We are not alone. That is the whole point. We belong together. How do we more fully realize our belonging?[8] Courses, conferences, workshops, books, films, religious organizations, social movements, spiritual teachers or groups, and often just very good friends can help us find our ways into deeper realizations of belonging.

Thich Nhat Hanh's Plum Village Monastery in southern France has become a global center to which spiritual pilgrims travel to practice the basics of engaged Buddhism, a spirituality grounded in deep reverence of earth and earth creatures. A practicing Lutheran Christian in America, Rasmussen has found students, companions, and fellow activists in courses, retreats, and conferences that have been largely but by no means exclusively Christian. Joanna Macy has led workshops and courses that have been grounded in the Buddha dharma and attended by those drawn to Buddhism for the same reason she herself was: its wholistic, nondualistic, reverence for all creation, including humans.

SHIFTS IN OUR LIVES

In part 2, we looked at Larry Rasmussen's descriptions of where and how human beings have lost our moral way on this planet. We return here to Rasmussen's proposals. Having suggested that morality is how we get from what is to what ought to be,[9] he offers some ways for lovers of the earth and earth creatures to proceed. Rasmussen proposes that there are five shifts we need to make in our lives collectively and individually if we are committed to belonging together, siblings in earth-honoring communities.

The first shift is *from consumerism to asceticism* as "something deep in the human spirit and a requirement of authentic humanity."[10] We live in the midst of consumerism; advanced capitalism wraps us in it. Sometimes, more often than perhaps we would choose, we are lured by the glitter and sparkle of fashion and food and fun things to do. Most days, we are simply busy with things we must do and, along the way, we become consumers of more than we realize—clothes, food, gadgets, things, and more things. Our time is spent, gone, and there is no quiet space or time for us. We become strangers to the ascetic, simple places, slow lanes, less cluttered spaces in which just to be. Our town in western North Carolina has become something of a hub for tourism during the summer, thanks to its rivers, waterfalls, summer camps, and renowned music center, and during the fall and spring because of spectacular leaf displays, banks of azaleas and mountain laurel, and the ever-more-popular sport of mountain biking. Recently, a public celebration was held in our town on behalf of a "contemplation path" that has been created downtown for passersby to take a break and walk quietly. This path was named for an Episcopal deacon, Diane Livingston, who had just retired and whose ministry had represented for many the spirituality of such a path. I tell you this little story because its context is a small, relatively quiet, easygoing town nestled in the Appalachian Mountains. At a glimpse, this town would epitomize a place of rest and relaxation in which a "contemplation path" would seem redundant. After all, we are not in one of our large-city neighbors like Atlanta or Charlotte, or even a smaller city like Asheville or Greenville, each located not far away. Even in small-town America, relatively rural and culturally conservative, people are seeking ways to slow down and breathe and not become exhausted by the consumerism that so easily fuels tourism.

The second shift is kin to the first. We must move *from commodification toward the sacred* (the divine, which is always present and often hidden in creation, including humanity and other creature-kind).[11] This is the distinction drawn by Martin Buber between "it" and "thou," a thing and a living being. For some reason—perhaps a sacred nudge—as I moved toward retirement, I decided to help launch a therapeutic horseback riding center on the outskirts of this same small mountain town. Free Rein, as we named it, became a source of renewable human and equine energies converging in the sacred work of healing. Bear in mind that therapy horses are healthy, happy equines (they must be well cared for to work in this way), but they are not being used by humans for recreation or entertainment. They are not show horses. They are not racehorses. They are not star athletes. They are not breeders. There is nothing commodified about a therapy horse. By the same token, children and adults who turn to therapeutic horseback riding as a resource for healing are often humans with special needs and disabilities of one form or another—physical, cognitive, mental, social—human beings often disregarded in a world that values glamour and wealth. Like therapy horses, the humans who seek their help cannot be commodified—that is, turned into objects of economic value. Anyone who has experienced the therapeutic connection between a horse, a dog, a cat, and a human being—or, for that matter, a therapeutic relation between humans—knows what Martin Buber was getting at in drawing the moral distinction between "I-it" and "I-thou" relationships. One is commodified. The other is sacred.

The third shift is *from alienation (roots in the rampant individualism that disconnects us from each other and our world) toward belonging or "interbeing"* (Thich Nhat Hanh's term) that can be realized only through the mystical practice of glimpsing that which is so often hidden in creation.[12] As we experience ourselves belonging together, we are better able to see through the eyes of God our connectedness to one another and to all creatures great and small. Interbeing cannot be taught in books or lectures. It comes through experience at the deepest levels of our humanity and creatureliness. And it comes as a sweet source of personal strength and hope in the context of the chaos that cloaks our interbeing and hides us from our true selves. It is no small wonder that so many Americans, often Christians and former Christians, have turned to Buddhist teachers like Thich Nhat Hanh and Joanna Macy, whose spiritual gifts to their students and friends are not primarily through lectures and words but through sitting together, walking, and quietly experiencing interbeing together. One of my dearest friends, and my chief spiritual mentor for almost forty years, is Janet Surrey, a clinical psychologist and a Jew who has become Buddhist. In retirement, Surrey has become an insight dialogue teacher in the modern insight meditation tradition. Giving and receiving energy from this practice, Jan not only teaches but has also become an environmentalist activist, working alongside others in the Dakota Access Pipeline protests.[13] Jan Surrey's life's work and that of her husband Steve Bergman, a psychiatrist and writer (pen name: Samuel Shem), reflect a steady determination to create paths through alienation more fully into interbeing.

The fourth shift we must make is *from oppression toward prophetic-liberative practices*.[14] This is the work of making justice throughout our society, contributing in whatever ways we can "to bring good news to the poor . . . to proclaim release to the captives and recovery of sight to the blind, to let the oppressed go free" (Luke 4:18 NRSV). In this fourth shift, Rasmussen places his advocacy for earth-honoring faith in the context of our efforts in these pages to better understand and respond to the "seven deadly sins of white Christian nationalism." A close colleague of Beverly Harrison, Delores Williams, James Cone, and other Christian activists, Rasmussen knows well the resistance that his work on behalf of the earth receives from many Christians and others under the spell of white supremacy, misogyny, capitalist spirituality, and the other deadly sins.

The fifth shift, simply put, is *from folly to wisdom*,[15] to invite Sophia—the Wisdom of God—into our collective midst. Wisdom's call constitutes the core of the book of Proverbs in Hebrew scripture. The lyrical Psalms are better known among most Christians than the sage teachings of Proverbs, but it is in the latter that we meet Sophia/Wisdom, likely the least known and most ignored manifestation of who and what God is in our midst:

> Does not wisdom call,
> and does not understanding raise her voice?
> On the heights, beside the way,
> at the crossroads she takes her stand;
> beside the gates in front of the town,
> at the entrance of the portals she cries out:
> "To you, O people, I call,
> and my cry is to all that live.
> O simple ones, learn prudence;
> acquire intelligence, you who lack it.
> Hear, for I will speak noble things,
> and from my lips will come what is right." (Prov. 8:1–6 NRSV)

In Rasmussen's view, "wisdom may be the biblical eco-theology and ethic."[16] In other words, having wisdom is the heart, mind, and soul of our belonging.

We must ask Sophia to teach us. Alison Cheek, sister priest (among the eleven women ordained "irregularly" in 1974) wrote a Sophia liturgy that she asked to be used as the basis for her own memorial service in 2019. Here is a small portion of this liturgy:

Gracious Sophia, you order the universe. You came forth from the mouth of the Most High and covered the earth like mist. Alone you encircled the vault of the sky and walked on the bottom of the deep. You deployed your strength and joy, and even your laughter, throughout the earth, ordering all things for good and promoting the well-being of all.

You moved among human beings and all creatures, infusing each with Wisdom of its own special kind. We give thanks that you dwell among us and make your ways known to us.

We live in a world and nation fraught with injustice, yet infused also with sparks of your Wisdom. We pray for each nation, each community, each group, and everyone who works for justice, freedom, and peace.

We thank you for the wonder and beauty of the world and we pray for an increase in our awareness and acceptance of our shared responsibility to care for your creation.[17]

THE POWER OF BELONGING

In a gripping testimony to the power of belonging, a Puerto Rican woman tells of returning to her native land after having lived for years and been educated in the United States. A nagging shoulder pain had been her cue to go home again, following her physical therapist's perception that "[your] pain is associated with feeling like you have no community."[18] Christine Nieves Rodriguez arrived in the mountain town of Mariana exactly nine months before Hurricane Maria hit on September 19, 2017. She tells a story of terror, displacement, confusion, and the death of almost three thousand people. Like the biblical slave woman Hagar driven into the wilderness by Sarah and Abraham, however, Nieves Rodriguez also tells a story of resilience, hope, and survival:

> [When] everything collapsed, it was crystal clear what was the real infrastructure and what was an insubstantial façade. When everything collapses, the life-saving infrastructure is our knowledge of one another's skills, our trust of one another, our capacity to forgive our neighbor, work with our neighbor, and mobilize. When everything collapses—no ATMs, no water, no food, no diesel, no communication—you have to tap into a pre-existing system of trust and dignity and reciprocity.[19]

It's all about belonging, our power-with one another, our call to "tap into a pre-existing system of trust and dignity and reciprocity." Christine Nieves Rodriguez, Alison Cheek, Larry Rasmussen, Joanna Macy, Thich Nhat Hanh are asking the same question: How do we find this sense of belonging, and share it as the sacred ground of our being, as if our lives and the well-being of our planet depend upon it, because they do?

DISCUSSION QUESTIONS

1. Do you think that we as a species are lost? Does it matter to those of us who inhabit the earth today whether or not humanity is bound for extinction due to our indifference to the health of our planet-home and our sibling creatures? Don't stop with yes or no answers. Talk about how your faith informs your responses.
2. Christian theologian Sallie McFague notes that while we humans need the earth, the earth does not need us. Respond. How does this make you feel—angry, accepting, relieved, sad, surprised?
3. To what extent are we "utilitarian" in relation to creation and earth creatures—that is, interested primarily in how we can "use" creation and other earth creatures? Give examples from your own lives. Can you also give some examples of where, when, and how you, or others, have regarded the earth and other creatures with mutual love and respect rather than primarily for their usefulness?
4. How can our congregation (or community) make the moral shifts noted by Larry Rasmussen, and how can we do so as individuals? Are there other shifts we might make to more fully belong?
5. Share whatever you can about your experiences of the Sophia/Wisdom of God and what you believe she can teach the church.
6. From what resources do you draw hope and resilience?
7. How do we find a sense of belonging, and share it as the sacred ground of our being, as if our lives and the well-being of our planet depend upon it? How might the churches deepen our senses of belonging?

Chapter 18

The Seventh Call

Breaking the Spiral of Violence

The goal of this chapter is to expose roots of the violence that pervades America as a grave moral challenge, and to urge specific actions toward breaking the spirals of violence in our common life, not only as Americans but also as global citizens.

> [God] shall judge between the nations, and shall arbitrate for many peoples; they shall beat their swords into plowshares, and their spears into pruning hooks; nation shall not lift up sword against nation, neither shall they learn war any more. (Isa. 2:4 NRSV)

> "Blessed are the peacemakers, for they will be called children of God." (Matt. 5:9 NRSV)

Both Jesus and the Hebrew prophets were strong advocates of peacemaking and nonviolence as foundational to our belonging. Why then is Christian history littered with violence near and far, in the home as well as between tribes, religions, cultures, and nations? Can we Christians understand and respond constructively to what Brazilian bishop and nonviolent activist Helder Camara (1909–1999) named "the spiral of violence"[1]—violence begetting violence leading to more violence, round and round we go, spiraling ruthlessly and relentlessly through Christian and American history as well as the history of civilization itself?

The seventh deadly sin of violence brings us full circle back to the beginning of our study of the sins. Here, as also in relation to the other deadly sins, the primary problem is listed first among the sins: the lust for power-over, control, or domination of a weaker being. Without this motive—to secure power-over another being, tribe, nation, species—violence would not be eliminated entirely of course, but it would be reduced to spontaneous outbursts by humans and other creatures that are angry; frightened; or seeking justice, food, shelter, or other life-sustaining resources. In such contexts, violence and the harm inflicted by humans upon others or on themselves can sometimes be mitigated through skillful interventions by personal or professional helpers. Through legal, spiritual, psychological, or social mediation, humans—unlike other creatures, as far as we can tell—can be encouraged to generate conditions for greater mutuality and possibilities of forgiveness rather than simply fueling our lust for vengeance and retribution, thereby igniting an unending spiral of violence. From a moral perspective, our ability to break the spiral of violence may be the primary difference between humans and other animals.

HOW IS GOD INVOLVED?[2]

Christians ought not envision an entirely violence-free society in America or anywhere else on the planet. As a matter of fact, neither testament in the Christian Bible assumes that a world without violence is within human reach. Hear Paul's admonition to the Romans: "If it is possible, so far as it depends on you, live peaceably with all" (Rom. 12:18 NRSV). This is sage counsel to the young church as well as to our churches today. This is wise counsel because we cannot eliminate all violence—human beings' violent, hurtful treatment of humans, other animals, and the earth;[3] or the earth's and other earth creatures' harsh, destructive treatment of humans and other creatures.

Animals, Creation, and "Natural" Evil

The latter—destructive actions by nature and animals—we usually do not regard as "violence," since violence is a moral category denoting immorality or evil, and most Christians do not attribute moral agency to the earth or nonhuman animals, although certain animals act in ways human beings view as loving, moral, or good.[4] However we may understand nature's destructive behavior in scorching forests, drowning villages, and blowing apart human and creature habitats, the fact is that earth, wind, water, and fire inflict enormous damage and suffering on humans and other animals. And it is beyond dispute that nonhuman animals often act violently toward each other as well as humans.

The violence or destructive activity that is not necessarily brought on by human activity is what Christian moral philosophers sometimes call "natural" evil as distinct from "social" or "moral" evil.[5] We witness savagery between animals that are hungry, frightened, territorial, or perhaps motivated by some of the other emotions they share with humans, such as anger and envy. There is no honest way to conclude that nature isn't violent. The best we can do, if our theologies allow, is blame it on God, who made the lions and the lambs, the foxes and the chickens, and who stirs the wind and troubles the waters.

Humans and "Moral" Evil

It is also God who made human beings and, however we may understand our freedom of will, do we humans not also, in some sense, act as agents of God, act with God's permission in history? If, as Dorothee Soelle insisted, our hands are God's hands in the world, where do we draw the moral lines between our reflecting divine goodness, including peacekeeping—and the more mysterious dimensions of divinity, God's involvement in our violence against animals, earth, and even perhaps other humans? Does God allow us to hunt and kill animals for food, and then encourage us to bless our meals? Does God permit us to slaughter other tribes for land that we need for our own families and then expect us to thank God for blessing our land? Are we acting on behalf of God's righteousness when we violently punish men, women, and children because they have done wrong to us or to our tribes, our races, our nation, our religion, and our God?

Where do we draw the line between other animals' violent behavior against each other and us—and our own violence, so often waged, we believe, in God's name? How do we decide what violence—ours and that of other creatures—is justified by God and what violence is not? How do we determine morally what is a just, defensive war, for example, and what is not? How do we understand the difference between offensive wars waged basically against innocent people who are simply defending themselves against our aggression—and those enemies whose violence against innocent people, us or others, we perceive to be ungodly or evil? These are huge moral questions with which Christians should be wrestling in the name of Jesus whenever we are working and praying together for justice and peace. What kind of God is it that permits, and even encourages, violence done by human and other creatures? How can such a God possibly be love?

Is All Violence Evil or Embedded in the Mystery of God?

Could it be that all violence is evil, all violence ungodly, regardless of who does it to whom, and regardless of whether it is done by humans or other animals? Perhaps, if we can dare suggest such a thing, violence is a tragic flaw in creation, a problem embedded in the mystery of the One who we believe is love.

When I imagine that God somehow authorizes and blesses violence and suffering, I hold an indictment of such a God in my soul, which I make with a clenched fist before the Wisdom/Sophia of God. I am angry at the possibility of such a God, Goddess, Source, Higher Power, Spirit of Life—and Spirit of Death. I slam my fist against the air, as I ask, Why? Why animal suffering? Why earth plundering? Why human violence against humans, earth, animals, and God?

Like all Christians and other believers in a monotheistic deity over the millennia, we are left with the question—why? We are left in anger and confusion as we try to untangle the mystery of the violence that shrouds our lives and our world, creating suffering that is somehow connected to God. Much of Holocaust survivor Elie Wiesel's life was spent interrogating God about what, where, or who God was as Jews were loaded into boxcars and hauled off to death camps to be gassed. Wiesel finally concluded that God was both in the victims and in their liberators.[6] God suffers, and God comes bearing freedom, liberation, and healing. Still, there is no adequate answer for Wiesel, or for me, about how to understand the relationship between a God of love and the presence of evil in history. I personally have been wrestling with this mystery ever since wrestling with it in my early book (and doctoral thesis), The Redemption of God, in which I suggest that love—the mutual relation at the heart of the Sacred—is indeed the greater power, the stronger force, always and eternally.

BLESSED ARE THE PEACEMAKERS

I believe that we too, like Wiesel, must be specific and clear about what is good and what is evil, if we dare to hope that, as human beings, we might diminish the violence in our life together. Our only hope, if we wish to break the spirals of violence, is to understand that human violence is a deadly sin, a uniquely human phenomenon, and a major moral problem for humans and all creation. God is love. Goodness. Mutuality. Healing. Liberation. There is nothing godly in human violence against humans, earth, or animals. Here then is the heart of our work as peacemakers: *earth and animals can be violent and terribly destructive, but humans are the only participants on the planet who can choose to break spirals of violence—and therein is our hope.*

If Christians do not condemn all human violence against other humans, the earth, and other earth creatures, where do we draw the line? If we are not peacemakers, as Jesus calls us to be in the Sermon on the Mount, how do we describe ourselves in relation to the violence around us and to the possibility of nonviolent responses to it? Do we envision ourselves as peacemakers who just cannot quite bring ourselves to make peace with our foes, or do we struggle to cultivate the courage to take Jesus at his word—and redouble our efforts to love our enemies? Where do Christians draw the line between resigning ourselves to the violence that permeates our life together and stepping up to the moral work of peacemaking?

We have teachers who span the ages—Isaiah, Jesus, Saints Francis and Clare, Abraham Lincoln, Gandhi, Martin Luther King, Albert Schweitzer, Thomas Merton, Dorothee Soelle, the Berrigan brothers, and so forth. Such mentors and so many more can help us if we are seriously interested in breaking the spirals of violence whenever we sense in our souls that we all belong. Whenever our consciences long for nonviolent alternatives, we can figure out how to work toward peace with one another. We can help each other cultivate that elusive peace that "surpasses all understanding" (Phil. 4:7 NRSV). We can take to heart the Beatitudes and do our best to embody them in our lives, not perfectly but as inspirations and guideposts going forward. We can be encouraged by scores of wise modern and contemporary men and women in the moral work of peacemaking.

Martin Luther King Jr. should be canonized as an American Christian saint for his unparalleled leadership in establishing the power of nonviolent action, including nonviolent civil disobedience, as a reliable strategy for social change. There were many others also who taught and practiced nonviolent civil disobedience in the American civil rights movement of the 1950s and 1960s; the anti–Vietnam War movement of the 1960s and 1970s; and the peace movements of the late twentieth and early twenty-first centuries.[7]

It is essential, if Christians seriously want to follow Jesus, that we commit ourselves to making peace and learn how to do it. As we move more deeply into the twenty-first century, we can discover together, as Christians, how to make peace. We can do so by wrestling together with some of the most critical questions of our time. These are questions that American churches should put at the center of sermons, liturgies, and education as well as social mission and action.

What will we do if America moves toward making war, yet again? Consider the possibility that our nation could slip into war with Iran, China, or possibly North Korea. Imagine that America might stealthily attack a small nation like Nicaragua (again), our southern neighbor currently under the oppressive rule of a ruthless autocrat who needs to be deposed by his own people? Or what if our country were to decide to return to Afghanistan or Iraq, ostensibly to continue fighting Islamic terrorists? In such situations as these, what should the Christian churches do and say? What should we do and say, as Christians? Can we imagine Christianity as a significant force for peacemaking in America? How might this happen? What are our roles? We do not have to be total pacifists (I, for one, am not) to want our country to learn how to make peace rather than spend so much of its time, energy, and money preparing for the next war. How can peacemaking be cultivated among us as a foundation of Christian faith and morality, especially young people, in parishes? (The above paragraph was written before Russia's war against Ukraine. Still, the questions for Christians are what should our churches be teaching and preaching in relation to peacemaking and war?)

How can we, in good faith, tolerate the proliferation of guns and gun violence in America? Put simply, we cannot. What then do Christians do about the gun culture that is growing exponentially all around us? Along with capitalist spirituality, the Second Amendment has become another golden calf that is perched in the middle of America, mocking victims of gun violence, daring Americans, including Christians, to topple it. What is God requiring Christians to do about gun violence in America? I assume that some readers of this book own guns and support responsible gun ownership. Though I don't own a gun or want one, I support others owning guns—with limits. I say this to acknowledge that, as with the issue of abortion, the matter of guns is contentious among Christians. We do not all agree, to say the least. But gun violence at rising epidemic levels in America poses a major health crisis and moral conundrum for American Christians whose deepest moral commitment, if we love Jesus, is to love our neighbor.

How can Christian churches in America wrestle honestly, respectfully, and intelligently with the deep, painful tensions between ownership and control of guns in America? It would be such a gift to American culture and politics—and much more to the lives of ordinary Americans, including many Christians—if our churches would take up this issue and study it as a significant moral problem that Americans need to solve through a combination of compassion and compromise.

What about the role of the police and the U.S. military in American society and around the world? Can we not build accountability into these institutions? Can we not respect and support our state and local police as well as the United States military without giving these public servants permission to use their own judgment with little accountability to anyone except others within the same organization? How do Christians hold *anyone* accountable for what they do—grocers, nurses, lawyers, doctors, teachers, cooks, auto mechanics, and police officers? Our churches should demand that law enforcement and military officers work on behalf of the common good. We should insist that the police and soldiers who do not enforce liberty and justice for all have no place in law enforcement or the U.S. military. What should our churches teach about the tensions between (predominantly white) law enforcement establishments and the Black American community? What are some strong, justice-loving, nonviolent responses that white American Christians can make to the slaughter of young men and women of color at the hands of the police?

Will American Christians continue to tolerate a for-profit criminal justice system? Our prison system has been designed to turn a profit as it punishes, breaks, and eventually destroys young Black and brown men and others deemed undesirable or expendable by wealthy white Christian men and their allies. The evil of this system is in its blatant placement of financial gain for stockholders over the lives and dignity of everyone in the penal system, especially the prisoners. American prisons have become violent, sadistic bastions of white supremacy and capitalism run amok. Christian ministers and congregations should seriously consider making criminal justice a priority issue for their educational and social justice missions. We should not tolerate what is intolerable. If we ask what Jesus would do, we can imagine Jesus condemning America's criminal justice system from top to bottom. The Supreme Court currently seems hostile to the well-being of prisoners and their rights to fair trials and to punishments that fit the crimes; and America has by far the highest incarceration rate of any nation in the world (639 per 100,000 in May 2021).[8] These are just examples of the deplorable state of our criminal justice system. It is time for our churches to speak and act.

Breaking the Spiral of Violence

This book is ending as it began—as a response to the violent insurrection at the U.S. Capitol on January 6, 2021. Having witnessed neo-Nazis, Proud Boys, and other hate groups lie, destroy property, and torture others in the name of Jesus, many of us knew deep in our bones that this moment was not an anomaly in U.S. history. We realized that its violence has roots deep in our national story. We also knew that the groups attacking the Capitol, like hate groups before them, were relying on most Americans and most Christians to provide them with legitimacy either by trivializing or shunning any connection with and responsibility for the insurrection. Furthermore, as research in the months after the attack has shown, many of the insurrectionists were not members of hate groups, but rather were average, mainstream American citizens. The January 6 riot demonstrated that violence is perfectly acceptable to white American Christians as a means of having their way, holding on to their power. This has proven itself to be not a fringe notion but an assumption as American as pumpkin pie. It also helps us understand why extremist ideologies have moved increasingly into the mainstream and how the Republican Party can get away with dismissing the insurrection as an unseemly public relations fiasco that ought to be talked about as little as possible to minimize its political impact on future elections.

An understandable response to the violence at the Capitol and the refusal by one of our two major political parties to take it seriously would be for large numbers of Americans to continue the spiral of violence. Who could condemn a violent response by women? Or by African Americans and other people of color? Or by gay, lesbian, and trans Americans; refugee and immigrant communities; people suffering from poverty, mental illness, and other social and personal disabilities; as well as by those white American men who stand with those on the margins? It is not hard to understand how violence begets violence in American and Christian history.

But any violence against the Republican Party and its white conservative, gun-loving, Christian male leadership would not only be foolish and stupid, it would be the wrong thing to do. If Americans of color and liberal white allies, or American women and other marginalized people were to smash down the doors of Republican-dominated statehouses and beat GOP legislators with American flags and the cross of Jesus, the rioters would be shot on the spot or arrested and would likely "disappear" into some of our country's insidious for-profit prisons. No slaps on the wrist, house confinement, or suspended sentences for such criminals. Waging violence against white America Christian men with power would be foolish, even suicidal.

More importantly from a moral perspective, for those most harmed by white supremacy, misogyny, and other deadly sins, to wage violence against conservative white American Christians would be the wrong thing to do morally and spiritually as well as socially, psychologically, and politically. It would be wrong because, until they are broken, spirals of violence only intensify. They generate hatred and revenge that burrow ever more deeply into the collective mindsets of those who have been violated and their descendants. As the prophet Jeremiah noted, "The parents have eaten sour grapes, and the children's teeth are set on edge" (Jer. 31:29 NRSV). The violence spirals, never ending.

This is why such contemporary leaders as Sikh spiritual teacher Valerie Kaur (b. 1981), young Pakistani activist Malala Yousafzai (b. 1997), and American civil rights icon John Lewis (1940–2020) have said no to violence as an effective or long-lasting response to the brutal violence they themselves have experienced. Such spiritual teachers have known that stronger and more durable will always be the grassroots movements in nonviolent civil disobedience. One such movement is being led today by William Barber (b. 1963) and Liz Theoharis (b. 1976) of the Poor People's Campaign's National Call for a Moral Revival.[9] There are hundreds of other international-, national-, state-, and local-level associations and movements devoted to nonviolent direct action in countless realms of justice making. Some of the better known are listed in the resources at the back of this book.

Grassroots education and activism are where Christians—wherever we are in America—need to provide leadership, attend workshops, plan worship, write letters, make phone calls, put together social media presentations, make art and play music, and put boots on the ground to move the struggle for justice-love as a collective, nonviolent effort to "let justice roll down like waters, and righteousness like an ever-flowing stream" (Amos 5:24 NRSV).

We also need to urge our churches collectively to take a stand on behalf of cultivating nonviolence and peacemaking as new American ways. American churches have major roles to play. Larger and smaller churches. More liberal and more conservative churches. Of course our churches won't have the same priorities, we won't adopt the same strategies, and we won't understand our mission in the same ways theologically. We probably won't belong to the same political parties—although we might often support the same candidates, depending upon the choices we have. We should all rally around candidates and leaders who share America's foundational commitments to generating greater liberty and justice for all of us, not some of us. This being our moral vision as Christians, we share spiritual calls and moral responsibilities to lift up and support the basic rights that belong to all Americans, which include absolute rights to food security, safe and clean housing, universal health care, and good public schools.

At this time in America, Christian churches should support in every possible way the irrepressible movement for voting rights for all Americans and women's rights to reproductive health, including access to safe, legal abortions. Christians do not agree across the board that abortion can be a moral choice, but we must find ways to compromise—helping make abortion a rare but safe and legal option that reflects the full personhood and moral capacity of women to make good choices.

The churches also must increasingly be among the leading activists for the well-being of the earth and its many varied creatures. This is likely to be the realm in which children will lead the way. This would not surprise Jesus. For the first time in American history, Christian churches must be among the loudest, clearest, and most unequivocal advocates of the earth's future, its health and sustainability, and its many varied creatures that need our protection and solidarity. Here too it may be the children who will teach us, lead us, and bless us most tenderly. We can hope, and pray.

It's imperative that we try to hold our concerns about violence in a global perspective. This could, and should, be of primary interest to our religious leaders, from Christian and other traditions. The violence in America both spawns and is spawned by violence throughout the world. It's all connected:

Violence against women in Iran and China and Britain and Peru is permitted by similar attitudes toward women as property and possessions, regardless of which if any religious traditions support these attitudes. Similarly, violence against gay, lesbian, bisexual, and trans people anywhere in the world has a common root in the deadly link between misogyny (gender-based hatred of women) and homo/transphobia (gender-based fear of diverse sexual identities and activities).

White supremacist violence, other manifestations of "colorist" violence, religious violence such as anti-Semitism and Islamophobia, and tribal violence of many kinds in Europe, the Americas, and other formerly European colonies in Africa, Asia, and the South Pacific has been generated historically by similar customs and laws based on attitudes and superstitions of anti-Blackness, antidarkness, and an obsession with purity over and against pollution and filth.

The glorification of weapons—guns, bombs, and other tools of terror—is a global phenomenon steeped undoubtedly in human beings' fears of real and imagined dangers and threats. To the extent that Christians and people of other faith and moral traditions can help minimize the imagined dangers and threats, the stronger our networks of nations, religions, and cultures can become, and the more hospitable our world can be for all people.

Can we learn from, rather than fight against, different customs and religions? Can we welcome rather than ban foreign people and languages? Can we simply wonder about, rather than obliterate, oddities that we don't understand, or maybe even like, but which do no harm to us or others? Is it possible that drones and other products of human inventiveness can become instruments more of scientific achievement, educational advancement, and recreation than of making war and mounting violence against our enemies?

Instead of viewing socialism as a threat to capitalism, could we imagine presenting it as a humanizing, earth-friendly companion piece to what is best about capitalism: the celebration of the visions and skills of individuals and small units (families, businesses) that are shaped to take care of themselves— but also, in a thriving spirit of neighbor-love, to help take care of the whole community of humans and earth? Our connectedness, our wholeness as an earth community, and as nations, is what is best about socialism. Could such a moral vision of mixed capitalist-socialist motives be envisioned by national and religious leaders as foundational to a world at peace?

Such dreaming is usually bracketed as utopic—nowhere yet—in the real world, the stuff of workshops in art and music; creative writing, novels, and drama; self-actualization efforts and spiritual yearning for those seeking a better world and clearer senses of themselves. But I became interested in religion, and later in becoming a Christian minister, many decades ago when a utopic spark got lit in me by the civil rights movement. I ask you and myself now: Were Rosa Parks and Fanny Lou Hamer utopic? Martin Luther King and Malcolm X—were they also utopic? Were Viola Liuzzo, James Reeb, and Jonathan Daniels utopic? James Cheney, Andrew Goodman, Michael Schwerner? Were Marian Anderson, Paul Robeson, Louis Armstrong, Woody Guthrie, Ronnie Gilbert, Pete Seeger utopic? And John Lewis—were he and the other young men and women utopic as they crossed the Edmund Pettus Bridge in Selma, Alabama, only to be met by clubs and hate-filled violence?

Yes indeed. Any significant social transformation in America or elsewhere in the world will always rely on prophetic eyes and courageous voices to lead us toward "nowhere yet"—and, in crossing those bridges, to join in bending the moral arc of the universe.

"YOU GIVE ME HOPE THAT THE TRUTH WILL GO ON"

In the spring of 2002, as my colleague and sister priest Sue Hiatt lay weak and dying from anaplastic thyroid cancer in a Watertown, Massachusetts, hospice, she asked if I would bring Archbishop Desmond Tutu to see her. Bishop Tutu was at the time a visiting scholar at the Episcopal Divinity School (EDS) in Cambridge, Massachusetts, where Sue and I had been on the faculty since 1975. The bishop was glad to join me at Sue's bedside, and I was honored to step into the background and simply observe what happened between these two spiritual leaders. Sue showed Desmond the "Desmond Tutu doll" that a South African student at EDS had brought her a year earlier, and he laughed. She then asked him to sing for her. At first he demurred, saying that he couldn't sing, but then, glancing around at me for support, he said he would sing if I would join him. I nodded, and he burst into a well-known version of the "Gloria Patri," which he sang with gusto and I did the same, albeit without much conviction, since both Sue and I had been working for three decades to clean up the sexist language of the liturgy. As the bishop and I sang, Sue giggled and I followed suit. I think the bishop did not notice.

The two of them then had a brief conversation about South Africa's Truth and Reconciliation Commission (TRC), which Tutu had chaired in its early years (starting in 1996) and still did at the time of his bedside meeting with Sue Hiatt. The TRC has been described as having "inspired other similar efforts around the world, even as the country has learned over time that working through a complicated past takes time, and is still taking time. It opened up a way to talk about the individual and systemic wrongs committed under 43 years of apartheid."[10]

Speaking to Sue and me, Desmond Tutu was emphatic that our only hope as a human race is to break the spiral of violence that is entirely capable of wiping out humanity and much of creation. Only insofar as those who've done violence can confess what they have done, he insisted, and only insofar as victims of the violence can forgive those who have hurt them, or worse, have killed their families and friends, only if both of these conditions are met can the spiral of violence be broken. Confession and repentance empower forgiveness.

In the wake of violence, there can be no reconciliation and very little chance of building a future together, unless there is forgiveness, and there can be no forgiveness that is deep and lasting unless there has been repentance and honest confession. This, Tutu had explained to one of my seminary classes several weeks earlier, was the theology behind the Truth and Reconciliation Commission—which, he noted, seemed to be functioning fairly well, although it was still at work and would be for another year or two. He drew this theological road map to reconciliation again, as he stood at the bedside of Sue Hiatt.

Sue and I listened spellbound to this earnest, faithful Christian leader. As he said his goodbyes to Sue and turned to leave, she asked for his blessing, which he gave—and then he asked for her blessing, which she gave. As Desmond Tutu walked toward the door, Sue thanked him for coming and said to him, "You give me hope that the truth will go on." Desmond Tutu and I drove home in silence and sadness and hope. We hugged as we parted in the seminary parking lot.

Discussion Questions

1. Spirals of violence intensify. They generate hatred and revenge that burrow ever more deeply into the collective mindsets of those who have been violated and their descendants. As the prophet Jeremiah noted, "The parents have eaten sour grapes, and the children's teeth are set on edge" (Jer. 31:29 NRSV). The violence spirals; it never ends. Give examples of spirals of violence that you have witnessed or heard about. Discuss Jeremiah 31:29. What does it mean to you?

2. Humans are the only participants on the planet who can choose to break spirals of violence—and therein is our hope. Discuss how you understand these affirmations.

3. Select and discuss one or more of the "questions that American churches should put at the center of sermons, liturgies, and education as well as social mission and action," listed in this chapter.

4. What do you know about South Africa's Truth and Reconciliation Commission (TRC), which Desmond Tutu had chaired in its early years, starting in 1996? The TRC opened up a way to talk about the individual and systemic wrongs committed under forty-three years of apartheid. The TRC established an essential connection between repentance/conversion and forgiveness in South Africa's reconciliation process. What might Americans learn from this in relation to our own needs for racial healing and reconciliation?

5. Discuss the bedside meeting between Sue Hiatt and Desmond Tutu. What stands out for you? What gives you hope that the truth will go on?

Notes

CHAPTER 1

1. Jeffrey Goldberg, "Mass Delusion in America," *Atlantic*, January 6, 2021, https://www.theatlantic.com/politics/archive/2021/01/among-insurrectionists/617580/.

2. NPR Staff, "The Capitol Siege: The Cases behind the Biggest Criminal Investigation in U.S. History," NPR, updated October 8, 2021, https://www.npr.org/2021/02/09/965472049/the-capitol-siege-the-arrested-and-their-stories.

3. Anthea Butler, *White Evangelical Racism: The Politics of Morality in America* (Chapel Hill: University of North Carolina Press, 2021), 10.

4. Adrienne Rich, *On Lies, Secrets, and Silences* (New York: Norton, 1979).

5. I identify today as a "Universalist Christian." My spirituality transcends any one religious tradition, but Christianity is my tradition and the Jesus story, buoyed by the most justice-loving teachings and practices of Christians over time, continues to feed my soul. As for all the hate done in Jesus's name, all the Christian garbage, it belongs in history's trash bins.

6. Andrew L. Whitehead and Samuel Perry, *Taking America Back for God: Christian Nationalism in the United States* (New York: Oxford University Press: 2020), 10.

7. Most of what I've written in my life has been steeped in these same themes: protests against male superiority, white supremacy, class elitism, economic exploitation, human domination of earth, and the nativist assumptions that America is always best, always right, and always worthy of uncritical affirmation. Together these themes constitute the basis of white Christian nationalism—what I am calling here "the deadly sins" of white Christian nationalism, themes that have sparked and spun their way through all of my books, essays, and sermons, starting with *A Priest Forever* (1976) about the "irregular" ordination of Episcopal women priests in 1974, right up to my most recent book, *Tears of Christepona* (2021), an imagined conversation between myself and my better angels on topics ranging from grief at the death of my horse Feather to the growth of authoritarianism in America and the culture of lies being built like a tall, thick wall around our national consciousness.

8. In conversation, 1981.

9. See, for example, *The Jewish Americans*, 2008, a documentary miniseries written and directed by David Grubin, 2008, PBS, www.pbs.org.

10. Two of the best explorations of Christian anti-Semitism by Christian theologians are Rosemary Radford Ruether, *Faith and Fratricide: Theological Roots of Anti-Semitism* (Eugene, OR: Wipf & Stock,1995), and James Carroll, *Constantine's Sword: The Church and the Jews* (New York: Mariner, 2002).

11. Jonathan Greenblatt, *It Could Happen Here: Why America Is Tipping from Hate to the Unthinkable—and How We Can Stop It* (New York: Mariner, 2022).

12. Isabel Fattal, "A Brief History of Anti-Semitic Violence in America," *Atlantic*, October 28, 2018, https://www.theatlantic.com/politics/archive/2018/10/brief-history -anti-semitic-violence-america/574228/.

13. Michiko Kakutani, "Examining T. S. Eliot and Anti-Semitism: How Bad Was It?," *New York Times*, August 22, 1989, https://www.nytimes.com/1989/08/22/books/ critic-s-notebook-examining-t-s-eliot-and-anti-semitism-how-bad-was-it.html.

14. Joe Killian, "GOP Pols Robinson, Walker, Cawthorn Align Themselves with Movement Seeking to End Separation of Church and State," North Carolina Policy Watch, October 7, 2021, www.ncpolicywatch.com/2021/10/07/gop-pols-robinson -walker-cawthorn-align-themselves-with-movement-seeking-to-end-separation-of -church-and-state.

15. Elie Wiesel, *The Town beyond the Wall* (New York: Schocken, 1995/1962).

16. Amanecida Collective, *Revolutionary Forgiveness: Feminist Reflections on Nicaragua*, ed. Carter Heyward and Anne B. Gilson, with foreword by Dorothee Soelle (Eugene, OR: Wipf & Stock, 2021 [Maryknoll, NY: Orbis, 1986]).

17. Mud Flower Collective, *God's Fierce Whimsy*(New York: Pilgrim, 1985).

18. Carter Heyward, *When Boundaries Betray Us* (Cleveland: Pilgrim, 1999/1993).

CHAPTER 2

1. Anthea Butler, *White Evangelical Racism: The Politics of Morality in America* (Chapel Hill: University of North Carolina Press, 2021), 73.

2. The 1619 Project was a "long-form journalism" piece produced by the *New York Times* as its magazine on August 17, 2019. It was written by a number of authors on different themes. Their single purpose was to reframe American history by showing how the institution of slavery has influenced and shaped the nation's economic, cultural, religious, and other realms of development ever since the arrival of the first slaves in 1619.

3. "When Jefferson wrote 'all men are created equal' in the preamble to the Declaration, he was not talking about individual equality. What he really meant was that the American colonists, *as a people*, had the same rights of self-government as other peoples, and hence could declare independence, create new governments, and assume their 'separate and equal station' among other nations. But after the Revolution succeeded, Americans began reading that famous phrase another way. It now became a statement of individual equality that everyone and every member of a deprived group could claim for himself or herself. With each passing generation, our notion

of who that statement covers has expanded. It is that promise of equality that has always defined our constitutional creed." Stanford historian Jack Rakove, interview by Melissa De Witte, Stanford News Service, July 1, 2020, https://news.stanford.edu /2020/07/01/meaning-declaration-independence-changed-time/.

4. The First Amendment to the U.S. Constitution has two clauses related to religion: one preventing the government from establishing any national religion ("the establishment clause") and the other protecting people's ability to freely exercise religious beliefs (the "free exercise clause."); see www.constitutioncenter.org/firstamendment.

5. David Goldfield, "Evangelical Religion and Evangelical Democracy in the Nineteenth Century," *Brewminate* (blog), March 3, 2019,https://brewminate.com/ evangelical-religion-and-evangelical-democracy-in-the-19th-century/.

6. Kristin Kobes Du Mez, *Jesus and John Wayne: How White Evangelicals Corrupted a Faith and Fractured a Nation* (New York: Liveright, 2020), 17–19.

7. Walter Rauschenbusch, *A Theology for the Social Gospel* (New York: Cross-Reach, 2017/1917).

8. Kevin M. Kruse, "How Corporate America Invented Christian America," *POLITICO*, April 16, 2015.

9. Kruse, "How Corporate America Invented Christian America."

10. Gary North, "The Intellectual Schizophrenia of the New Christian Right," in *The Failure of the American Baptist Culture*, Christianity and Civilization, ed. James B. Jordan (Tyler, TX: Geneva Divinity School, 1982), 25.

11. Anne Bathurst Gilson, *The Battle for America's Families: A Feminist Response to the Religious Right* (Cleveland, OH: Pilgrim, 1999).

12. J. Edgar Hoover and his longtime companion Clyde Tolson were a well-known couple in underground "lavender" circles in Washington, DC. The same was true of the fiercely antihomosexual, anti-Communist, and anti–civil rights lawyer Roy Cohn, counsel to white Christian nationalists from Hoover himself to the younger tycoon Donald Trump. The homosexuality and hypocrisy of J. Edgar Hoover and Roy Cohn were well known to the gay and lesbian community in the late 1960s and 1970s as increasingly numbers of us were "coming out."

13. *Muhammad Ali*, four-part documentary written and directed by Ken Burns, Sarah Burns, and David McMahon, PBS, September 2021, www.pbs.com/muhammadali/ sept19-222020.

14. See Guylin Cummins, "The Fairness Doctrine Redux?," *Communications Lawyer* 26, no. 2 (March 2009), https://www.americanbar.org/content/dam/aba/publishing /communications_lawyer/mar09/chair.authcheckdam.pdf.

15. "Post September 11 Attitudes," Pew Research Center, December 6, 2001, https: //www.pewresearch.org/politics/2001/12/06/post-september-11-attitudes/.

16. Bonnie Kristian, "Why 9/11 Brought Neither Unity nor Revival," *Christianity Today*, September 10, 2021, https://www.christianitytoday.com/ct/2021/september -web-only/september-11-why-911-brought-neither-unity-nor-revival.html.

17. Laurie Goodstein, "After the Attacks: Finding Fault; Falwell's Finger Pointing Inappropriate, Bush Says," *New York Times*, September 19, 2001, 11, 31.

18. www.splc.org/terrorism/reports/

19. Martin Luther King Jr., "I Have a Dream," August 28, 1963, speech found at https://www.americanrhetoric.com/speeches/mlkihaveadream.htm.

20. January 21, 2020, marked a decade since the *Supreme Court's ruling in Citizens United v. Federal Election Commission,* a controversial decision that reversed century-old campaign finance restrictions and enabled corporations and other outside groups to spend unlimited funds on elections. While wealthy donors, corporations, and special interest groups have long had an outsized influence in elections, that sway has dramatically expanded since the *Citizens United* decision, with negative repercussions for American democracy and the fight against political corruption. www.brennancenter.org/

21. This part of Ginsburg's dissent was cited in both *Mother Jones* and the *New York Times* on June 30, 2014.

22. Sonia Sotomayor, "Sotomayor's Defiant Dissent," *The Nation,* September 3, 2021, https://www.thenation.com/article/society/sotomayor-abortion-dissent/.

23. Megan Briggs, "Beth Moore: Trumpism is the Most 'Seductive & Dangerous' Thing I've Seen," December 14, 2020, ChurchLeaders.com, https://churchleaders .com/news/386834-beth-moore-trumpism-is-the-most-seductive-dangerous-thing-ive -seen.html.

CHAPTER 3

1. Anne B. Gilson, *The Battle for America's Families* (Cleveland, OH: Pilgrim, 1999) is a useful introduction to many of the conservative evangelical Christian groups operating in late twentieth-century American politics. Susan Lefler has researched some of the more recent groups to have emerged, including groups like Pink Incense, Proud Boys, 3 Percenters, and other Christian groups that were involved in, or supported, the January 6, 2021, insurrection.

2. From the earliest days, most Christians understood "sin" as a collective problem. The Roman and later Orthodox Churches have tried, with varying degree of success, to balance the collective root of "original sin" with the individual's need for salvation. From the Protestant Reformation in the sixteenth century onward, Protestant Christianity has placed salvation of each human soul almost entirely in the context of the individual person's spirituality.

3. What have come down to us as the seven deadly sins apparently took root first among the Desert Fathers, a monastic group in northern Africa, in about the fourth century CE. In the sixth century, Pope Gregory I adopted and formalized seven deadly sins as pride, greed, wrath, envy, lust, gluttony, and sloth. This particular list of sins has been passed down through the ages among Christians of most traditions, including Roman Catholics, Eastern Orthodox, and Protestants.

4. Theologian Denise Ackerman, speaking with me in the early 1990s about her life as a white South African, said that apartheid was in the air she woke up breathing every day; there was no escaping its toxic effects regardless of who, or what color, you were. This is true in America as well.

5. I discuss sin and evil at length in *The Redemption of God: A Theology of Mutual Relation* (Eugene, OR: Wipf & Stock, 2010/1982). In fact, my particular interest in sin and evil led me to focus my graduate research on it. *The Redemption of God* was my doctoral dissertation.

CHAPTER 4

1. Heather Cox Richardson, "January 19, 2022," *Letters to an American* (blog), January 19, 2022, https://heathercoxrichardson.substack.com/p/january-19-2021-a53?s=r.

2. In his Farewell Address to the nation on January 17, 1961, President Eisenhower warned, "In the councils of government, we must guard against the acquisition of unwarranted influence, whether sought or unsought, by the military-industrial complex. The potential for the disastrous rise of misplaced power exists and will persist." https://www.npr.org/2011/01/17/132942244/ikes-warning-of-military-expansion-50-years-later.

3. See my *Redemption of God* (Eugene, OR: Wipf & Stock, 2010/1982). I would argue that the doctrine of divine omnipotence itself reflects a mistaken understanding of God, a key spiritual and moral question that will be addressed in part 3. I submit that if God is truly loving—the dynamic root of all justice making, mutuality, and compassion in our life together—God does not exert power-over us but rather is the sacred energy by which we generate and experience power-with one another. I believe that is how God loves us and that is how we love God and one another.

4. Sam Gillette and Kim Hubbard, "Margaret Atwood on Why *The Handmaid's Tale* Resonates in the Trump Era: It's 'No Longer a Fantasy Fiction,'" *People*, May 5, 2017, https://people.com/books/margaret-atwood-talks-handmaids-tale-trump-era/.

5. Christopher Krebs, "Trump Fired Me for Saying This, but I'll Say It Again: The Election Wasn't Rigged," *Washington Post*, December 1, 2020.

6. Christine Todd Whitman and Miles Taylor, "We Are Republicans: There's Only One Way to Save Our Party from Pro-Trump Extremists," Opinion Guest Essay, *New York Times*, October 11, 2021.

7. Jamelle Bouie, "Slavery Was Not a Secondary Part of Our History," Opinion, *New York Times*, August 23, 2019. Bouie and fellow collaborators develop this theme in the 1619 Project.

8. Adam M. Schor, "Conversion by the Numbers: Benefits and Pitfalls of Quantitative Modelling in the Study of Early Christian Growth," *Journal of Religious History* 33, no. 4 (2009): 472–98, http://dx.doi.org/10.1111/j.1467-9809.2009.00826.x.

9. The First Amendment (ratified 1791) to the United States Constitution prevents the government from making laws that would regulate an *establishment of religion* or that would prohibit the *free exercise of religion.*

10. Molly Olmstead, "'God Have Mercy on and Help Us All': How Prominent Evangelicals Reacted to the Storming of the U.S. Capitol." *Slate*, January 7, 2021, https://slate.com/human-interest/2021/01/trump-capitol-riot-evangelical-leaders-reactions.html.

11. Olmstead, "God Have Mercy."

12. Jack Jenkins, "Evangelicals Denounce 'Radicalized Christian Nationalism,'" *Religion News Service*, February 25, 2021.

13. Aaron Blake, "Nearly 4 Out of 10 Who Say Election Was Stolen from Trump Say Violence Might Be Needed to Save America," *Washington Post*, November 1, 2021.

14. The Mueller Commission was authorized by the United States Justice Department under the auspices of Deputy Attorney General Rod Rosenstein. A "coup" is an illegal seizure of power.

15. Vanessa Reimer, "Theologizing the Evangelical Purity Dialectic" (PhD diss., York University, February 2016), https://core.ac.uk/download/pdf/77106449.pdf, and Angie Hong, "The Flaw at the Center of Purity Culture," *Atlantic*, March 28, 2021, examine damaging effects of religious emphases on purity on Christian women and girls in general and, in Hong's essay, especially Korean Christian females.

CHAPTER 5

1. Nikole Hannah-Jones, *The 1619 Project: A New Origin Story*, ed. Nikole Hannah-Jones, Caitlin Roper, Ilena Silverman, and Jake Silverstein (New York: One World, 2021/2019).

2. Most American feminists cite the publication of Betty Friedan's *The Feminine Mystique* (New York: Norton, 1963) as the literary event that launched the women's movement in the second half of the twentieth century.

3. Alice Walker coined the term "womanist" in *In Search of Our Mothers' Gardens: Womanist Prose* (San Diego, CA: Harcourt Brace Jovanovich, 1983).

4. For examples of Latina, Asian American, and Indigenous women writers in late twentieth century, see Ada Maria Isasi Diaz, *Mujerista Theology: A Theology for the 21st Century* (Maryknoll, NY: Orbis, 1996); Daisy L. Machado, ed., *A Reader in Latina Feminist Theology: Religion and Justice* (Austin: University of Texas Press, 2002); Amy Tan, *The Joy Luck Club* (New York: Putnam, 1989); Kwok Pui-lan, *Introducing Asian Feminist Theology* (Sheffield, UK: Sheffield, 2000); Heid E. Erdrich and Laura Tohe, eds., *Sister Nations: Native American Women Writers on Community (Native Voices)* (St. Paul: Minnesota Historical Society, 2002).

5. In my *Touching Our Strength: The Power of the Erotic and the Love of God* (San Francisco: Harper, 1989), I make a theological case for sexual diversity as good and right. I do not explore transgender here. That would come later, especially in the bold work of Virginia Ramey Mollenkott. See Mollenkott's *Transgender: A Trans-religious Approach* (Cleveland, OH: Pilgrim, 2001), for a compelling study of transgender. Mollenkott was among the first Christian theologians to explore transgender as an identity. Though most of her life a prominent feminist woman theologian, Mollenkott themselves had begun to identify as trans by the time of their death in 2020. A decade after Mollenkott's work on transgender, Patrick S. Cheng's *Radical Love: An Introduction to Queer Theology* (New York: Seabury, 2011) became a leading resource for Christian leaders on queer matters, including trans identity. See also

Marvin M. Ellison, *Same Sex Marriage? A Christian Ethical Analysis* (Cleveland, OH: Pilgrim, 2004), for an excellent presentation of the contentious issue of same-sex marriage.

6. Bill McKibben, *The End of Nature* (New York: Norton, 1989), and Andrew Linzey, *Animal Theology* (Urbana: University of Indiana Press, 1995) are exemplary studies in environmentalism and animal well-being, respectively.

7. Melissa Denchak, "Flint Water Crisis: Everything You Need to Know," National Resources Defense Council, November 8, 2018, https://www.nrdc.org/stories/flint-water-crisis-everything-you-need-know.

8. www.npr.org/pipeline3/june2021

9. In an unpublished piece of research, my friend and colleague, the writer Susan Lefler, discusses the frenzy of the conservative Christian "Jericho Marches," the urgency of many Christian women leaders to "stop the steal" of the 2020 election, and the determination of influential Christian Republicans like James Dobson, evangelical founder of Focus on the Family, and Bill Barr, Trump's attorney general, to turn back the tides of diversity in order to restore America to its greatness. Lefler has been consulting with me on this book.

10. Critical race theory was conceptualized by Harvard professor and civil rights attorney Derrick Bell in the early 1980s. See Jelani Cobb, "The Man behind Critical Race Theory," *New Yorker*, September 13, 2021, https://www.newyorker.com/magazine/2021/09/20/the-man-behind-critical-race-theory. More recently, over the past two decades, lawyer and professor Kimberlé Williams Crenshaw of UCLA and Columbia University School of Law has become a leading advocate of critical race theory.

11. American historian, professor, and blogger Heather Cox Richardson discusses the backlash against the 1619 Project. www.heathercoxrichardson@substack.com

12. See Philip Shenon, "'A Threat to Democracy': William Barr's Speech on Religious Freedom Alarms Liberal Catholics," October 20, 2019, *Guardian*, on William Barr's speech at Notre Dame on September 16, 2019, in which Barr blasted "militant secularists" as "a threat to democracy" and said that America should be governed by "natural law," a classical Roman Catholic concept suggesting a "natural" hierarchy of power and privilege: https://www.theguardian.com/us-news/2019/oct/19/william-barr-attorney-general-catholic-conservative-speech.

13. Laurie Goodstein, "Falwell: Blame Abortionists, Feminists and Gays," *Guardian*, September 19, 2001.

CHAPTER 6

1. According to Pew Research, 85 percent of white evangelical Protestants and 63 percent of Catholics who attend church regularly voted for Trump in 2020. See Justin Nortey, "Most White Americans Who Regularly Attend Worship Services Voted for Trump in 2020," Pew Research, August 30, 2021, https://www.pewresearch.org/fact-tank/2021/08/30/most-white-americans-who-regularly-attend-worship-services-voted-for-trump-in-2020/. There was little difference in the findings between how

these same groups voted in 2020 and 2016. If anything, there was a slight tick upward toward Trump in both groups. See Jessica Martinez and Gregory A. Smith, "How the Faithful Voted: A Preliminary 2016 Analysis," Pew Research, November 9, 2016, https://www.pewresearch.org/fact-tank/2016/11/09/how-the-faithful-voted-a-preliminary-2016-analysis/.

2. The 1619 Project, a long-form journalism piece, was published in the *New York Times Magazine* in August 2019. It was conceived by Nikole Hannah-Jones, a journalism professor, scholar, and American historian, who was joined in this undertaking by several dozen other Black writers, scholars, and poets.

3. To refute the claims of the 1619 Project, the Trump administration authorized the publication of *1776.* According to the Trump White House's press release on January 18, 2021, "1776 Commission—comprised of some of America's most distinguished scholars and historians—has released a report presenting a definitive chronicle of the American founding, a powerful description of the effect the principles of the Declaration of Independence have had on this Nation's history, and a dispositive rebuttal of reckless 're-education' attempts that seek to reframe American history around the idea that the United States is not an exceptional country but an evil one." https://trumpwhitehouse.archives.gov/briefings-statements/1776-commission-takes-historic-scholarly-step-restore-understanding-greatness-american-founding/.

4. Amy Forliti, "Teen Who Recorded Floyd's Arrest, Death Wins Pulitzer Nod," AP News, June 11, 2021, https://apnews.com/article/pulitzer-prize-2021-citation-darnella-frazier-george-floyd-dce128319a373ef5360237f4c80dc9bb.

5. Leonard Pitts, "Kyle Rittenhouse Was Presumed Innocent until Proven Innocent. Must Be Nice," *Miami Herald*, November 19, 2021.

6. Sakshi Venkatraman, "Anti-Asian Hate Crimes Rose 73% Last Year, Updated FBI Data Says," October 25, 2021, NBC News, https://www.nbcnews.com/news/asian-america/anti-asian-hate-crimes-rose-73-last-year-updated-fbi-data-says-rcna3741.

7. *The Head of Christ*, or the Sallman Head, is a 1940 painting of Jesus of Nazareth by American artist Warner Sallman (1892–1968). An extraordinarily popular work of Christian devotional art, it had been reproduced over half a billion times worldwide by the end of the twentieth century.

8. Isabel Wilkerson, *Caste: The Origins of Our Discontents* (New York: Random House, 2020), 17.

9. Wilkerson, *Caste*, 17–19.

10. Audre Lorde, "The Transformation of Silence into Language and Action," in *Sister Outsider: Essays and Speeches* (Trumansburg, NY: Crossing, 1984), 40–44. See also Audre Lorde, *Your Silence Will Not Protect You* (London: Silver, 2017), posthumous collection.

11. Wilkerson, *Caste*, 101–4.

12. See Genesis 9:20–27.

13. Wilkerson, *Caste*, 103

14. Wilkerson, *Caste*, 115–30.

15. www.bbc.com/muhammadali. Also cited in documentary by Ken Burns in *Muhammad Ali*, four-part documentary written and directed by Ken Burns, Sarah

Burns, and David McMahon, PBS, September 2021, www.pbs.com/muhammadali/sept19-222020.

16. Adam Serwer, "The Fight over the 1619 Project Is Not about the Facts," *Atlantic*, December 23, 2019, www.theatlantic.com.

17. Serwer, "Fight over the 1619 Project."

18. Nineteenth-century transcendentalist and Unitarian minister Theodore Parker (1810–1860) originated this saying that has been attributed famously to Martin Luther King Jr. Preaching in 2006, the Rev. Susan Manker-Seale said, "One of Martin Luther King, Jr.'s, common quotes was given during a speech at the Fourth Continental Convention of the AFL-CIO in 1961: 'I'm convinced,' he said, 'that we shall overcome because the arc of the universe is long but it bends toward justice.' When he said that, he was quoting our Unitarian forebear, Theodore Parker who preached in 1853, 'I do not pretend to understand the moral universe; the arc is a long one. . . . And from what I see I am sure it bends toward justice.'" www.uucnwt.org/sermons/TheMoralArcOfTheUniverse/1-15-06.

19. Nikole Hannah-Jones, "The 1619 Project," *New York Times Magazine*, August 19, 2019, 15.

20. Hannah-Jones, "The 1619 Project," 17.

21. Nikole Hannah-Jones, preface to *The 1619 Project: A New Origin Story*, ed. Nikole Hannah-Jones, Caitlin Roper, Ilena Silverman, and Jake Silverstein (New York: One World, 2021/2019), xxvi.

22. Hannah-Jones, preface, xxvi.

CHAPTER 7

1. Audre Lorde, *Selected Works of Audre Lorde*, ed. Roxanne Gay (New York: Norton, 2020); and Adrienne Rich, *On Lies, Secrets, and Silence: Selected Prose 1966–1978* (New York: Norton, 1979).

2. Akasha (Gloria T.) Hull, Patricia Bell-Scott, and Barbara Smith, eds., *All the Women Are White, All the Blacks are Men, but Some of Us Are Brave* (New York: Feminist, 1982).

3. Mihee Kim-Kort, "I'm a Scholar of Religion. Here's What I See in the Atlanta Shootings," *New York Times*, March 24, 2021.

4. The *Oxford English Dictionary* revised its definition of "misogyny" in 2002, changing it from "hatred of women" to "hatred of, or dislike of, or prejudice against, women."

5. Beverly Wildung Harrison, "Homophobia and Misogyny: the Unexplored Connection," in *Making the Connections: Essays in Feminist Social Ethics*, ed. Carol S. Robb (Boston: Beacon, 1985).

6. Augustine, *On Marriage and Concupiscence, Book I* (Aeterna, 2014), written 419–420 CE. In this treatise, Augustine says that concupiscence or sexual lust is "wholly evil," a result of original sin, and is not in the nature of marriage itself, which is redeemed through the bearing of children.

7. Among the various forms of violence on display during the U.S. Capitol insurrection, one has been largely overlooked: misogyny, or hatred toward women. Yet behaviors and symbols of white male power were striking and persistent features of the riots. Members of the overwhelmingly male crowds defending a president well known for his sexist attacks, embraced male supremacist ideologies, wore military gear, and bared their chests in shows of masculine bravado. They even destroyed display cabinets holding historical books on women in politics. Actions targeting House Speaker Nancy Pelosi give the clearest illustration. Members of the mob broke into her office and vandalized it. Items like mail, signs and even her lectern proved to be particularly popular trophies—symbolizing an attack on Democrats and the House Speaker, but also against one of the most powerful women in American politics. www .theconversation.com/Jan13-2021/.

8. Elisabeth Schussler Fiorenza, *In Memory of Her: A Feminist Reconstruction of Christian Origins* (New York: Herder & Herder, 1994/1983) is among the best feminist resources for understanding women's lives and roles in the early church, and for refuting traditional treatments women as either absent from or irrelevant to the early Jesus movement.

9. Feminist, womanist, mujerista, and queer Christian leaders in late twentieth-century America such as Rosemary Radford Ruether, Beverly W. Harrison, Sally Bentley Doely (Sarah Bentley), Sheila D. Collins, Ada Maria Asasi Diaz, Kwok Pui-lan, Delores S. Williams, Katie Geneva Cannon, Joan Martin, Barbara Lundblad, Chung Hyun Kyung, Miriam Acevedo, Gale Yee, Kelly Brown Douglas, Barbara C. Harris, Janie Spahr, Janet Walton, Virginia Ramey Mollenkott, and Melanie Morrison were (and are) among the many brave women struggling to change Christianity from within.

10. Renny Golden and Sheila D. Collins, *Struggle Is a Name for Hope* (Albuquerque, NM: West End, 1982).

11. Ntozake Shange, *For Colored Girls Who Have Considered Suicide / When the Rainbow Is Enuf* (New York: Simon & Schuster, 1975). This brilliant choreopoem continues to be filmed (*For Colored Girls*, 2010) and staged. An announcement has been made that it will open at the Booth Theater in New York City in March 2022.

12. Alice Walker, *In Search of Our Mothers' Gardens: Womanist Prose* (New York: Harvest/Harcourt, 2003/1982).

13. James Carroll, *The Truth at the Heart of the Lie: How the Catholic Church Lost Its Soul—A Memoir of Faith* (New York: Random House, 2021).

14. Carroll, *Truth*, 170.

15. Antoinette Brown, later Blackwell, was ordained in 1851 to minister at a Congregational church in South Butler, New York.

16. The author was among the Philadelphia Eleven. See Carter Heyward, *A Priest Forever: Formation of a Woman and a Priest* (New York: Harper and Row, 1976). Also Darlene O'Dell, *The Story of the Philadelphia Eleven* (New York: Church Publishing Group, 2014).

17. Susan M. Shaw, "How Women in the Southern Baptist Convention Have Fought for Decades to Be Ordained," The Conversation, June 1, 2021, https://theconversation

.com/how-women-in-the-southern-baptist-convention-have-fought-for-decades-to-be -ordained-161061.

18. See Fiorenza, *In Memory of Her*; Luise Schottroff, *Lydia's Impatient Sisters: A Feminist Social History of Early Christianity* (Louisville, KY: Westminster John Knox, 1995); also Ross Shepard Kraemer and Mary Rose D'Angelo, eds., *Women and Christian Origins*, 1st ed. (New York: Oxford University Press, 1999).

19. Gordon Light, "She Comes Sailing on the Wind" ("She Flies On"), copyright 1985, Common Cup Co., https://www.umcdiscipleship.org/resources/history-of -hymns-she-comes-sailing-on-the-wind.

20. Sophia/Wisdom introduces herself in Prov. 8:22–23 (NRSV): "The Lord created me at the beginning of his work, the first of his acts of long ago. Ages ago I was set up, at the first, before the beginning of the earth."

CHAPTER 8

1. Beverly Wildung Harrison, *Justice in the Making: Feminist Social Ethics*, ed. E. M. Bounds, P. K. Brubaker, J. E. Hicks, M.J. Legge, R. T. Peters, and T. C. West (Louisville, KY: Westminster John Knox 2004), 165.

2. Stories from a work in progress by Darlene O'Dell. Her extended essay is on various incidents that illuminate white Christian nationalism over a period of about 150 years in her hometown of Union, South Carolina. O'Dell is working with a university press on the publication of this piece, and she has been a primary consultant with me on this book.

3. The Chicago school of economics was founded in the 1920s but rose to prominence midcentury in the neoclassical theories of Milton Friedman, George Stigler, and other members of the economics faculty. Central tenets of neoclassical theory are that consumer perception of a product's value (not the cost of production) is the chief factor in its pricing, and that the less government regulation of the economy, the healthier it is.

4. British economist John Maynard Keynes (1883–1946), considered Britain's premier economist in the twentieth century, believed that the market requires some government regulation in order to function effectively. Friedman, Stigler, and the neoclassical economists disagreed and opposed Keynesian economics in the second half of the twentieth century. Keynesian economics made a comeback in the wake of the 2008 crisis but is predictably opposed by the Republican Party in America and its conservative counterparts in Europe and elsewhere.

5. Bernie Sanders, Elizabeth Warren, Sherrod Brown, Alexandria Ocasio-Cortez, Rashida Tlaib, Ilhan Omar, Karen Bass, and a handful of other legislators in the U.S. Congress are democratic socialists. A number of other legislators probably share their goals but, for political reasons, don't use the label "democratic socialist."

6. This seems so obvious. Corporations own the government, not vice versa, in today's political economy. Beverly Harrison warned that this was going to happen long before the Supreme Court's infamous *Citizens United* in 2010.

7. Beverly Wildung Harrison's three books are *Our Right to Choose: Toward an Ethic of Abortion* (Boston: Beacon, 1983); *Making the Connections: Essays in Feminist Social Ethics*, ed. Carol S. Robb (Boston: Beacon, 1985); and *Justice in the Making*.

8. Scottish philosopher Adam Smith's *The Wealth of Nations*, first published in 1796, is widely accepted as the introduction to capitalism as an economic alternative to European feudalism. *The Wealth of Nations* was republished in 2019 by Ixia Press.

9. www.cpost@uchicago.edu/demographics-of-rioters-on-Jan6. The University of Chicago Project on Security and Threats has found that many of the insurrectionists were older white men (and some women), employed, financially secure, and that the main factors motivating their participation were anxiety about Black and Hispanic people gaining power in their communities, which in turn may help explain their enthusiasm for Trump.

10. "Speaking at a fundraiser in New York City on Friday [Sept 9, 2016], Hillary Clinton said half of Donald Trump's supporters belong in a 'basket of deplorables' characterized by racist, sexist, homophobic, xenophobic, Islamaphobic views." www.time.com/katie-reilly/september-10-2016/12:27-pm/ET.

11. From "Service of Holy Baptism," *The Book of Common Prayer*, according to the use of The Episcopal Church (New York: Church Hymnal Corporation and Seabury Press, 1977), 302.

CHAPTER 9

1. Robert Brennan, "Dominion over Nature—Is Traditional Christianity Really the Eco-villain?" ISCAST.org, August 2014; and Matthew Cavedon, "Dominion and Stewardship: Imaging God in Creation," December 14, 2013, SSRN: https://ssrn.com/abstract=2566374 or http://dx.doi.org/10.2139/ssrn.2566374.

2. "Sikh Ecology," Interfaith Center for Sustainable Development, n.d., www.interfaithsustain.com/Sikh-ecology.

3. See Naomi Klein's essay "On Fire" in *All We Can Save: Truth, Courage, and Solutions for the Climate Crisis*, ed. Ayana Elizabeth Johnson and Katharine K. Wilkinson (New York: One Word 2020), 39–48.

4. "The Nobel Peace Prize 2007," NobelPrize.org, https://www.nobelprize.org/prizes/peace/2007/summary/.

5. "Millions Attend Global Climate Strike," BBC News, September 20, 2019, https://www.bbc.com/news/in-pictures-49767747.

6. Rosemary Radford Ruether, *Gaia and God: An Ecofeminist Theology* (San Francisco: HarperCollins, 1992).

7. Sallie McFague, *The Body of God: An Ecological Theology* (Minneapolis, MN: Fortress, 1993).

8. Daniel T. Spencer, *Gay and Gaia: Ethics, Ecology, and the Erotic* (Cleveland, OH: Pilgrim, 1996).

9. Larry L. Rasmussen, *Earth-Honoring Faith: Religious Ethics in a New Key* (New York: Oxford University Press, 2013).

10. Rasmussen, *Earth-Honoring Faith*, 239–54.

11. Rasmussen, *Earth-Honoring Faith*, 255–84.

12. This is a central tenet of the 1619 Project—that slavery continues to shape our society in ways that white Americans often do not notice.

13. Rasmussen, *Earth-Honoring Faith*, 285–304.

14. Rasmussen, *Earth-Honoring Faith*, 308.

15. Rasmussen, *Earth-Honoring Faith*, 332–56.

16. "Co-dependent arising" or "interdependent co-arising" is a radically relational Buddhist concept that refers to the interconnectivity of all life and the constancy of our interdependencies on one another—humans and all creatures. Nothing that we do is simply on our own or no one else's business, because everything we do affects others. This is what I refer to in my theological work as "mutual relation." See Carter Heyward, *The Redemption of God: A Theology of Mutual Relation* (Eugene, OR: Wipf & Stock, 2010/1982).

17. Jane Goodall and Douglas Abrams, *The Book of Hope: A Survival Guide for Trying Times* (New York: Celadon, 2021).

18. Douglas Abrams was coauthor with the Dalai Lama and Desmond Tutu of *The Book of Joy: Lasting Happiness in a Changing World* (New York: Cornerstone, 2016).

19. Watch "Jane Goodall on the Threat of Animal Agriculture, GOP Climate Change Denial & Why She's a Vegetarian," January 14, 2016, on www.democracynow.org.

20. Michael Pollan, *The Omnivore's Dilemma: A Natural History of Four Meals* (New York: Penguin, 2006). See other Pollan resources on www.michaelpollan.com.

CHAPTER 10

1. Bob Dylan, "With God on Our Side," Copyright © 1963 by Warner Bros. Inc.; renewed 1991 by Special Rider Music. www.bobdylan.com/.

2. Reis Thebault, Joe Fox, and Andrew Ba Tran, "2020 Was the Deadliest Gun Violence Year in Decades. So Far, 2021 Is Worse," *Washington Post*, June 14, 2021.

3. www.politifact.com/2017 and www.USAToday/Ipsos/2021

4. Tommy Beer, "Majority of Republicans Believe the QAnon Conspiracy Theory Is Partly or Mostly True, Survey Finds," Forbes, September 2, 2020, https://www .forbes.com/sites/tommybeer/2020/09/02/majority-of-republicans-believe-the-qanon -conspiracy-theory-is-partly-or-mostly-true-survey-finds/?sh=7a8d76be5231.

5. Thomas B. Edsall, "Why Millions Think It Is Trump Who Cannot Tell a Lie," *New York Times*, January 19, 2022.

6. The Quincy Institute, founded in 2019, believes "that a foreign policy that emphasizes military restraint and diplomatic engagement and cooperation with other nations will serve American interests and values better than policies that prioritize the maintenance of U.S. global dominance through force" (https://quincyinst.org/ about/). Andrew J. Bacevich, a professor emeritus of history at Boston University, is one of the Quincy Institute's lead writers and is an excellent and reliable resource on America's culture of violence, especially war. His most recent book is *After the Apocalypse: America's Role in a World Transformed* (New York: Henry Holt, 2021).

7. See Miroslav Volf, director of the Yale Center for Faith and Culture, "Christianity and Violence," *Reflections*, Winter 2004, https://reflections.yale.edu/article/violence-and-theology/christianity-and-violence/2004; see also Volf's "Sedition in the Capitol," Yale Center for Faith and Culture, January 7, 2021, https://faith.yale.edu/media/riot-in-the-capitol.

8. National Council of Churches, "The Dangers of Christian Nationalism in the United States: A Policy Statement of the National Council of Churches," updated April 22, 2021, https://nationalcouncilofchurches.us/common-witness-ncc/the-dangers-of-christian-nationalism-in-the-united-states-a-policy-statement-of-the-national-council-of-churches/.

9. Dietrich Bonhoeffer, *Letters and Papers from Prison*, ed. Eberhard Bethge (New York: Touchstone, 1997/1953).

10. Martin Luther King Jr., *Where Do We Go from Here: Chaos or Community?* (Boston: Beacon, 1968), 58.

11. Bonnie Steinbock, "Should Pro-Choice Advocates Compromise on Abortion?" The Hastings Center, Bioethics Forum, October 25, 2021, https://www.thehastingscenter.org/should-pro-choice-advocates-compromise-on-abortion/.

12. Christian feminist writer Darlene O'Dell, who has consulted with me throughout this project, warns that "compromise" can be used against the powerless in any situation and that safeguards need to be in place to prevent this.

13. I am especially indebted for these insights to friends of color in our local mountain community—Black Americans Robert Kilgore, Tommy Kilgore, Sheila Mooney, Patience Camp, Spencer Jones, the late Curtis Cash; Pakistani American Zaibun Jangda; Chinese American Yang Li Chin; and Puerto Ricans Pedro Sandin, Rosalynd Storer, and Elly Andujar.

14. For Helder Camara's small 1971 book, *Spiral of Violence*, go to http://www.alastairmcintosh.com/general/spiral-of-violence.htm.

15. Reinhold Niebuhr, *Moral Man and Immoral Society: A Study in Ethics and Politics* (Louisville, KY: Westminster John Knox, 2021) (originally published New York: Charles Scribner's, 1932).

CHAPTER 11

1. There are many groups and organizations, including those led by Christians, working hard on justice matters today. Among the older groups are the NAACP, the Poor People's Campaign, Planned Parenthood, Human Rights Watch, the Human Rights Campaign, and the Sierra Club. Some of the younger movements are gun control efforts such as #Whatif, #NeverAgain, #MeNext, #MarchForOurLives, and #EndGun Violence; and youth-led environmental movements such as the Sunrise Movement in the United States, the Extinction Rebellion in Britain, and any number of Black environmental activists and movements—see https://sustainability.yale.edu/blog/9-black-environmentalists-follow. A few organizations founded to resist hate in America, and the written work of many justice leaders over the last couple of decades, are listed in the resources and bibliography at the end of this book.

2. Marvin M. Ellison and Sylvia Thorson-Smith, eds., *Body and Soul: Rethinking Sexuality as Justice-Love* (Cleveland, OH: Pilgrim, 2003).

CHAPTER 12

1. Augustine, *The City of God*, ed. Paul A Boer Sr., (Hyde Park, NY: New City), 2012.

2. Augustine, *De Trinitate* (On the Trinity), ed. Paul A. Boer Sr. (Edmond, OK: Veritatis Splendor, 2012), XV.17.24.

3. Frederick Denison Maurice, *Theological Essays* (Miami, FL: HardPress, 2017/1853).

4. Dorothee Soelle, *Christ the Representative: An Essay in Theology after the Death of God* (Philadelphia: Fortress, 1967).

5. Dietrich Bonhoeffer, *Letters and Papers from Prison*, ed. Eberhard Bethge (New York: Touchstone, 1997/1953).

CHAPTER 13

1. Richard Rohr, "Preaching 'On the Mount,'" Center for Action and Contemplation, Daily Meditation, July 20, 2021.

2. Martin Luther King Jr., "Pride versus Humility: The Parable of the Pharisee and the Publican" (September 25, 1955), Dexter Avenue Baptist Church, Montgomery, AL, in *The Papers of Martin Luther King, Jr. Volume VI: Advocate of the Social Gospel, September 1948–March 1963*, ed. Clayborne Carson, Susan Carson, Susan Englander, Troy Jackson, and Gerald L. Smith (Stanford, CA: Martin Luther King Jr. Research and Education Institute).

3. King, "Pride versus Humility."

CHAPTER 14

1. The term "colorism" is attributed to Alice Walker. See Kimberly Jade Norwood, "'If You Is White, You's Alright. . . . ': Stories about Colorism in America," *Washington University Global Studies Law Review* 14, no. 4 (2015), https://openscholarship.wustl.edu/law_globalstudies/vol14/iss4/8/.

2. Nikole Hannah-Jones, *The 1619 Project: A New Origin Story*, ed. Nikole Hannah-Jones, Caitlin Roper, Ilena Silverman, and Jake Silverstein (New York: One World, 2021/2019).

3. James H. Cone, *Black Theology and Black Power* (Maryknoll, NY: Orbis, 1969), and *A Black Theology of Liberation* (Maryknoll, NY: Orbis, 1970). Over the years, Cone moved away from his early focus on Blackness. Two of his best-known books, *The Spirituals and the Blues* (1992) and *The Cross and the Lynching Tree* (2013), both

published by Orbis, illustrated Cone's growing interest in analyzing themes, symbols, and cultural representations of life among African Americans.

4. Some other Black colleagues and inspirations in my life as a teacher and theologian earlier in my work included Jacquelyn Grant, Kelly Brown Douglas, James Washington, and Cornel West at Union Seminary; Walter Dennis, Ed Rodman, Bunchie Rodman, and Byron Rushing in the Episcopal Church; and Katie Geneva Cannon, Robert Bennett, Joan Martin, Irene Monroe, Ruby Sales, Karen Montagno, Eston Collins, and Stephanie Spellers at the Episcopal Divinity School. I am sure there are many others. The point is: I am grateful to having been introduced to the Blackness of God by many Black colleagues and friends over time, starting in the 1970s.

5. One of Cone's colleagues, the Christian feminist ethicist Beverly Wildung Harrison, titled her inaugural address at Union Seminary in 1980 "The Power of Anger in the Work of Love," included in *Making the Connections: Essays in Feminist Social Ethics* (Boston: Beacon, 1985). In this essay Harrison—like James Cone and many of her Black male and female colleagues, and her white feminist cohorts—suggests that anger often is a signal that something is wrong and needs to be fixed. Like Cone, Harrison taught that anger has a loving role to place in relation to white supremacy, misogyny, and other structures of injustice.

6. "Durham's Malcolm X Liberation University," North Carolina Department of Natural and Cultural Resources, October 25, 2016, https://www.ncdcr.gov/blog/2016 /10/25/durhams-malcolm-x-liberation-university.

CHAPTER 15

1. Katie G. Cannon, foreword to twentieth anniversary edition of Delores S. Williams, *Sisters in the Wilderness: The Challenge of Womanist God-Talk* (Maryknoll, NY: Orbis, 2013/1993), x.

2. Delores S. Williams, *Sisters in the Wilderness: The Challenge of Womanist God-Talk* (Maryknoll, NY: Orbis, 1993), 6.

3. Cannon, foreword to Williams, *Sisters in the Wilderness* (2013), xi.

4. Jean-Yves Leloup, *The Gospel of Mary Magdalene*, English translation and notes by Joseph Rowe (Rochester, VT: Inner Traditions, 2002), 14.

5. Karen L. King, *The Gospel of Mary of Magdala: Jesus and the First Woman Apostle* (Santa Rosa, CA: Polebridge,) 2003.

6. Cynthia Bourgeault, *The Meaning of Mary Magdalene: Discovering the Woman at the Heart of Christianity* (Boston: Shambhala, 2010), ix.

7. The victims of the spa shootings in Atlanta on March 16, 2021, were Delaina Ashley Yaun, Paul Andre Michels, Xiaojie Tan, Daoyou Feng, Soon Chung Park, Hyun Jung Grant, Suncha Kim, and Yong Ae Yue.

8. Angie Hong, "The Flaw at the Center of Purity Culture," *Atlantic*, March 28, 2021.

9. Hong, "Flaw at the Center of Purity Culture."

10. The Equal Rights Amendment (ERA), which guarantees basic rights to Americans regardless of sex, had been first drafted in 1923 and had languished in Congress. In 1971, the ERA was introduced into the Congress where it easily passed in both houses but ran into trouble over the decade as its advocates sought its ratification by the necessary number of states (thirty-eight or two-thirds). Over the decade, an anti-ERA momentum had built among those men and, especially women like Phyllis Schlafly, who argued that the ERA would strip women of special rights such as exemption from the draft, alimony, preference in child custody cases, and protection in the labor force. Although Congress has extended the date for ratification several times, several states have rescinded their original ratification and although several have also ratified, the status of the ERA remains unclear in 2021.

11. Christian feminist Beverly W. Harrison's *Our Right to Choose: A New Ethic of Abortion* (Boston: Beacon, 1983), was heralded among liberal Christians as a definitive study on the ethics of abortion. In 2006, Harrison was honored by North Americans Catholics for Choice at a meeting in Mexico City, where a Spanish translation of this book was celebrated.

12. This now-famous quip was printed in the *New York Times* on August 16, 1981, which reported that Frank had made the statement a week earlier at a meeting of the American Bar Association. The quip has taken on a life of its own and has become a mantra among those who support a woman's right to choose.

13. Beverly W. Harrison, "Misogyny and Homophobia: The Unexplored Connections," in *Making the Connections: Essays in Feminist Social Ethics*, ed. Carol S. Robb (Boston: Beacon, 1985), 135–51.

14. Matt. 12:46–50, Mark 3:31, Luke 8:19, John 2:12, Acts 1:14, 1 Cor. 9:5. Paul refers to someone named James as "the Lord's brother" in Gal. 1:19.

15. Sigmund Freud, *The Three Essays on the Theory of Sexuality* (New York: Basic, 2000/1905). In the second essay on infantile sexuality, Freud makes his case for bisexuality as a universal human capacity and yearning.

16. Julian of Norwich, *Revelations of Divine Love* (London: Penguin, 1998). Many scholars believe that Julian's ongoing lifelong perception of Jesus as her Mother took root in her serious illness as a young woman and Christ's appearance to her to feed her with his blood.

CHAPTER 16

1. In an 1880 exchange with Jules Guerde, one of the organizers of Parti Ouvrier (the French Workers' Party), Marx was put off by Guerde's insistence that capitalism could not be reformed—that is, used as a vehicle to promote revolutionary change. In their meeting, Marx is reported to have said words to the effect that "if you [Guerde] are a Marxist, then I myself am not." Marx believed that capitalism could, and must, be reformed, not completely obliterated. Marx also was implying, in this statement, that even his own theory—Marxism—was liable to various interpretations and, therefore, like all theory, was idealistic—that is, it was in danger of floating around primarily in the world of ideas rather than in the actual embodiment of social struggle and

change. Another way of putting it is that Marx preferred struggle itself to the "idea" of struggle. This preference for the processes of actual activity ("praxis") is the theory behind liberation theology's insistence on the interplay of "theory" and "praxis" in all theology. Marx's famous remark about not being a Marxist was quoted by Friedrich Engels in a letter to Eduard Bernstein and can be found in Marx and Engels, *Werke (Works)*, vol. 35, and is cited in https://wikirouge.net/texts/en/The_Programme_of_the_Parti_Ouvrier_(1880).

2. Some important distinctions among terms: *Marxism* is named after Karl Marx (1818–1883), the *economic* theory developed by Marx and Friedrich Engels (1820–1895) that class struggle is the heart of social discord. They believed that class struggle would culminate in social revolution through which the means of production—for example, factories and other institutions, processes, and materials by which people manufacture and receive goods and services—would be owned collectively by those who actually do the work rather than by the individuals, the families, or—in advanced capitalism—the corporations controlled by those who control and profit from the wealth that is actually, materially, generated by the workers.

Communism is the *political* practice of Marxism in the Soviet Union, China, and other nations around the world in the twentieth century. As a political system, as distinct from Marxism itself as an economic theory, Communism has shown itself to be an authoritarian, basically one-party, system.

Democratic socialism challenges the authoritarian political system of Communism, democratic socialists believe, following Marx, that the state should be responsible for meeting many basic economic needs of its citizens—that is, food, housing, medical care, education; and that this economic system can be maintained through a democratic political system, in which people vote for their leaders, who represent different views on how to achieve the nation's economic goals. The political debate is not about whether the goals themselves are important but rather about how most effectively and efficiently to meet them—to provide food for everyone, health care for all, excellent education for all children, and so forth.

Christian socialism is an idealistic view, similar to democratic socialism, but with an explicitly Christian motive: love of neighbor. Also assumes a democratic political system, in which people vote for their leaders, who represent different views on how to achieve the nation's economic goals. As with democratic socialism, the political debate is not about whether these goals are important but rather about how to meet them.

Social democracy is a major political party in much of Europe, where socialism is not as greatly caricatured and feared as it is in the United States of America. Social democrats resemble liberal Democrats in America. Social democrats in Europe, like liberal Democrats in America, tend to advocate providing basic economic resources to everyone; and they believe strongly in democracy, voting rights for all, at least two political parties, and so forth.

Social democrats in Europe, *liberal Democrats* in America, and *democratic socialists* in America share basic economic aims, democratic values, and differ largely in strategies about how to achieve their aims and honor their values.

3. Amanecida Collective, *Revolutionary Forgiveness: Feminist Reflections on Nicaragua*, ed. Carter Heyward and Anne B. Gilson (Maryknoll, NY: Orbis, 1986).

4. Diane Maria Pella, "As We Are United in One: Frederick Denison Maurice and Christian Socialism" (PhD diss., Fordham University, 1999), https://research.library .fordham.edu/dissertations/AAI9941916/.

5. For pastors, priests, and other Christian teachers, a recent publication, reviewed quite positively by liberal Roman Catholic and Protestant leaders, is Raymond F. Collins, *Wealth, Wages, and the Wealthy: New Testament Insight for Preachers and Teachers* (Collegeville, MN: Liturgical, 2017).

6. Kirstin Downey, *The Woman behind the New Deal: The Life and Legacy of Frances Perkins; Social Security, Unemployment Insurance and the Minimum Wage* (New York: Anchor, 2010).

CHAPTER 17

1. Larry L. Rasmussen, *Earth-Honoring Faith: Religious Ethics in a New Key* (New York: Oxford University Press, 2013), 4.

2. Rasmussen, *Earth-Honoring Faith*, 17.

3. See Sallie McFague, *The Body of God: An Ecological Theology* (Minneapolis, MN: Fortress, 1993); *Super, Natural Christians: How We Should Love Nature* (Minneapolis, MN: Fortress, 1997); and *A New Climate for Theology: God, the World, and Global Warming* (Minneapolis, MN: Fortress, 2008).

4. See Pierre Teilhard de Chardin, *Pierre Teilhard de Chardin: Writings*, Modern Spiritual Masters (Maryknoll, NY: Orbis, 1999).

5. Christian ecoliberation theologians Rosemary Radford Ruether, Sallie McFague, and Daniel Spencer, and animal rights activists Jay McDaniel, Andrew Linzey, and Carol Adams have been among many Christian leaders over the last several decades raising their voices eloquently on behalf of the earth and its many varied creatures.

6. Thich Nhat Hanh, foreword to Joanna Macy's *World as Lover, World as Self* (Berkeley, CA: Parallax, 1991), vii–viii.

7. Joanna Macy, *A Wild Love for the World: Joanna Macy and the Work of Our Time*, ed. Stephanie Kaza (Boulder, CO: Shambhala, 2020), 6.

8. Rasmussen, *Earth-Honoring Faith*, 26–36.

9. Rasmussen, *Earth-Honoring Faith*, 36.

10. Rasmussen, *Earth-Honoring Faith*, 240.

11. Rasmussen, *Earth-Honoring Faith*, 258.

12. Rasmussen, *Earth-Honoring Faith*, 258.

13. The Dakota Access Pipeline, which stretches across the Dakotas into Kansas, at the service of several oil companies in Canada and the United States, including Enbridge and Marathon Petroleum, has drawn upward of fifteen thousand protesters since 2019. The protesters have been in solidarity with Indigenous residents of the Standing Rock Sioux Reservation, whose land is at risk from the oil moving through the pipeline.

14. Rasmussen, *Earth-Honoring Faith*, 305–31.

15. Rasmussen, *Earth-Honoring Faith*, 332–56.

16. Rasmussen, *Earth-Honoring Faith*, 332.

17. From *Memorial Celebration of the Life and Witness of Alison M. Cheek*, St. Philip's Episcopal Church, Brevard, NC, November 2, 2019. Unpublished.

18. Christine E. Nieves Rodriguez, "Community Is Our Best Chance," in *All We Can Save: Truth, Courage, and Solutions for the Climate Crisis*, ed. Ayana Elizabeth Johnson and Katharine K. Wilkinson (New York: One World, 2020), 364.

19. Nieves Rodriguez, "Community Is Our Best Chance," 366.

CHAPTER 18

1. Helder Camara, *The Spiral of Violence* (London: Sheed and Ward, 1971); not in print; available as PDF download: https://www.alastairmcintosh.com/general/spiral -of-violence.htm.

2. See Dorothee Soelle, *Suffering* (Philadelphia: Fortress, 1984); and Carter Heyward, *The Redemption of God: A Theology of Mutual Relation* (Eugene, OR: Wipf & Stock, 2010/1982), for connections between God, violence, and suffering.

3. In realms of violence, there is a link between how humans have treated animals through the ages and how we have treated each other. Psychologists and legal workers have shown connections between the abuse of animals and abuse of people. Some of the most notorious killers in modern American society began their sadistic rampages with cruelty toward animals. See "The Link between Cruelty to Animals and Violence toward Humans," Animal Legal Defense Fund, n.d., https://aldf.org/article/the-link -between-cruelty-to-animals-and-violence-toward-humans-2/.

4. Tia Ghose, "5 Animals with a Moral Compass," LiveScience, November 15, 2012, https://www.livescience.com/24800-animals-emotions-morality.html; and Joanne Kennell, "Empathy Is More Common in the Animal Kingdom Than Thought," The Science Explorer, January 26, 2016, http://thescienceexplorer.com/nature/ empathy-more-common-animal-kingdom-thought.

5. See John Hick, *Evil and the God of Love* (New York: Palgrave, 2021/1966) for helpful discussion of "social" and "natural" evil, as well as Heyward, *Redemption of God*. Consult City University of NY (CUNY) online to read Philip A. Pecorino, "The Problem of Evil: The Nature of Evil," 2001, https://www.qcc.cuny.edu/socialsciences /ppecorino/phil_of_religion_text/CHAPTER_6_PROBLEM_of_EVIL/Nature_of _Evil.htm.

6. Wrestling with Elie Wiesel's novel *The Town beyond the Wall* (New York: Schocken, 1995/1962), was one of the most important experiences in my theological education. This is the book in which Wiesel suggests that evil is done by the spectators, those who watch and do nothing, as much as by the active perpetrators.

7. To name a few representatives from the civil rights struggle, there were Rosa Parks, Fannie Lou Hamer, Ella Baker, Bayard Rustin, and John Lewis, as well as martyrs Andrew Goodman, James Chaney, Michael Schwerner, Jonathan Daniels, Viola Liuzzo, James Reeb, and others. There were also the members of organizations—SNCC (Student Non-violent Coordinating Committee), CORE (Congress on

Racial Equality), and the SCLC (Southern Christian Leadership Conference). Other nonviolent leaders in recent American history include Dorothy Day, Cesar Chavez, Delores Huerta, Catholic priests Dan and Phil Berrigan, Sister Elisabeth McCallister, Muhammad Ali, Joan Baez, Noam Chomsky, Sister Helen Prejean, and Sister Simone Campbell. Two contemporary leaders in nonviolence are the young Pakistani Malala Yousafzai and the American Sikh spiritual teacher Valerie Kaur.

8. "Incarceration Rates by Country 2021," World Population Review, https://worldpopulationreview.com/country-rankings/incarceration-rates-by-country.

9. Poor People's Campaign: A National Call for Moral Revival, https://www.poorpeoplescampaign.org.

10. Mary Kay Magistad, "Truth & Reconciliation in South Africa, Revisited," *Whose Century Is It?* (podcast), April 6, 2017, https://whosecenturyisit.com/truth-reconciliation-in-south-africa-revisited. The TRC of South Africa, as it happens, was not the first such commission to be set up in the twentieth and twenty-first centuries to provide encourage truth telling and reconciliation, but it seems to have been among the commissions that operated on a theological assumption that reconciliation requires forgiveness and that forgiveness requires repentance and honest confession of wrongdoing.

Resources and Selected Bibliography

ANTI-HATE ACTIVIST AND WATCHDOG ORGANIZATIONS

Anti-Defamation League (fighting anti-Semitism): https://www.adl.org
Center for American Progress: https://www.americanprogress.org/topic/anti-hate/
Christians against Christian Nationalism: https://www.christiansagainstchristiannationalism.org
Counter Extremism Project: https://www.counterextremism.com/hate-groups
Faithful America: https://faithfulamerica.org
Human Rights Campaign: https://www.hrc.org
Institute for Christian Socialism: https://christiansocialism.com/
Interfaith Alliance: https://interfaithalliance.org
Jewish Voices for Peace (fighting hate against Palestinians in Israel/Palestine): https://jewishvoiceforpeace.org
NAACP Legal Defense Fund: https://www.naacp/legaldefensefund.org
P-Flag: https://www.pflag.org
Planned Parenthood: https://www.plannedparenthood.org
Southern Poverty Law Center: https://www.splcenter.org
Stop AAPI Hate: https://www.stopaapihate.org
United against Hate: https://www.united-against-hate.org
Vote Common Good: https://www.votecommongood.com

WHITE CHRISTIAN NATIONALISM AND RELIGIOUS-BASED VIOLENCE

Applebaum, Anne. *Twilight of Democracy: The Seductive Lure of Authoritarianism.* New York: Doubleday, 2020.
Butler, Anthea. *White Evangelical Racism: The Politics of Morality in America.* Chapel Hill: University of North Carolina Press, 2021.

Carroll, James. *Constantine's Cross: The Church and the Jews.* New York: Mariner, 2002.

Du Mez, Kristin Kobes. *Jesus and John Wayne: How White Evangelicals Corrupted a Faith and Fractured a Nation.* New York: Liveright, 2020.

Ellis, Marc H. *Unholy Alliance: Religion and Atrocity in Our Time.* Minneapolis, MN: Fortress, 1997.

Fletcher, Jeannine Hill. *The Sin of White Supremacy: Christianity, Racism, & Religious Diversity in America.* Maryknoll, NY: Orbis, 2017.

Gilson, Anne Bathurst. *The Battle for America's Families: A Feminist Response to the Religious Right.* Cleveland, OH: Pilgrim, 1999.

Greenblatt, Jonathan. *It Could Happen Here: Why America Is Tipping from Hate to the Unthinkable—and How We Can Stop It.* New York: Mariner, 2022.

Heyward, Carter. *Saving Jesus from Those Who Are Right: Rethinking What It Means to Be Christian.* Minneapolis, MN: Fortress, 1999.

Jones, Robert P. *The End of White Christian America.* New York: Simon & Schuster, 2016.

———. *White Too Long: The Legacy of White Supremacy in American Christianity.* New York: Simon & Schuster, 2020.

Posner, Sarah. *Unholy: Why White Evangelicals Worship at the Altar of Donald Trump.* New York: Random House, 2020.

Ruether, Rosemary Radford. *Faith and Fratricide: Theological Roots of Anti-Semitism.* Eugene, OR: Wipf & Stock, 1995/1974.

Snyder, Timothy. *On Tyranny: Twenty Lessons from the Twentieth Century.* New York: Tim Duggan, 2017.

Stewart, Katherine. *The Power Worshippers: Inside the Dangerous Rise of Religious Nationalism.* New York: Bloomsbury, 2019.

Thistlethwaite, Susan. *When Demons Float: A Novel.* Eugene, OR: Resources, 2020.

Whitehead, Andrew L., and Samuel Perry. *Taking America Back for God: Christian Nationalism in the United States.* New York: Oxford University Press, 2020.

ON THEMES IN THIS BOOK

On Mutuality/Power-With

Bergman, Stephen, and Janet L. Surrey. *Bill W. and Dr. Bob—A Play.* New York: Samuel French, 2010.

Buber, Martin. *I and Thou.* New York: Scribner, 1958.

Cardenal, Ernesto. *The Gospel in Solentiname.* Vols. 1–3. Translated by Donald D. Walsh. Maryknoll, NY: Orbis, 1977–1979.

Curry, Michael. *Love Is the Way: Holding On to Hope in Troubling Times.* New York: Avery/Penguin, 2020.

Dalai Lama and Desmond Tutu. *The Book of Joy: Lasting Happiness in a Changing World.* New York: Avery, 2016.

Driver, Tom F. *Christ in a Changing World: Toward an Ethical Christology.* New York: Crossroad, 1981.

Heyward, Carter. *The Redemption of God: A Theology of Mutual Relation.* 2nd ed., with preface by Janet L. Surrey. Eugene, OR: Wipf & Stock, 2010. 1st ed. 1982.

———. *Tears of Christepona: Mystical Musings on Grief, Evil, and Godding.* Eugene, OR: Resources, 2021.

Kaur, Valerie. *See No Stranger: A Memoir and Manifesto of Revolutionary Love.* London: One World, 2021.

Sandin-Fremaint, Pedro A. *The Holy Gospel of Uncertainty.* Brevard, NC: Self-published, 2017.

Soelle, Dorothee. *Against the Wind: Memoir of a Radical Christian.* Translated by Barbara and Martin Rumscheidt. Minneapolis, MN: Fortress, 1999.

Varghese, Winnie. *Church Meets World.* New York: Morehouse, 2016.

On Racial Justice

Anzaldua, Gloria. *Borderlands / La Frontera: The New Mestiza.* San Francisco: Aunt Lute, 2012.

Baldwin, James. *The Fire Next Time.* New York: Vintage International/Random House, 1992/1963.

Bonilla-Silva, Eduardo. *Racism without Racists: Color-Blind Racism and the Persistence of Racial Inequality in the United States.* 2nd ed. Lanham, MD: Rowman & Littlefield, 2006.

Coates, Ta-Nehisi. *Between the World and Me.* New York: Spiegel & Grau, 2015.

———. *We Were Eight Years in Power: An American Tragedy.* New York: Random House, 2017.

Cone, James H. *A Black Theology of Liberation.* 40th anniv. ed. Maryknoll, NY: Orbis, 2011.

Diangelo, Robin. *White Fragility: Why It's So Hard for White People to Talk about Racism.* Boston: Beacon, 2018.

Douglas, Kelly Brown. *Resurrection Hope: A Future Where Black Lives Matter.* Maryknoll, NY: Orbis, 2021.

———. *Stand Your Ground: Black Bodies and the Justice of God.* Maryknoll, NY: Orbis, 2015.

Hannah-Jones, Nikole, creator. *The 1619 Project: A New Origin Story.* Edited by Nikole Hannah-Jones, Caitlin Roper, Ilena Silverman, and Jake Silverstein. New York: One World, 2021 (expanded version of 2019 publication).

Kendi, Ibram X, and Keisha N. Blain, eds. *Four Hundred Souls: A Community History of African America: 1619–2019.* New York: One World, 2021.

King, Martin Luther, Jr. "Pride versus Humility: The Parable of the Pharisee and the Publican" (September 25, 1955), Dexter Avenue Baptist Church, Montgomery, AL. In *The Papers of Martin Luther King Jr. Volume VI: Advocate of the Social Gospel, September 1948–March 1963.* Edited by Clayborne Carson, Susan Carson, Susan Englander, Troy Jackson, and Gerald L. Smith. Stanford, CA: Martin Luther King Jr. Research and Education Institute.

———. *A Testament of Hope: The Essential Writings and Speeches.* San Francisco: HarperOne, 2003.

Lorde, Audre. *The Selected Works of Audre Lorde.* Edited by Roxanne Gay. New York: Norton, 2020.

Pui-lan, Kwok. *Postcolonial Politics and Theology: Unraveling Empire for a Global World.* Louisville, KY: Westminster John Knox, 2021.

Spellers, Stephanie. *The Church Cracked Open: Disruption, Decline, and New Hope for Beloved Community.* New York: Church Publishing, 2021.

Vega, Carlos V. *Our Hispanic Roots: What History Failed to Tell Us.* 2nd ed. Santa Maria, CA: Janaway, 2013.

Wilkerson, Isabel. *Caste: The Origins of Our Discontents.* New York: Random House, 2020.

Williams, Delores S. *Sisters in the Wilderness: The Challenge of Womanist God-Talk.* New York: Orbis, 1993.

On Gender and Sexual Justice

Bolz-Weber, Nadia. *Shameless: A Sexual Reformation.* New York: Convergent, 2019.

Bourgeault, Cynthia. *Mary Magdalene: Discovering the Woman at the Heart of Christianity.* Boston: Shambhala, 2010.

Carroll, James. *The Truth at the Heart of the Lie: How the Catholic Church Lost Its Soul—A Memoir of Faith.* New York: Random House, 2021.

Cheng, Patrick S. *Rainbow Theology: Bridging Race, Sexuality, and Spirit.* New York: Seabury, 2013.

Douglas, Kelly Brown. *Sexuality and the Black Church.* Maryknoll, NY: Orbis, 1999.

Ellison, Marvin M. *Same-Sex Marriage? A Christian Ethical Analysis.* Cleveland, OH: Pilgrim, 2004.

Ellison, Marvin M., and Kelly Brown Douglas, eds. *Sexuality and the Sacred: Sources for Theological Reflection.* 2nd ed, foreword by James B. Nelson. Louisville, KY: Westminster John Knox, 2010/2004.

Ellison, Marvin M., and Sylvia Thorson-Smith, eds. *Body and Soul: Rethinking Sexuality as Justice-Love.* Cleveland, OH: Pilgrim, 2003.

Fujiwara, Lynn, and Shireen Roshanravan, eds. *Asian American Feminisms and Women of Color Politics: Decolonizing Feminisms.* Seattle: University of Washington Press, 2018.

Harrison, Beverly Wildung. *Making the Connections: Essays in Feminist Social Ethics.* Edited by Carol S. Robb. Boston: Beacon, 1985.

———. *Our Right to Choose: Toward an Ethic of Abortion.* Boston: Beacon, 1983.

Heyward, Carter. *Touching Our Strength: The Power of the Erotic and the Love of God.* San Francisco: Harper, 1989.

Leloup, Jean-Yves. *The Gospel of Mary Magdalene.* English translation and notes by Joseph Rowe. Rochester, VT: Inner Traditions, 2002.

Mollenkott, Virginia Ramey. *Omnigender: A Trans-religious Approach.* Cleveland, OH: Pilgrim, 2007.

Pui-lan, Kwok. *Postcolonial Imagination & Feminist Theology.* Louisville, KY: Westminster John Knox, 2005.

Shore-Goss, Robert, Thomas Bohache, Patrick S. Cheng, and Ramona Faye West, eds. *Queering Christianity: Finding a Place at the Table for LGBTQI Christians.* Santa Barbara, CA: Praeger, 2013.

On Economic Justice

Barber, William J., II. *We Are Called to Be a Movement.* New York: Workman, 2020.

Collins, Raymond F. *Wealth, Wages, and the Wealthy: New Testament Insight for Preachers and Teachers.* Collegeville, MN: Liturgical, 2017.

Dorien, Gary. *American Democratic Socialism: History, Politics, Religion, and Theory.* New Haven, CT: Yale University Press, 2021.

Downey, Kristin. *The Woman behind the New Deal: The Life and Legacy of Frances Perkins; Social Security, Unemployment Insurance and the Minimum Wage.* New York: Anchor, 2010.

Gutierrez, Gustavo. *A Theology of Liberation: History, Politics and Salvation.* Translated and edited by Sister Caridad Inda and John Eagleson. Maryknoll, NY: Orbis, 1973/1971.

Harrison, Beverly Wildung. *Justice in the Making: Feminist Social Ethics.* Edited by E. M. Bounds, P. K. Brubaker, J. E. Hicks, M. J. Legge, R. T. Peters, and T. C. West. Louisville, KY: Westminster John Knox, 2004.

Pella, Diane Maria. "As We Are United in One: Frederick Denison Maurice and Christian Socialism." PhD diss., Fordham University, 1999. https://research.library .fordham.edu/dissertations/AAI9941916. https://kingscollections.org/exhibitions/ archives/maurice/christian-socialism

Reich, Robert. *The System: Who Rigged It, How We Fix It.* New York: Vintage, 2020.

Soelle, Dorothee. *The Silent Cry: Mysticism and Resistance.* Translated by Barbara and Martin Rumscheidt. Minneapolis, MN: Fortress, 2001.

Temple, William. *Christianity and Social Order.* New York: Pelican, 2019/1942.

On Environmental Justice

Adams, Carol J. *The Sexual Politics of Meat: A Feminist-Vegetarian Critical Theory.* 25th anniv. ed. London: Bloomsbury Academic, 2015.

Adams, Carol J., and Virginia Messina. *Protest Kitchen: Fight Injustice, Save the Planet, and Fuel Your Resistance One Meal at a Time.* Newburyport, MA: Red Wheel, 2018.

Goodall, Jane, and Douglas Abrams. *The Book of Hope: A Survival Guide for Trying Times.* New York: Celadon, 2021.

Goodall, Jane, with Gary McAvoy and Gail Hudson. *Harvest for Hope: A Guide to Mindful Eating.* New York: Warner, 2005.

Heyward, Carter. *Flying Changes: Horses as Spiritual Teachers.* Cleveland, OH: Pilgrim, 2005.

Johnson, Ayana Elizabeth, and Katharine K. Wilkinson, eds. *All We Can Save: Truth, Courage, and Solutions for the Climate Crisis.* New York: One World, 2020.

Linzey, Andrew. *Why Animal Suffering Matters: Philosophy, Theology, and Practical Ethics.* New York: Oxford University Press, 2009.

Macy, Joanna. *A Wild Love for the World: Joanna Macy and the Work of Our Time.* Edited by Stephanie Kaza. Boulder, CO: Shambhala, 2020.

———. *World as Lover, World as Self.* Foreword by Thich Nhat Hanh. Berkeley, CA: Parallax, 1991.

McDaniel, Jay B. *Of God and Pelicans: A Theology of Reverence for Life.* Louisville, KY: Westminster John Knox, 1989.

McFague, Sallie. *The Body of God: An Ecological Theology.* Minneapolis, MN: Fortress, 1993.

———. *Super, Natural Christians: How We Should Love Nature.* Minneapolis, MN: Fortress, 1997.

McKibben, Bill. *Falter: Has the Human Game Begun to Play Itself Out?* Melbourne, Australia: Black Inc., 2019.

Newberry, Alice Kurima. "8 Black Environmentalists You Need to Know." Greenpeace.org. February 8, 2021.

Phillips, Jan. *No Ordinary Time: The Rise of Spiritual Intelligence and Evolutionary Creativity; A Book of Hours for a Prophetic Age.* San Diego, CA: Livingkindness Foundation, 2011.

Pollan, Michael. *The Omnivore's Dilemma: A Natural History of Four Meals.* New York: Penguin, 2006.

Rasmussen, Larry L. *Earth-Honoring Faith: Religious Ethics in a New Key.* New York: Oxford University Press, 2013.

Ruether, Rosemary Radford. *Gaia and God: An Ecofeminist Theology of Earth Healing.* San Francisco: HarperCollins, 1992.

Spencer, Daniel T. *Gay and Gaia: Ethics, Ecology, and the Erotic.* Cleveland, OH: Pilgrim, 1996.

Waldau, Paul, and Kimberley Patton, eds. *A Communion of Subjects: Animals in Religion, Science and Ethics.* New York: Columbia University Press, 2006.

Wilson, David Sloan. *Darwin's Cathedral: Evolution, Religion, and the Nature of Science.* Chicago: University of Chicago Press, 2006.

On Nonviolence and Peacemaking

Amanecida Collective. *Revolutionary Forgiveness: Feminist Reflections on Nicaragua.* Edited by Carter Heyward and Anne B. Gilson, with foreword by Dorothee Soelle. Eugene, OR: Wipf & Stock, 2021 (Maryknoll, NY: Orbis, 1986).

Bonhoeffer, Dietrich. *Letters and Papers from Prison.* Edited by Eberhard Bethge. New York: Touchstone, 1997/1953.

Brock, Rita Nakashima, and Rebecca Ann Parker. *Saving Paradise: How Christianity Traded Love of This World for Crucifixion and Empire.* Boston: Beacon, 2008.

Camara, Helder. *Dom Helder Camara: Essential Writings.* Modern Spiritual Masters. Maryknoll, NY: Orbis, 2009.

Ellis, Marc H. *Unholy Alliance: Religion and Atrocity in Our Time.* Minneapolis, MN: Fortress, 1997.

Nhat Hanh, Thich. *How to Love: Mindfulness Essentials, Book 3.* Berkeley, CA: Parallax, 2014.

King, Martin Luther, Jr. *Where Do We Go from Here: Chaos or Community?* Boston: Beacon, 1968.

Macy, Joanna, and Chris Johnstone. *Active Hope: How to Face the Mess We're In without Going Crazy.* San Francisco: New World Library, 2012.

Merton, Thomas. *Thomas Merton: Essential Writings.* Modern Spiritual Masters. Maryknoll, NY: Orbis, 2000.

Niebuhr, Reinhold. *Moral Man and Immoral Society: A Study in Ethics and Politics.* Louisville, KY: Westminster John Knox, 2021. Originally published New York: Charles Scribner's, 1932.

Rohr, Richard. *What Do We Do with Evil?* Albuquerque, NM: CAC, 2019.

Ruether, Rosemary Radford. *America, Amerikka: Elect Nation and Imperial Violence.* London: Equinox, 2007.

Soelle, Dorothee. *Dorothee Soelle: Essential Writings.* With Dianne L. Oliver. Modern Spiritual Masters. Maryknoll, NY: Orbis, 2006.

Turner, Toko-pa. *Belonging: Remembering Ourselves Home.* Salt Spring Island, BC, Canada: Her Own Room, 2017.

Tutu, Desmond. *No Future without Forgiveness.* New York: Image/Doubleday, 2000.

Wink, Walter. *The Powers That Be: Theology for a New Millennium.* New York: Doubleday, 1999.

Index

abortion, 29–30, 95–97, 135, 188–90, 193–94, 247n11
Abrams, Douglas, 124–25
Ackerman, Denise, 144, 234n4
activism: by African Americans, 52–53; for Black Lives Matter, 133; by children, 119; in civil rights movement, 250n7; globalization of, 213–14; by Jesus Christ, 143–44; in LGBTQ movement, 181; for minorities, 136–37; protests, 28–29, 60–62, 78–79; psychology and, 15–16; in religion, 60–61
addiction, 16–17, 157
Affordable Care Act (Obamacare), 111, 205
Afghanistan, 31–33, 223
Africa, 19–20, 68, 72
African Americans: activism by, 52–53; *Brown v. Board of Education* for, 29–30, 73; in Christianity, 182–83; civil rights movement for, 68; Commission to Study and Develop Reparation Proposals for African Americans Act, 177; culture of, 246n3; discrimination against, 84–86; in history, 86–88; leadership of, 26, 172; Malcolm X for, 26–28; March on Washington

by, 26–27; with minorities, 79–81; Native Americans and, 21; Obama to, 33–34; oppression of, 71–72; race of, 165; racism against, 8–9, 77–79; segregation of, 29–30; slavery of, 20–21; social justice for, 136–37; Tulsa Massacre of, 77. *See also* Blackness
Alcoholics Anonymous, 16, 157
Ali, Muhammad, 27–28, 71, 85
alienation, 121–22, 215
Allende, Salvador, 60, 197, 199
American Renewal Project (ARP), 14–15
Anderson, Marian, 46, 228
animals, 7–8, 117–26, 209–12, 220–21, 250n3
Antifa, 59
anti-Semitism, 12–14, 38, 131–32, 201
Anzaldua, Gloria, 95
apartheid, 144, 228–30, 234n4, 251n10
Aquinas, Thomas, 190–91
Armstrong, Louis, 228
ARP. *See* American Renewal Project
Asians, 80, 85, 165–66, 187–88, 193, 197, 236n15
Atwood, Margaret, 53, 64, 184–85
Augustine (saint), 100, 149–50, 239n6
authoritarianism, 231n7

Bacevich, Andrew J., 243n6
Baker, Ella, 172
Baldwin, James, 68
Bannon, Steve, 59
Barber, William, 136, 226
Barr, William, 53, 72–73,
    237n9, 237n12
Batista, Fulgencio, 197
Beatitudes, 159–60
Bell, Derrick, 237n10
belonging, 211–12
Bentham, Jeremy, 124–25
Bernstein, Eduard, 247n16
Bible: in Christianity, 220–22; God in,
    146–48, 209–10; Good Samaritan
    parable, 151–53, 156; Hagar in,
    182–86, 188, 193, 217; Jesus Christ
    in, 67–68, 75, 158; Mary Magdalene
    in, 182, 186–88; Sermon on the
    Mount, 159–60; sexism in, 103;
    sexual orientation in, 191; socialism
    in, 202–3; spirituality in, 144–45
Biden, Joe: for Democratic Party, 61;
    Harris, K., and, 55; Obama and, 129;
    as President, 28, 30, 77, 113–14;
    religion of, 43
Big Lie, 37–39, 54–55, 59, 127, 129
bin Laden, Osama, 32, 80
birth control, 36–37, 96–98,
    188, 193–94
Black Lives Matter, 78–79, 81, 133, 166
Blackness: to Cone, 246n3; of God,
    165–66, 171–75, 178–79; reparations
    and, 177–78; spirituality of, 175–76;
    in U.S., 166–71
Black Panthers, 174
Black women, 68–69, 89
Blake, Jacob, 34
Bonhoeffer, Dietrich, 134, 154–55
Boogaloo Bois, 34, 92
Bourgeault, Cynthia, 187
Brown, John, 174
Brown v. Board of Education, 29–30, 73
Buber, Martin, 155–56, 214–15
Buddhism, 212–13, 243n16

Bulkin, Elly, 95
Burwell v. Hobby Lobby, 36–37
Bush, Barbara, 96
Bush, George H. W., 96
Butler, Anthea, 4

Camara, Dom Helder, 137–38, 219–20
Canada, 249n13
Cannon, Katie Geneva, 186
capitalism: in Christianity, 203–4;
    globalization of, 111–12, 118;
    insurrection related to, 114–16; to
    Marx, 247n16; reform in, 195, 206–
    7; socialism and, 196–97; spirituality
    and, 105–14, 120–21, 126, 202–3
Cardenal, Ernesto, 197–98
Carroll, James, 97–99, 103–4
Carter, Mary Ann, 7, 9, 107
caste, 83–84
Castro, Fidel, 197–99
Catholicism. *See* Christianity
Cawthorn, Madison, 14–15
Chardin, Pierre Teilhard de, 118, 212
charity, 136–37
Charlottesville riots, 12–13, 78
Cheek, Alison, 216–17
Cheney, James, 228
Cheney, Liz, 50
Cheng, Patrick S., 236n5
Chicago school of economics, 241n3
children, 6–11, 119–20
Chile, 60–61, 197–99
China, 28, 105, 196, 227
Christianity: African Americans in, 182–
    83; to Asians, 236n15; Bible in, 220–
    22; capitalism in, 203–4; Christian
    anti-Semitism, 12–14; Christian
    Coalition, 72; Christian socialism,
    151, 248n2; Christofascism, 11–15;
    class in, 106–9; in culture, 5–6;
    culture of, 147, 166–71; ecology
    in, 117–18, 249n5; economics in,
    202–3; education in, 25; entitlement
    in, 68–69, 122–23; in Europe, 86;
    evangelical Christians, 19–20,

23–24; feminism in, 123, 240n9; God in, 22–23, 52–53, 65, 74, 82, 177–78, 211–12; history and, 45–47, 234n3; homophobia in, 181–82; humility in, 157–64; identity in, 192–93; insurrection and, 57–62; Jesus Christ in, 219–20; Jews in, 131, 186; leadership in, 61–62; LGBTQ movement to, 191–92; love in, 149–56; misogyny in, 92–93, 97–98; morality of, 109–12, 211–12; original sin in, 234n2; patriarchy in, 99, 188; peacemakers in, 222–30; philosophy and, 62–63, 144–45; politics in, 100–102, 143–44; purity in, 84–86; racism in, 80–81; repentance in, 177; in Republican Party, 114–15, 129, 237n9; responsibility in, 48; SBC, 99–100; sexism in, 188–90; sexual orientation in, 194; socialism in, 198–202; social justice in, 187, 244n1; spirituality in, 7, 24; theology of, 13, 45–47, 120–23, 236n5; Trump and, 237n1; Universalist, 11, 231n5; in U.S., 3–5, 15–16, 57–63, 65–66, 146–48, 193, 212–13; violence in, 131–34; whiteness in, 83–84; women in, 240n8. *See also specific topics*
Christ the Representative (Soelle), 154–56
cisgender, 17, 192, 194
Citizens United v. Federal Election Commission, 234n20
civil rights movement, 26–27, 68–69, 85, 96, 189, 223, 250n7
Civil War, 22–23, 54, 133
Clare of Assisi, 117
class, 7, 105–9
Clay, Cassius. *See* Ali
climate change, 117–26
Clinton, Bill, 30, 110–11
Clinton, Hillary, 55, 115, 129–30, 242n10
colonialism, 20–21, 68, 201

Commission to Study and Develop Reparation Proposals for African Americans Act, 177
commodification, 121, 214–15
communication, 57–63
Communism: culture and, 197–201; in globalization, 105; McCarthy, J., against, 26, 73; New Deal compared to, 113; in politics, 248n2; religion to, 132; terrorism and, 133; to U.S., 26, 68, 71, 73, 196–97
compromise, 244n12
Concerned Women for America, 72
Cone, James H., 172, 174, 246n3
Congregation Beth Israel, 13
Constitution, 14, 21, 35–36, 233n4, 235n9
consumerism, 121, 214
conversion, 177
corporations, 121–22, 242n6
corruption, 51–52
Counter Extremism Project, 34
coup, 236n14
COVID-19, 37–39, 125
Crenshaw, Kimberlé Williams, 237n10
criminal justice system, 163, 224–25
critical race theory, 70–73, 174–75, 237n10
Cuba, 197–99
Cybersecurity and Infrastructure Security Agency, 55

Dakota Access Pipeline, 249n13
Daniels, Jonathan, 68, 228
Davis, Angela, 174
Declaration of Independence, 145–46, 232n3
Defense of Marriage Act (DOMA), 35
democracy: democratic socialism, 241n5, 248n2; nationalism and, 132; philosophy of, 145–46; SDS, 72; to Supreme Court, 234n20; to theocracy, 54; in U.S., 237n12
Democratic Party: Biden for, 61; identity in, 50–51, 95–96;

insurrection to, 240n7; leadership of, 46–47, 55; liberals in, 60–62; Obama for, 30; Republican Party and, 49–52, 113–14, 176

DeWitt, Bob, 210

discrimination, 55–56, 79–82, 84–86

Disney, Walt, 25

District of Columbia v. Heller, 35–36

diversity, 181–82, 190–94, 236n5

Dobbs v. Jackson (MS) Women's Health Organization, 97

Dobson, James, 237n9

DOMA. *See* Defense of Marriage Act

domestic terrorism, 33–34

Douglass, Frederick, 70

Duke, David, 78

Earth, 117–26

ecology: animals in, 211–12; in Christianity, 117–18, 249n5; of food, 124–26; humans and, 16, 119–20; morality of, 209–11; power of, 217–18; psychology for, 215–17; in religion, 120–23, 212–13; theology and, 123–24; in U.S., 118–19

economics: Chicago school of economics, 241n3; in Christianity, 202–3; crisis in, 109–12; Great Depression, 24, 56; Jesus Christ on, 203–4, 207; Keynesian, 241n4; New Deal, 24, 30, 56, 113; philosophy of, 112–14; politics and, 34–35, 105–6, 234n20; in psychology, 106–9; spirituality and, 114–16; trickle down, 30, 109–10; of white Christian nationalism, 24–25

education: in Christianity, 25; critical race theory, 70–73, 174–75, 237n10; entitlement in, 70–73; about love, 168; racism in, 173; religion in, 101; segregation, 29–30; 1619 Project, 86–88; of slavery, 86–88; social justice and, 61–62

Einstein, Albert, 124–25

Eisenhower, Dwight, 51, 235n2

elections: Big Lie, 37–39, 54–55, 59, 127, 129; voting rights, 36, 55–56, 96, 176; Voting Rights Act, 96, 189; white Christian nationalism in, 19–20

Eliot, T. S., 12

elitism, 115

empowerment, 158–59, 181–90

Engels, Friedrich, 247n16

entitlement: in Christianity, 68–69, 122–23; in education, 70–73; to minorities, 163; after 9/11 attacks, 73–76; privilege and, 65–68; psychology of, 69–70

Equal Rights Amendment, 189, 247n10

Europe: Christianity in, 86; colonialism by, 20–21; culture of, 69; U.S., and, 44, 169; violence in, 227; whiteness from, 165–66; World War II for, 155–56

evangelical Christians, 19–20, 23–26

evil, 134–35, 220–22

factory farming, 124–25

Fairness Doctrine, 31

Falwell, Jerry, 32, 72, 73

Family Research Council, 44

fascism, 11–15, 60–61

Fattal, Isabel, 12

Fauci, Anthony, 37–38

Federal Communications Commission (FCC), 31

feminism, 9, 93–95, 123, 190, 240n9

Fifield, James W., Jr., 24

Fiorenza, Elisabeth Schussler, 240n8

First Amendment, 21, 233n4, 235n9

Floyd, George, 78–79, 81, 162

Flynn, Michael, 53, 59

food, 124–26

For Colored Girls Who Have Considered Suicide (Shange), 94

Ford, Christine Blasey, 10

foreign policy, 243n6

Francis (pope), 38

Francis (saint), 117

Frank, Barney, 189

Frank, Leo, 13
Frazier, Darnella, 78–79
Freud, Sigmund, 192, 194
Friedman, Milton, 110, 113, 241n3
Fugitive Slave Acts, 70
Fuller, Charles E., 25

Gay rights, 33–35
gender: cisgender, 17, 192, 194;
    diversity, 181–82, 190–94; in
    LGBTQ movement, 204–5;
    psychology of, 6–7; purity
    and, 102–4; race and, 6–7, 15;
    transgender, 236n5
genocide, 155
Germany, 12–13, 138
Gilbert, Ronnie, 228
Gilded Age, 23–24
Gilead, 53
Ginsburg, Ruth Bader, 36–37
Go, Michelle Alyssa, 80
God: in Bible, 146–48, 209–10;
    Blackness of, 165–66, 171–75, 178–
    79; in Christianity, 22–23, 52–53,
    65, 74, 82, 177–78, 211–12; in civil
    rights movement, 85; enemies of,
    131–34; to humans, 138–39; Jesus
    Christ and, 70, 100, 115, 168; MLK
    on, 174; omnipotence of, 235n3;
    philosophy of, 7–8, 46, 66–67,
    100–102, 116, 193; in politics, 54,
    62–63; power of, 149–56; in U.S.,
    163; violence and, 220–22
Goldberg, Jeffrey, 4
Golden, Renny, 93
Goodall, Jane, 124–25
Goodman, Andrew, 228
Good Samaritan parable, 151–53, 156
Gore, Al, Jr., 119

The Gospel of Mary Magdalene
    (Leloup), 186

Graham, Billy, 19–20, 24–25,
    71, 113, 196

Grand Old Party. *See* Republican Party
Great Depression, 24, 56
Greear, J. D., 58–59
Greenblatt, Jonathan, 12
Guerde, Jules, 247n16
guilt, 175–76
guns, 34–36, 119, 127–28, 135, 223–24
Guthrie, Woody, 228

Haake, Alfred, 24
Hagar, 182–86, 188, 193, 217
Haiti, 78
Hamer, Fannie Lou, 68, 228

The Handmaid's Tale (Atwood), 53,
    64, 184–85

Hannah-Jones, Nikole, 86–88, 238n2
Harris, Barbara C., 173
Harris, Kamala, 55, 129–30
Harrison, Beverly Wildung, 105–6, 108,
    112–13, 138–39, 190, 246n5, 247n11
hate groups, 33–34, 63–64, 92, 127–30
health care, 36–39, 111, 125, 177, 188–
    90, 193–94, 205
Heritage Foundation, 44
Heyward, Bob, 7, 9, 107
Hiatt, Sue, 210, 228–30
Hicks, Mary Ellen, 88
Hildegard of Bingen, 117, 212
Hill, Anita, 10
Hippo, 100
history. *See specific topics*
Hitler, Adolf, 60, 138
Ho Chi Minh, 28–29
homophobia, 33–34, 91–92, 120–21,
    181–82, 233n12
Hong, Angie, 187–88, 193, 236n15
Hoover, Herbert, 24
Hoover, J. Edgar, 26, 233n12
Howard University, 88
humans: alienation by, 215; animals
    and, 209–11, 250n3; in Buddhism,
    243n16; ecology and, 16, 119–20;
    evil and, 221; food for, 124–26; God

to, 138–39; Industrial Revolution for, 22–23; Jesus Christ on, 56–57, 151–52; pride of, 161; secular humanism, 73; sin of, 47–48; in theology, 17–18
humility, 157–64

I and Thou (Buber), 155–56
identity: in Blackness, 172; in Catholicism, 11, 15, 53, 73; in Christianity, 192–93; culture and, 43–48; in Democratic Party, 50–51, 95–96; to LGBTQ movement, 102–3; politics, 16–17; psychology of, 158, 167–68; sexual, 181–82, 190–94; with sexual orientation, 173–74
"I Have a Dream" speech (MLK), 27
imagination, 7–8, 17–18, 128–29
immigration, 33, 51, 79–80
Indian Removal Act, 70
individualism, 204–5
Industrial Revolution, 22–23
injustice, 122
In Memory of Her (Fiorenza), 240n8
insurrection: capitalism related to, 114–16; Christianity and, 57–62; guns at, 127–28; psychology of, 3–4, 143; research on, 242n9; rioters in, 11; violence in, 225–26, 240n7
Intergovernmental Panel on Climate Change (IPCC), 119
intersectionality, 17–18
IPCC. *See* Intergovernmental Panel on Climate Change
Iran, 227
Iraq, 31–33, 223
Islam, 27, 31–33, 132, 174

Jefferson, Thomas, 21, 70, 232n3
Jesus Christ: activism by, 143–44; Beatitudes, 159–60; in Bible, 67–68, 75, 158; in Christianity, 219–20; in culture, 238n7; on economics, 203–4, 207; family of, 101; God and, 70, 100, 115, 168; on humans, 56–57, 151–52; "The Lord's Prayer"

to, 159–60; philosophy of, 62–63; questions by, 152–53; Smith, A., and, 114–15; spirituality of, 120. *See also* Christianity
Jewish Anti-Defamation League, 12
Jews, 9, 12–14, 38, 131–32, 186, 201
Jim Crow laws, 9–11, 171
Johnson, Lyndon, 28, 113, 205
John XXIII (pope), 98
Julian of Norwich, 150, 192–93, 247n16
justice. *See specific topics*

Kaur, Valerie, 226
Kavanaugh, Brett, 10
Kennedy, John, 28, 198
Keynes, John Maynard, 241n4
Kim-Kort, Mihee, 90
King, Karen L., 186–87
King, Martin Luther, Jr. (MLK): in civil rights movement, 26–27; on God, 174; in history, 189; on humility, 161–64; leadership of, 34, 44, 68, 71, 172, 175, 223; Malcolm X and, 228; nonviolence to, 134; to Parker, 86; Parker and, 239n18
Kinzinger, Adam, 50
Krebs, Christopher, 55

Lane, David, 14
Latin America, 72, 197–202, 207
LatinX communities, 51, 85
Lawrence v. Texas, 35
Lee, Sheila Jackson, 177
Lefler, Susan, 234n1, 237n9
Leloup, Jean-Yves, 186
Letters and Papers from Prison (Bonhoeffer), 155
Lewis, John, 68, 172, 228
LGBTQ movement: activism in, 181; to Christianity, 191–92; gender in, 204–5; history of, 13; identity to, 102–3; NAACP and, 136–37; oppression against, 62, 97; politics of, 43; whiteness and, 173–74
liberals, 60–62

Limbaugh, Rush, 31
Lincoln, Abraham, 3, 18, 38,
    46, 108, 222
Lincoln, C. Eric, 173
Lindbergh, Charles, 12
Linzey, Andrew, 124
Liuzzo, Viola, 68, 228
Lorde, Audre, 83–84, 89, 95
"The Lord's Prayer," 159–60
love, 149–56, 168, 200
lust, 239n6

MacArthur, Douglas, 25
Macy, Joanna, 124, 212–13, 215, 217
Malcolm X, 26–28, 71, 174, 178, 228
Manchin, Joe, 51
Manifest Destiny, 22
Manker-Seale, Susan, 239n18
March on Washington, 26–27
Marshall, Thurgood, 172
Martin, Trayvon, 79
Marx, Karl, 151, 196, 200, 207,
    247n1, 248n2
Marxism, 248n2
Mary Magdalene, 182, 186–88
Mary of Magdala (King, K.), 186–87
masculinity, 9–10, 25
mass psychology, 44–48
Maurice, Frederick Denison, 150–51,
    156, 199–203, 207
McCarriston, Linda, 124
McCarthy, Joseph, 26, 73, 196
McCarthy, Kevin, 55
McConnell, Mitch, 50, 55
McDaniel, Jay, 124
McDonald v. Chicago, 35–36
McFague, Sallie, 120, 212, 218
McVeigh, Timothy, 34
Meacham, Jon, 44

The Meaning of Mary Magdalene
    (Bourgeault), 187

Merton, Thomas, 150
Michigan Civil Rights Commission, 69

Middle East, 32–33, 79–80, 85, 165–66
military, 32–33, 51–52
militias, 49–50
Milliken, Roger, 106, 113
Mink, Patsy, 95
minorities: activism for, 136–37;
    African Americans with, 79–81;
    Asians as, 165–66; Civil Rights Act
    for, 96, 189; critical race theory for,
    70–73; entitlement to, 163; Equal
    Rights Amendment for, 189, 247n10;
    globalization of, 227–28; history
    of, 127–30; leadership of, 250n7;
    oppression of, 55–56, 127; 1619
    Project for, 171; social justice for, 60
misogyny: in Christianity, 92–93,
    97–98; in culture, 10; feminism
    against, 93–95; homophobia and,
    120–21; from omnipotence, 99;
    oppression from, 102–4; patriarchy
    and, 100–102; philosophy of, 90–92;
    in politics, 95–97, 129–30; in U.S.,
    181–90; violence from, 89–90
MLK. *See* King, Martin Luther, Jr.
Mohler, R. Albert, Jr., 58–59
molestation, 8–10
Mollenkott, Virginia Ramey, 236n5
monotheism, 188
Moore, Beth, 39
Moraga, Cherrie, 95
morality: of Christianity, 109–12, 211–
    12; evil in, 221; in philosophy, 124–
    25, 134–35; of Rasmussen, L., 209,
    213–14, 217–18; in religion, 132–34;
    spirituality and, 137–38, 175–76; of
    white Christian nationalism, 147–48
Moral Majority, 72
Moral Man and Immoral Society
    (Niebuhr), 138
Morgan, Robin, 95
Mother Emmanuel Church, 34
Muhammad, Elijah, 174
Murray, Pauli, 172–73

National Association for the Advancement of Colored People (NAACP), 136–37
National Association of Manufacturers, 24
nationalism, 4–5, 11, 54, 84–86, 132. *See also* white Christian nationalism
National Rifle Association, 128
Native Americans, 21, 70, 173, 249n13
nature, 117–26
Nazis, 4, 12–15
neo-Nazis, 4, 14–15
New Deal, 24, 30, 56, 113
Newton, Huey, 174
Nicaragua, 16, 61, 197–99
Nichols, Terry, 34
Niebuhr, Reinhold, 138–39
9/11 attacks, 31–33, 73–76
1984 (Orwell), 64
Nixon, Richard, 96
nonviolence, 134, 137–39, 223
normalization, 166–71
North, Gary, 25–26
North Korea, 223

Oath Keepers, 92
Obama, Barack: Biden and, 129; Clinton, B., and, 110–11; culture after, 128; for Democratic Party, 30; Obamacare, 111, 205; as President, 33–34; Trump and, 33–34, 77–78
Obergefell v. Hodges, 35
Ocasio-Cortez, Alexandria, 51
O'Dell, Darlene, 106, 135, 241n2, 244n12
O'Donohue, John, 124
Oklahoma City Federal Building attack, 34
Old Fashioned Revival Hour (radio show), 25
Oliver, Mary, 124
Olmstead, Molly, 58
omnipotence: of God, 235n3; lust for, 49–52; misogyny from, 99; in politics, 54–56; power and, 47–48,

56–57, 62–64; religion and, 57–62; theocracy and, 52–53
oppression: of African Americans, 71–72; injustice and, 122; against LGBTQ movement, 62, 97; of minorities, 55–56, 127; from misogyny, 102–4; of race, 173; in religion, 15; social justice against, 181–82, 215–17; in U.S., 77–79
Orban, Viktor, 38
original sin, 234n2
Ortega, Daniel, 197–99
Orwell, George, 64
O'Sullivan, John L., 22
Our Right to Choose (Harrison), 247n11

Parker, Theodore, 86, 239n18
Parks, Rosa, 26, 46, 68, 172, 174, 228
patriarchy: birth control to, 96–97; in Christianity, 99, 188; misogyny and, 100–102; philosophy of, 190–91; privilege in, 167; sexual orientation to, 93–94; white male supremacy, 150–51
patriotism, 54, 123
peacemakers, 222–30
Pellauer, Mary, 109
Pelosi, Nancy, 240n7
Pence, Mike, 3
Penney, J. C., 25
Perry, Samuel, 11
Peru, 227
Pew, J. Howard, 24
philosophy. *See specific topics*
piety, 146
Pinochet, Augusto, 60–61, 197, 199
Pitts, Leonard, 79
Pledge of Allegiance, 24
police, 8–11, 78–79, 163, 224
politics: of abortion, 29–30, 188–90; ARP, 14–15; Blackness in, 176–77; in Christianity, 100–102, 143–44; Communism in, 248n2; corporations in, 242n6; corruption in, 51–52; coup in, 236n14; economics and,

34–35, 105–6, 234n20; of Equal Rights Amendment, 247n10; of evangelical Christians, 24–25, 26; of foreign policy, 243n6; God in, 54, 62–63; homophobia in, 233n12; identity, 16–17; in Latin America, 197–202; of LGBTQ movement, 43; of McCarthy, J., 196; in Middle East, 32–33; misogyny in, 95–97, 129–30; omnipotence in, 54–56; progressive, 24; of protests, 60; psychology and, 136; QAnon, 128–29; of reform, 163; of refugees, 79–80; religion and, 11, 14, 39, 66; of Republican Party, 3–4; of *Roe v. Wade*, 29–30, 96–97, 135; of scholarship, 15–16; science and, 84–85; silence in, 8–10; social, 50–51; terrorism in, 74–76; in U.S., 176–77; violence and, 136–37; of voting rights, 36; of white Christian nationalism, 26, 29–30, 132–34. *See also specific topics*
Pollan, Michael, 125
Poor People's Campaign, 136
Poor People's Campaign's National Call for a Moral Revival, 226
Pound, Ezra, 12
poverty, 111
power: of ecology, 217–18; empowerment, 158–59, 181–90; of God, 149–56; of love, 200; masculinity and, 10; omnipotence and, 47–48, 56–57, 62–64; in theology, 210–11
"The Power of Anger in the Work of Love" (Harrison), 246n5
pride, 161
prison, 224–25
privilege, 65–68, 167
professional theology, 123–24
progressive politics, 24, 60–62
Promise Keepers, 44
Protestant Reformation, 150
protests, 28–29, 60, 61–62, 78–79, 163
Proud Boys, 4, 34, 92

psychology: activism and, 15–16; addiction, 16–17, 157; of children, 119–20; of class, 7; of consumerism, 214; for ecology, 215–17; economics in, 106–9; from empowerment, 158–59; of entitlement, 69–70; Freud in, 192, 194; of gender, 6–7; guilt, 175–76; in hate groups, 63–64, 127–30; of identity, 158, 167–68; of insurrection, 3–4, 143; from intersectionality, 17–18; mass, 44–48; of molestation, 8–9; politics and, 136; projection, 90–91; of race, 5–6; of secrets, 8–10; shame, 175–76; of silence, 10–11; storytelling for, 9–10; of violence, 134–35, 250n3; of white Christian nationalism, 216; of whiteness, 77–79; in World War II, 12–13
Puerto Rico, 217
purity, 63–64, 84–86, 102–4, 187–88, 236n15
Putin, Vladimir, 196

QAnon, 128–29
Quincy Institute, 243n6

race: of African Americans, 165; caste and, 83–84; gender and, 6–7, 15; immigration and, 33; oppression of, 173; psychology of, 5–6; religion and, 44; violence and, 10–11; women and, 93–95
racism: against African Americans, 8–9, 77–79; apartheid, 144, 228–30, 234n4, 251n10; in Christianity, 80–81; in education, 173; history of, 83–84; against Middle East, 79–80; purity and, 63–64; sexism and, 18; systemic, 82; in U.S., 79–82; violence from, 81–82, 89–90
Radical Love (Cheng), 236n5
rape, 47
Rasmussen, Larry, 121–22, 125, 209, 211–14, 216–18

Rasmussen, Nyla, 121
Rauschenbusch, Walter, 23–24
Reagan, Nancy, 96
Reagan, Ronald, 30, 44, 96, 110–11, 189, 205
Reeb, James, 228
reform, 163, 195, 205, 206–7
refugees, 79–80
religion: activism in, 60–61; of Biden, 43; Buddhism, 212–13; to Communism, 132; ecology in, 120–23, 212–13; in education, 101; in elections, 55; hierarchies in, 56–57; history of, 172; Islam, 27; leadership in, 152–54, 222–23; masculinity in, 25; monotheism, 188; morality in, 132–34; omnipotence and, 57–62; oppression in, 15; philosophy and, 4–5, 48; politics and, 11, 14, 39, 66; purity in, 236n15; race and, 44; sexism in, 23–24; sexual orientation in, 149–50; in slavery, 130; in U.S., 11–12, 17, 21–22, 235n9; to white Christian nationalism, 27–28, 56–57
reparations, 177–78
repentance, 177
repression, 103–4
Republican Party: abortion to, 95–97, 188–89; Big Lie to, 54–55; Christianity in, 114–15, 129, 237n9; Democratic Party and, 49–52, 113–14, 176; discrimination to, 55–56; fascism and, 60–61; health care to, 205; leadership of, 46–47, 50; politics of, 3–4; *Roe v. Wade* to, 29–30, 96–97; 1619 Project to, 78; Supreme Court with, 111–12; traditional, 38; after Trump, 37–38; whiteness in, 225–26. *See also specific topics*
Rich, Adrienne, 9, 95
Richardson, Heather Cox, 44, 50
Rittenhouse, Kyle, 34, 79, 134
Roberts, John, 36
Robertson, Pat, 32, 73

Robeson, Paul, 228
Rodriguez, Christine Nieves, 217
Roe v. Wade, 29–30, 89, 96–97, 135, 189–90
Rohr, Richard, 150, 159–60
Romney, George, 96
Romney, Mitt, 96
Roof, Dylann, 34
Roosevelt, Eleanor, 46
Roosevelt, Franklin, 24, 44, 56, 113, 205
Ruether, Rosemary Radford, 120
Russia, 28, 196

Sanders, Bernie, 51, 68
SBC. *See* Southern Baptist Convention
Schor, A. M., 57
Schumer, Chuck, 31
Schweitzer, Albert, 124–25
Schwerner, Michael, 228
science, 84–85
SDS. *See* Students for a Democratic Society
Seale, Bobby, 174
Second Amendment, 35–36
secular humanism, 73
Seeger, Pete, 228
segregation, 29–30
Sermon on the Mount, 159–60
Serwer, Adam, 86–87
sexism, 6–7, 18, 23–24, 89, 90–92, 103, 188–90. *See also* misogyny
sexual diversity, 236n5
sexual identity, 181–82, 190–94
sexual impurity, 102–4
sexual orientation, 93–94, 103–4, 149–50, 173–74, 191, 194. *See also specific topics*
shame, 175–76
Shange, Ntozake, 94
Sheen, Fulton, 196
Shelby County (AL) v. Holder, 36
silence, 8–11
sin. *See specific topics*
Sinema, Krysten, 51

Sisters in the Wilderness
(Williams), 182–84
1619 Project, 78, 86–88, 171,
232n2, 238nn2–3
slavery, 20–21, 70, 86–88, 130–31, 133,
174, 232n2
Smith, Adam, 114–15
Smith, Barbara, 95
social democracy, 248n2
socialism, 105, 151, 196–203, 206–7,
241n5, 248n2. *See also* capitalism
social justice: for African Americans,
136–37; in Christianity, 187, 244n1;
consciousness for, 16–17; in criminal
justice system, 163; education and,
61–62; in health care, 177; history
of, 13–14, 145–46; for minorities,
60; against oppression, 181–82,
215–17; in U.S., 17–18
social media, 31
social politics, 50–51
Soelle, Dorothee, 11–12, 16, 109,
149–50, 154–56
Somoza, Anastasio, 197
Soros, George, 38
Sotomayor, Sonia, 37
South Africa, 144, 228–30,
234n4, 251n10
Southern Baptist Convention
(SBC), 99–100
Southern Poverty Law Center, 34
Soviet Union, 198
Spencer, Daniel T., 120–21
Spiral of Violence (Camara),
137–38, 219–20
spirituality: in Bible, 144–45; of
Blackness, 175–76; capitalism and,
105–14, 120–21, 126, 202–3; charity
in, 136–37; in Christianity, 7, 24;
consciousness and, 7–8; economics
and, 114–16; of Jesus Christ, 120;
lies in, 161; morality and, 137–38,
175–76; philosophy and, 143–44;
white Christian nationalism and,
22–24, 43–44

Stabenow, Debbie, 31
Stalin, Josef, 60
Steinem, Gloria, 95
Stewart, Jimmy, 25
Stigler, George, 241n3
story-telling, 9–10
Students for a Democratic
Society (SDS), 72
Sunday, Billy, 23–24
Sun Oil Company, 24
Supreme Court, 10, 34–37, 111–12,
189, 224–25, 234n20. *See also*
specific cases
Surrey, Janet, 124, 215
systemic racism, 82

terrorism, 13–15, 33–34, 59,
74–76, 132–33
Texas, 37, 70–73
Thatcher, Margaret, 30, 110
theocracy, 52–54
Theoharis, Liz, 136, 226
theology: of Christianity, 13, 45–47,
120–23, 236n5; ecology and,
123–24; history of, 11–12; humans
in, 17–18; philosophy and, 15, 57–63, 154–56; power
in, 210–11; professional, 123–24;
Union Theological Seminary,
172–73; violence in, 130–31; of
whiteness, 166–71

A Theology for the Social Gospel
(Rauschenbusch), 23

Thich Nhat Hahn, 124, 212–
13, 215, 217
think tanks, 44
Thomas, Clarence, 10
3 percenters, 34, 92, 234
Thunberg, Greta, 119
Thurman, Howard, 172
Tolson, Clyde, 233n12
The Town beyond the Wall
(Wiesel), 250n6

Transgender (Mollenkott), 236n5
Tree of Life Synagogue, 12
trickle down economics, 30, 109–10
Truman, Harry, 19, 25, 205
Trump, Donald: abortion to, 97; Big
    Lie and, 37–39, 54–55, 59, 127, 129;
    Christianity and, 237n1; Clinton,
    H., and, 115; Fauci and, 37–38;
    influences of, 233n12; leadership
    of, 19, 61, 133; Obama and, 33–34,
    77–78; Reagan, R., and, 44, 110–11;
    reputation of, 54, 143, 242n10;
    1619 Project to, 238n3; slogans of,
    14; supporters of, 3–4, 14–15, 33,
    49–50, 55, 58–60, 129; Supreme
    Court of, 36
Truth and Reconciliation Commission,
    229–30, 251n10
Tulsa Massacre, 77
Turner, Nat, 174
Tutu, Desmond, 228–30

Union Theological Seminary, 172–73
United States (U.S.): anti-Semitism
    in, 38, 131–32; Asians in, 80;
    authoritarianism in, 231n7;
    Blackness in, 166–71; Canada
    and, 249n13; Capitol, 3–4, 11;
    Christianity in, 3–5, 15–16, 57–63,
    65–66, 146–48, 193, 212–13; civil
    rights movement, 26–27, 68–69,
    85; class in, 105–9; Commission
    to Study and Develop Reparation
    Proposals for African Americans
    Act, 177; Communism to, 26, 68,
    71, 73, 196–97; corporations in,
    121–22, 242n6; criminal justice
    system in, 163, 224–25; culture of,
    83–84, 145–46, 166; Declaration
    of Independence, 145–46, 232n3;
    democracy in, 237n12; ecology
    in, 118–19; Europe and, 44, 169;
    Fairness Doctrine, 31; Gilded Age
    in, 23–24; in globalization, 60–61,
    243n6; God in, 163; health care

in, 205; history of, 47–48, 170;
    immigration in, 51; Islam in, 27;
    Jewish Anti-Defamation League in,
    12; Jim Crow laws in, 9–11, 171;
    Latin America and, 207; militias
    in, 49–50; misogyny in, 181–90;
    New Deal, 24, 30, 56, 113; 9/11
    attacks, 31–33; oppression in,
    77–79; patriotism in, 123; police in,
    224; politics in, 176–77; racism in,
    79–82; religion in, 11–12, 17, 21–22,
    235n9; 1619 Project in, 86–88;
    socialism in, 105, 195, 241n5;
    social justice in, 17–18; Supreme
    Court, 10; in Vietnam War, 27–29;
    violence in, 127–30; voting rights
    in, 176; white Christian nationalism
    in, 25–26; women in, 64; World
    War II to, 66–68, 106–7. *See also*
    specific topics
Universalist Christianity, 11, 231n5
U.S. *See* United States

Vietnam War, 27–29, 60, 71
violence: abuse and, 8; Camara on,
    137–38, 219–20; in Christianity,
    131–34; in Europe, 227; as evil,
    221–22; globalization of, 13–14;
    God and, 220–22; from guns,
    34–36, 119, 128, 135, 223–24; in
    insurrection, 225–26, 240n7; against
    Jews, 12–13; masculinity and, 9;
    from misogyny, 89–90; nonviolence,
    134, 137–39; to peacemakers,
    222–30; by police, 78–79; politics
    and, 136–37; psychology of, 134–35,
    250n3; race and, 10–11; from racism,
    81–82, 89–90; rape, 47; spiral of,
    137–38, 219–20, 225–30; terrorism
    and, 59; in theology, 130–31; in U.S.,
    127–30; violent lone rangers, 33–34;
    in war, 31–33; against women,
    90–91, 129–30
Volf, Miroslav, 130

voting rights, 36, 55–56, 96, 176, 179, 189

Walker, Alice, 95
Walker, Mark, 14–15
Warren, Elizabeth, 68
Washington, George, 70
Washington, Paul, 173
Weyrich, Paul, 20
white Christian nationalism: civil rights movement to, 26–27; during COVID-19, 37–39; economics of, 24–25; in elections, 19–20; history of, 19–22; on Internet, 33–34; in military, 51–52; morality of, 147–48; 9/11 attacks to, 31–33; Obama to, 33–34; to O'Dell, 241n2; politics of, 26, 29–30, 132–34; psychology of, 216; Reagan, R., to, 30; religion to, 27–28, 56–57; spirituality and, 22–24, 43–44; stereotypes of, 63; Supreme Court and, 34–37; in U.S., 25–26; Vietnam War and, 27–29. *See also specific topics*
Whitehead, Andrew, 11
whiteness: in Christianity, 83–84; discrimination and, 81–82; from Europe, 165–66; history of, 79–81, 86–88; LGBTQ movement and, 173–74; nationalism and, 84–86; psychology of, 77–79; in Republican Party, 225–26; slavery and, 131; theology of, 166–71; white male supremacy, 150–51; for women, 157
white supremacy. *See specific topics*
Whole Women's Health v. Jackson (TX), 37
Wiesel, Elie, 15–16, 222, 250n6
Wildung, Adelia, 112
Wilkerson, Isabel, 83–84
Williams, Delores S., 173, 182–84
Willie, Charles, 173
Windsor v. United States, 35
wisdom, 216–17

women: Black, 68–69, 89; in Christianity, 240n8; Concerned Women for America, 72; in culture, 10–11; empowerment of, 181–90; hate groups against, 92; health care for, 188–90, 193–94; legal issues of, 37, 97, 189; race and, 93–95; in Texas, 37; in U.S., 64; violence against, 90–91, 129–30; whiteness for, 157; women's rights, 93–95
World War II, 12–13, 61, 66–68, 71, 106–7, 155–56

Xi Jinping, 196

Yousafzai, Malala, 226

About the Author

Carter Heyward is a Christian theologian who taught feminist, Black, Latin American, LGBTQ, ecological, and other liberation theologies for thirty years at the Episcopal Divinity School in Cambridge, Massachusetts. In 1974, she was one of the eleven women ordained "irregularly" to the Episcopal priesthood; and in 1979, Heyward was among the first religious leaders in America to "come out" as lesbian. As a priest and teacher, she has spent her life working on the boundaries of organized religion with those who also live and work on borders of church and world and with groups representing different identities, ideologies, and issues. She has written or edited sixteen books, including *The Redemption of God: A Theology of Mutual Relation*, *Touching Our Strength: The Erotic as Power and the Love of God*, *Saving Jesus from Those Who Are Right: Rethinking What It Means to Be Christian*, and *Tears of Christepona: Mystical Musings on Evil, Grief, and Godding*.

Over four decades, Carter Heyward has spoken and led workshops nationally and internationally on matters of gender and sexual justice and Christian theology; the christic presence of Jesus in our life together; and horses as spiritual teachers. Since retiring from seminary teaching in 2005, Heyward has lived in an intentional community in the mountains of North Carolina, twenty miles from her childhood home. During this time, she has written four books and many essays; preached at dozens of ordinations, weddings, and funerals; and mentored countless Christians and others wrestling at intersections of spirituality and politics. In this latter period, Heyward also founded and has helped shape a therapeutic horseback riding center in her small mountain town and has served as a founder and leader of her local chapter of the NAACP. For ten years, Carter was fiddler in the Bold Gray Mares, a women's old-time (Appalachian) music string band. From her own perspective, *The Seven Deadly Sins of White Christian Nationalism: A Call to Action* is her most consequential book.